GENDER, MANUMISSION, AND THE ROMAN FREEDWOMAN

This book examines the distinct problem posed by the manumission of female slaves in ancient Rome. The sexual identities of a female slave and a female citizen were fundamentally incompatible, as the former was principally defined by her sexual availability and the latter by her sexual integrity. Accordingly, those evaluating the manumission process needed to reconcile a woman's experiences as a slave with the expectations and moral rigor required of the female citizen. The figure of the freedwoman – fictionalized and real – provides an extraordinary lens into the matter of how Romans understood, debated, and experienced the sheer magnitude of the transition from slave to citizen; the various social factors that impinged upon this process; and the community stakes in the institution of manumission.

Matthew J. Perry is Assistant Professor of History at John Jay College of Criminal Justice, City University of New York. His research focuses on Roman social history, especially issues related to gender, sexuality, law, and social status.

GENDER, MANUMISSION, AND THE ROMAN FREEDWOMAN

Matthew J. Perry

Assistant Professor of History
John Jay College of Criminal Justice

CAMBRIDGE
UNIVERSITY PRESS

CAMBRIDGE
UNIVERSITY PRESS

University Printing House, Cambridge CB2 8BS, United Kingdom

One Liberty Plaza, 20th Floor, New York, NY 10006, USA

477 Williamstown Road, Port Melbourne, VIC 3207, Australia

314-321, 3rd Floor, Plot 3, Splendor Forum, Jasola District Centre, New Delhi - 110025, India

79 Anson Road, #06-04/06, Singapore 079906

Cambridge University Press is part of the University of Cambridge.

It furthers the University's mission by disseminating knowledge in the pursuit of education, learning and research at the highest international levels of excellence.

www.cambridge.org
Information on this title: www.cambridge.org/9781107697638

© Matthew J. Perry 2014

First published 2014
First paperback edition 2018

A catalogue record for this publication is available from the British Library

Library of Congress Cataloging in Publication data
Perry, Matthew J., 1973–
Gender, manumission, and the Roman freedwoman / Matthew J. Perry, Assistant Professor of History, John Jay College of Criminal Justice, City University of New York.
    pages   cm
Includes bibliographical references and index.
ISBN 978-1-107-04031-1 (hardback)
1. Women slaves – Rome – History.   2. Slaves – Emancipation – Rome – History.   3. Rome – Social conditions.   4. Rome – History.   I. Title.
HT863.P47   2014
306.3'62082–dc23   2013022246

ISBN 978-1-107-04031-1 Hardback
ISBN 978-1-107-69763-8 Paperback

For my family

Contents

Acknowledgments   *page* ix

   Introduction   1

1. Gender, Sexuality, and the Status of Female Slaves   8

2. Gender, Labor, and the Manumission of Female Slaves   43

3. The Patron-Freedwoman Relationship in Roman Law   69

4. The Patron-Freedwoman Relationship in Funerary
   Inscriptions   96

5. The Slavish Free Woman and the Citizen Community   129

   Conclusion   155

Appendix A. Approximate Dates for Jurists Mentioned in the Text   161
Appendix B. Inscriptions from CIL 6 Commemorating "Patrons" and
   "Husbands"   162
Appendix C. Inscriptions from CIL 6 Commemorating an Individual
   as "Patron and Husband" or "Freedwoman and Wife"   164
Notes   167
Bibliography   237
Index of Sources   255
Subject Index   265

Acknowledgments

It is a pleasure to thank the many people whose efforts and insights helped me to write this book. This project began as a Ph.D. dissertation at the University of Chicago, and my advisor, Richard Saller, always made time to discuss new ideas, suggest invaluable critiques, and provide much-appreciated encouragement and guidance. Jonathan Hall, Cam Grey, and David Wray offered comments, advice, and support in equal measure. Emily Brunner, Fanny Dolansky, and Cameron Hawkins helped me better articulate my ideas and directed me toward useful sources. More recently, Lisa Andersen and Sara McDougall read the entire manuscript and prompted me to think more broadly about slavery and gender. Moderators and fellow panelists at meetings of the American Philological Association and the Association of Ancient Historians, as well as members of the University of Chicago Ancient Societies Workshop, raised numerous questions that prompted me to refine my ideas. My editor, Beatrice Rehl, and her staff supportively guided the manuscript through production. Finally, I would like to thank the anonymous readers from Cambridge University Press. Their detailed and thoughtful comments were extremely helpful in bringing this book to its final form.

Support for this project was provided by a PSC-CUNY Award, jointly funded by the Professional Staff Congress and the City University of New York. I would also like to thank the Interlibrary Loan staff at John Jay College, whose efforts went above and beyond the call of duty.

Finally, I would like to offer my deepest thanks to all of my family and friends, whose love and support made this project possible.

Introduction

Manumission was an institution that reconciled the categories of "slave" and "citizen," which were otherwise in a dialectical relationship, as the slave defined what the citizen was not, and vice versa. Since slaves lacked personal agency, bodily integrity, official kin, and a social identity independent of their owner, they could fulfill duties and roles deemed inappropriate for citizens. This deficiency was the fundamental difference between freedpersons and individuals descended from ex-slaves. While the descendants of a freedperson may still have suffered a moderate stigma from their slavish ancestry, they had always been Roman citizens, never having experienced the degrading lifestyle of slaves – a lifestyle that defined them as not being citizens.[1]

Historians have meticulously explored the matter of how men navigated the manumission process, but freedwomen's histories – and the ideas that made these histories possible – have been relatively under-investigated. Gendered attitudes toward morality, sexual conduct, and social status complicated a woman's manumission and passage to citizenship, as lawmakers and social commentators needed to reconcile her experiences as a slave with the expectations and moral rigor required of the female citizen. In a woman's case, the primary obstacle was that the sexual identities of a female slave and a female citizen were fundamentally incompatible, as the former was principally defined by her sexual availability and the latter by her sexual integrity. A woman's sexual conduct was so critical to evaluating her standing and moral worth that it completely overshadowed and nearly subsumed all of her other virtues or positive personal qualities. This is not to say either that sexuality was not an important component in determining male social status or that female status was unaffected by any other factors. Rather, I would argue that sexuality was a singularly important factor in judging female value and standing in the classical world, especially when authors considered virtue in a more abstract sense. While sexual honor was an essential indicator of male social status, it did not subsume other masculine virtues to the same extent. Just as men's and women's citizenship had different modes, so too did the manumission process of men and women.

In seeking to gain insight into the puzzle of why women were manumitted, and, if manumitted, why they were granted citizenship, my project draws upon ancient sources grouped into three very broadly defined categories: literary texts (nonlegal writing published for public consumption), legal texts (primarily juridical opinions), and epigraphic texts (primarily funerary epitaphs). This book is principally concerned with the laws, attitudes, and experiences of Roman citizens and their slaves during the classical era (ca. 200 BCE to 235 CE). While concentrated primarily on Italy and the city of Rome, the geographical focus of the project necessarily changes with the expansion of Roman culture and citizenship. I draw upon a wide range of textual source material, and the specific type of material influences the extent to which I am able to account for change over time. For example, the discursive nature of legal sources allows for a more diachronic analysis, whereas the lack of precise dating for most funerary epitaphs, the primary type of epigraphic source considered in this project, requires a more synchronic approach.

Yet even with all this breadth in the sources' genres, there are scant documents pertaining to the experiences of female slaves, with still-fewer about how freedwomen themselves viewed their progression from slavery to citizenship. Modern historians are uncertain even as to the number of female slaves made into free citizens, or about the ratio of women to men manumitted. The problems posed by the meagerness of the source base are compounded by the elite male bias inherent to most of the surviving texts. Some individuals, by virtue of their birth, talent, wealth, or achievements, possessed greater prestige and access to power than other Romans, and these were the people whose voices dominate in preserved historical documents. I am pushing the boundaries of "elite" a little beyond its traditional association with individuals of elevated status (where status is one's recognized place in the community) in order to signify those who possessed the means to shape and influence societal beliefs and customs. All of this leaves historians to sift through the limited evidence containing an elite male bias, peppered with intriguing but mostly elusive voices from freedwomen themselves.

While it is unsatisfying not to have more evidence of freedwomen's experiences and attitudes, the available sources are still useful for gleaning something significant regarding the gendered *ideology* of manumission. This book's primary focus is an analysis of the powerful beliefs, assumptions, and desires embedded in the vast and complex institution of Roman manumission. I have sought to interpret the discourse about a woman's transition from slavery to freedom, which must have been, at least in part, shaped by reality and at the same time contributed to shaping the real life opportunities and limitations confronted by individuals.[2] It is my hope that I contribute to scholars' understanding of how slavery and manumission worked in intellectual, cultural, and legal registers, and that I do so without denying the variety of freedwomen experiences that must have existed, including those that required reinterpreting or resisting the dominant ideology, or the diverse ways in which such women viewed themselves and were viewed by others.

The figure of the freedwoman represented in the ancient sources provides an extraordinary lens into how Romans understood, debated, and experienced the sheer magnitude of the transition from slave to citizen; the various social factors that impinged upon this process; and the community stakes in the practice of manumission. By invoking images of sexualized and scandalous freedwomen, literary authors linked them to slaves, calling attention to their servile origins and their separation from respectable free citizens. This depiction is intriguingly at odds with the more respectable and relatively ordinary freedwomen appearing in legal and epigraphic sources. While representations of these women still distinguish them from freeborn citizens, they nonetheless suggest a more inclusive vision of freedwomen. When taken all together, the sources on freedwomen suggest pervasive anxieties among the Roman elite regarding their success at transforming ex-slaves into authentic citizens.

At stake in these anxieties was the concept of "citizenship" itself. In his monumental study of Roman citizenship, A. N. Sherwin-White argues that all the motives commonly used to explain Roman manumission practices were to a degree inadequate because they failed to account for the enfranchisement of ex-slaves. He maintains that these rational explanations would have applied equally well to the grant of freedom without citizenship.[3] My book analyzes citizenship not just as an aspect of the manumission process, but as its central component; the bestowal of citizenship was critical to Romans' understanding of manumission as societal institution. It was the creation of citizenship that made manumission such a significant transition, and that deeply invested a society of people not necessarily directly involved with the transaction. Rome was unique among classical polities in that it bestowed full citizenship on freed slaves, granting them rights nearly equal to those of freeborn individuals. This practice was all the more remarkable given that Romans attached substantial meaning to citizenship, routinely hesitating to bestow full citizen rights upon freeborn foreigners.[4]

This book contributes to a rising field of scholarship that examines manumission not only in terms of the motivations of individual actors, both owners and slaves, but also as an institution designed to incorporate outsiders into the citizen community. Often responding to earlier theories premised on individual goodwill or an ethical/religious stimulus, historians writing in the late twentieth century have prioritized rational aims such as masters' economic incentives, the maximization of slave labor, and the creation of large, exploitable client groups.[5] While recognizing the importance of these individual motives, some scholars have emphasized the wider social meanings of manumission, focusing on the legally mandated lifelong relationship between freedpersons and their former masters. Andrew Wallace-Hadrill pragmatically reasons that patrons were essential conduits for social and legal knowledge, which consisted largely of orally transmitted custom.[6] Jane Gardner, in turn, argues that freedpersons' ongoing relationships with their ex-masters provided a link to an established Roman *familia*, which served as a means of social control as well as integration.[7] Most recently, Henrik Mouritsen stresses the importance of the patron-freedperson relationship as both a familial and a financial institution, and highlights its critical role in the Roman economy.[8] These historians have persuasively argued that, although a particular manumission might have intensely personal meanings for the slave/freedperson and the owner/patron, these meanings existed within, and thus were informed by, the wider social implications of the institution. Roman manumission cannot be understood simply as a transaction between two individuals, but must be examined within a larger social and political context, and as a process that required and received support from the Roman people as a whole.

The process of making slaves into citizens takes on additional significance from the frequency with which manumission took place over the course of centuries. Although the precise percentage of slaves who were ever freed has been much debated by modern scholars, the ancient sources clearly suggest that manumission was routine and commonplace in the Roman world. The very simplicity of the manumission process suggests that however much Romans might have been conflicted about the process of making slaves – both male and female – into citizens, they were also deeply committed to continuing this practice. Nonetheless, the ease by which manumission was legally executed magnified, rather than diminished, the underlying complexity of its social meanings, meanings that Romans themselves explored with not only anxiety but also enthusiasm.

It is this book's focus on gender and status, and its analysis of a female manumission model, that distinguishes it from previous works. Even as it destabilized the idea of the benevolent master, modern scholarship analyzing the transition from slavery to freedom has remained overwhelmingly male-normative, in that authors have treated the male experience as the definitive version, from which others are deviations. Thus, women appear only as a series of scattered "exceptions" throughout the narrative. (In this respect, modern studies reflect the treatment of the topic by the bulk of the ancient source material.)[9] This mode of scholarship continues to advance our understanding of the experiences of slaves and freedpersons, but it does not fully account for the impact of gender on this process. In this book, I build upon this scholarship, drawing heavily upon research that has explored how gendered attitudes and understandings influenced the peculiar experiences and representations of female slaves and freedwomen.[10]

Tracing the stages in a woman's manumission journey from property to citizen, this book begins by demonstrating how gendered assumptions about the relationship between sexual conduct and social status shaped Roman authors' and lawmakers' interpretation of female slaves' standing and worth. The second chapter explores how the relationship between gender and labor impacted a woman's experiences as a slave, her chances for manumission, and her assimilation into the category of female citizens. Chapter 3 investigates the legal relationship between freedwomen and their ex-owners, analyzing how Roman lawmakers and jurists carefully structured and limited the obligations in order to protect freedwomen's ability to live as respectable citizens. Chapter 4 continues the examination of the patron-freedwoman relationship by considering epigraphic evidence and the various ways that ex-slaves represented themselves, and were represented by their patrons. In particular, it focuses on descriptions of the patron-freedwoman relationship, and the work this reference did in depicting an ex-slave as an individual worthy of citizenship. In the final chapter, I examine various representations of freedwomen as a discrete rank, distinct from and socially inferior to freeborn women, and how this status meant something different in literature and law.

The institution of manumission prompted a peculiar understanding among the Roman elite of what slavery was or could be. It urged them to draw upon the gendered dimensions of sexuality, labor, and social relations in order to reinterpret and recast the experiences from a freedwoman's slave life in ways that illuminated her deservedness of citizenship. Having freedom as its outcome encouraged elite Romans to come to understand slavery as a process that did not necessarily make a woman unredeemable. A female slave was without honor rather than dishonored. To this end, Romans used legal codes articulating a particular understanding of the patron and his or her responsibilities to institutionalize a relationship that provided a former slave with a connection to the citizen community. This connection meant perpetual obligation and exploitation for women, but also the possibility of intimacy and legitimacy. Through these mechanisms, manumission achieved widespread – though never absolute – acceptance among Romans who might have otherwise challenged its capacity to produce authentic female citizens.

Once manumitted, the freedwoman remained a subject for debate among literary authors, jurists, patrons, and freedwomen themselves, all of whom investigated the meaning of slave and freedwoman sexuality, the rights and legal protections granted to ex-slaves, and the significance of freedwomen's continuing obligations to their former masters. Ultimately, I argue, it was the idea of marriage that could best assure the integrity of a freedwoman's citizenship by ascribing to her the responsibilities and respectability of the Roman matron. By creating an absolute set of boundaries that defined a woman as respectable, marriage alone solved the perceived ambiguity in the status of a freedwoman, effectively completing her transformation from slave to citizen. Or at least so went the discourse.

I Gender, Sexuality, and the Status of Female Slaves

On the basis of the nearly unquestioned principle that sexual activity was a gendered characteristic, Roman society elevated women whose sexuality was restricted and denigrated those who usurped the masculine prerogative of promiscuity.[1] This chapter explores how assumptions about gender and status shaped the meanings of female sexual behavior in ancient Rome, and how a woman's legal status as a slave complicated the boundaries separating illicit from acceptable behavior. There was a potential tension wrought by a female slave's sexuality that was rooted in the conflict between the feminine ideal of chastity and the servile obligation to acquiesce to the carnal demands of one's master. This question about how female slaves *should* behave speaks to two critical issues in Roman social history: ideas of respectability and status among individuals who had minimal legal agency and the persistence of gendered social conventions across categories of women.

Literary authors and legal policy makers consistently and systematically excluded female slaves from the category of "Roman women," holding female slaves outside the social expectations and bodily rights of free individuals. A free woman possessed a sexual honor that needed protection, lest she and her relatives incur shame and disgrace. In contrast, female slaves were owned property and therefore lacked such honor, as was manifest in their expected performance of sexual duties and their inability to protect their own physical integrity. Their degraded status meant that sexual conduct deemed shameful for free women was not shameful for female slaves in the same way. At the same time, the routine sexual exploitation of slaves, both in real acts occurring in daily life and in images reproduced in cultural texts, reinforced and validated their debased status, acutely distinguishing these individuals from free Roman women. Essentially, there was a circular logic buttressing assumptions about slave sexuality and status in ancient Rome: female slaves experienced forms of sexual conduct unsuitable for free women because of their degraded legal status, but female slaves possessed a degraded legal status because (at least in part) they experienced degrading sexual conduct.

Although modern scholars have well noted how sexual standards, particularly a lack of sexual honor, distinguished female slaves from free women, they have left largely unexplored how these same standards determined the standing of female slaves relative to each other.[2] Sexual standards for female slaves were not rooted solely in the assumption that chastity was superior to promiscuity, but were also shaped by expectations that correlated with the women's status as owned property. A model of licit sexuality, similar to that governing free women but adjusted to allow for sexual duties expected of female slaves, shaped perceptions of the standing of slaves and their worth as individuals. Only by understanding slaves' dual natures and the expectations governing their duties is it possible to comprehend the relationship between their sexual conduct and their perceived economic and moral worth.

HONOR-SHAME AND THE DEGRADATION OF FEMALE SLAVES

The principles of honor and shame provide an invaluable model for evaluating the social meanings of particular types of behavior by formalizing an assumed relationship between sexuality, gender identity, and social standing in the Roman world. Several modern scholars have asserted the usefulness of the honor-shame model (sometimes referred to as the honor-shame syndrome) for understanding the relationship between sexual conduct and social standing in the Greco-Roman world.[3] In its most basic sense, honor is an individual's estimation of his or her self-worth, and the larger society's recognition of that worth.[4] Individuals accumulated and maintained honor, which contributed to their prestige and status, by satisfying various cultural principles and societal requirements. Failing to meet prescribed standards or transgressing certain social norms could lead to shame – both an internal sense of failure and a public devaluation of worth – which could cause a decrease in honor, and thus a decrease in social standing.[5]

Honor and shame are not purely personal qualities in this model; an individual's honor is determined not only by his or her own behavior, but also by the conduct of close affiliates: spouse, children, kin, and even slaves. And an individual's behavior also affected the honor and shame of family and kin in turn. This interconnectedness, effectively localized these qualities in the household. Accordingly, a man's honor depended in good part on his ability to protect the integrity and reputation of his female family members.[6]

Although there has been substantial criticism of the honor-shame model, most of the critiques hinge on modern scholars' understanding and application of the model rather than the validity of the constitutive concepts themselves. Criticism of the model in general has largely focused on two issues: (1) the reification (or potential reification) of the Mediterranean as a socially homogeneous region and (2) the gendered association of honor with men and shame with women. In the first case, critics have noted that many scholarly proponents of the model treat it as a product – and often as a unifying product – of a shared Mediterranean culture. They argue that, in doing so, proponents do not take enough account of the diverse beliefs and practices of different Mediterranean communities and effectively misinterpret evidence as they attempt to fit beliefs and practices to a "universal"paradigm.[7] This mode of criticism has led to reservations about whether the honor-shame model, which was originally developed from anthropological studies of rural agrarian communities, is applicable to more urbanized societies (including ancient Rome).[8] The second point of criticism has called attention to proponents' assignation, either intentional or unintentional, of honor as a masculine virtue/trait and shame as feminine, which, critics argue, effectively masks and/or discredits female agency.[9] While these critiques all have significant merit, they have more to do with precisely how modern scholars wield the concepts of honor and shame rather than the validity of the fundamental principles of the model itself. Accordingly, I believe that the basic structure of the honor-shame model – namely, the existence of the interrelated (and perhaps analogous) concepts of honor and shame, and the interconnectedness of the honor and shame of family members – remains a compelling and useful tool for analyzing Roman society.[10]

Elite male Romans, whose ideals and beliefs are best attested in the surviving sources, defined feminine honor primarily in terms of a woman's sexual behavior.[11] There was an expectation that a respectable woman would refrain from any sexual conduct outside marriage; young girls were to remain chaste until they wed, and wives were to have no sexual partners other than their husbands.[12] Perhaps the best evidence for the significance of sexuality in the formulation of feminine honor is the fact that the standard injuries to women mentioned in Roman law were infringements on their sexual integrity and/or repute.[13] Yet, as critics of the honor-shame model have emphasized, there are numerous cases where social reality did not fully correspond with the expressed ideals. Two common examples are the lack of application or enforcement of the idealized social norms and the possession of divergent conceptions of honor and shame by a particular segment of the population (such as women or nonelite men).[14] Again, these criticisms are valid, but rather than disproving the existence of a Roman honor-shame model, they highlight the importance of understanding the boundaries of subjectivity and practice when applying this model in studies of Roman society. Accepting that the ideals of feminine sexual conduct and honor espoused by the Roman elite were not always enforced and were not necessarily embraced by all segments of the population does not eliminate their influence over (nor their historical insight into) attitudes and practices, especially those concerning manumission.

Literary authors and legal analysts drew heavily upon the concepts of *pudicitia*, *stuprum*, and *pudor* to explain the sexual integrity and honor of Roman women. The concept of *pudicitia* (often translated into English as "chastity") contained the ideas of sexual inviolability and virtue, both in action and in appearance.[15] Not only were Roman women required to maintain chaste standards of sexual conduct, but they were also expected to display their *pudicitia* through their nonsexual behavior.[16] Reputable women were to wear proper garments and travel with a female slave attendant in public, preferably one unattractive enough not to attract inappropriate attention from male bystanders.[17] In response to any violation of one's *pudicitia*, a respectable Roman woman suffered *pudor* (generally translated as "shame") – a sense that one's personal worth, and possibly even one's esteem in the eyes of the wider community, has diminished.[18]

In primary opposition to *pudicitia* was *stuprum*, a physical act that violated a woman's sexual integrity.[19] Although in general usage *stuprum* could refer to any type of illicit sexual conduct, it predominantly functioned as a legal term that denoted the sexual penetration of any Roman citizen, male or female.[20] While *stuprum* was originally a matter for the *pater familias*, offenders eventually became liable to penalties under Roman law, most likely through the notoriously ill-attested *lex Scantinia* in the mid-second century BCE.[21] The *lex Iulia de adulteriis coercendis* (c. 18 BCE) is the first definitive evidence of the criminalization of *stuprum* (or at least certain forms of *stuprum*, most notably adultery). As a key element in Augustus's social reform program, the creation of this law highlighted the sexual integrity of female citizens as a public concern.[22] In addition to sexual acts classified as *stuprum*, individuals could damage a woman's honor by public offenses, such as following her, shouting at her, or seducing/harassing her accompanying attendants.[23] It is clear that a woman could suffer shame and dishonor not only from physical violation or assault, but also from any display or conduct that questioned or besmirched her public façade of respectability.

Women could suffer shame and dishonor from conduct or events even if they were unwilling victims. The semimythical story of Lucretia vividly illustrates this point. Ostensibly taking place at the end of the monarchical period, the tale became a critical text for Augustan authors to convey contemporary ideals regarding feminine morality and civic virtue.[24] As the narrative goes, Lucretia refuses to submit to the sexual demands of Sextus Tarquinius when the prince menaces her with his sword; she only acquiesces after he threatens to fabricate evidence of an adulterous affair between her and a slave. Her husband and other male associates declare her innocence by pointing out her lack of intent, but Lucretia ultimately kills herself, according to Livy, as "punishment" (*supplicium*) for her *impudicitia* (1.58.10).[25] In this version of the story, Lucretia not only is aware that Tarquinius devalued her social worth through his sexual assault, but also sees herself as complicit in the offense, even though she and her relatives (and her readers) unequivocally know that she was an unwilling participant.[26] Both Roman law and social convention differentiated between voluntary and involuntary offenses, and in cases where a woman was assaulted or insulted, neither legal nor popular opinion sought to divorce the injuring party from blame and repercussions.[27] Yet victims like Lucretia still suffered a measure of shame – albeit mitigated by their lack of intent – that could trump their lack of culpability. Roman women had the right and the responsibility to protect their own sexual integrity, and suffered shame and dishonor if they failed to adhere to the chaste standards of reputable conduct.[28]

In stark contrast to the ideal of the chaste Roman woman, female slaves were overtly sexualized in textual sources. Generally speaking, Romans expected female slaves to be sexually active and by and large accepted such conduct as a positive and beneficial social practice. Living within a world that prized a woman's chastity, female slaves provided a socially appropriate outlet for male sexual energy. Literary authors closely associated female slaves as a group with sexual conduct, representing these women as accessible and readily available partners for men. Moreover, writers characterized sexual affairs with female slaves as being routine and rather banal, suggesting the perceived commonness of such encounters. Martial expressed this sentiment when he humorously ranked both free women and freedwomen as more desirable partners:

> Ingenuam malo, sed si tamen illa negetur,
> libertina mihi proxuma condicio est:
> extremo est ancilla loco: sed vincet utramque,
> si facie nobis haec erit ingenua.

> I prefer a freeborn woman, but if that should be denied, a freedwoman is
>   the next option for me:
> a female slave is in the last spot: but if one surmounts the others in
>   appearance, she will be freeborn to me (3.33).[29]

While the punch line of the epigram is that appearance ultimately takes precedence over legal status, the author still reinforced a hierarchy of sexual value, especially by the repeated use of *ingenua* in the last line as a metonym for the top rank in his appraisal.

A similar devaluation of slave sexuality appears in a declamation attributed to Quintilian that discusses the case of a rich dinner guest who raped his host's daughter. The host conceded that he identified his daughter as a slave (*ancilla*) to his guest, but maintained: "Nevertheless

I am not persuaded that he believed me. For an *ancilla* would not have been able to excite his opulent desires (*delicatas cupidines*) ... he raped her as if a free woman" (*Dec. Min.* 301.7).[30] The implication of such an accusation was that a man of lavish and luxurious tastes would not have been excited at the prospect of having sex with a slave because such an act was common – both frequent and low; whereas a sexual affair with a free woman represented something unique and exhilarating.

Other authors identified the commonness of slave sexuality as a benefit because of the ease and simplicity of such affairs. Horace satirically chastised those men who disdained the sexual company of slaves in favor of higher-status partners.

> Num, tibi cum faucis urit sitis, aurea quaeris
> pocula? Num esuriens fastidis omnia praeter
> pavonem rhombumque? Tument tibi cum inguina, num, si
> ancilla aut verna est praesto puer, impetus in quem
> continuo fiat, malis tentigine rumpi?
> Non ego: namque parabilem amo Venerem facilemque.

> When thirst burns your throat, surely you do not ask for golden cups? When hungry, surely you do not disdain everything except peacock and turbot? When your loins swell, surely you do not prefer to be burst apart by your erection, if a home-born slave girl or boy – someone whom you could take right then and there – is present? Not I: for I love sex that is easily attainable (*Sat.* 1.2.114–119).

The poet's use of rarities such as gold and food delicacies as counterexamples emphasized the everyday aspect of slave sexuality. He recognized that the commonness of slaves made them less desirable partners, but proclaimed that their accessibility ultimately made them advantageous tools for satisfying a man's regular sexual desires. The poet Rufinus also advocated the selection of female slaves as sexual partners rather than more highborn women – including one's wife – because slaves were more accessible and less complicated as a result of their lack of pretension (*AP* 5.18). For Horace and Rufinus, the banality of slave sexual partners made them desirable, as such liaisons were readily attainable and straightforward, especially in comparison to relationships with free women.

Some literature emphasized the baseness rather than the ease of sexual affairs with female slaves, implicitly classifying these women as disreputable and low. When Ovid defended himself from the charge of having an affair with his girlfriend's slave, he assured Corinna, "What free man would enter into a love affair with a female slave and embrace a back cut by the whip?" For any man who fell in love with a slave "lacked a good mind" (*Am.* 2.7.21-22, 2.8.9-10).[31] Emphasizing his own position as a free man, Ovid disparaged the slave as a potential partner, who was made less desirable because she possessed a degraded legal and social status, symbolized by her subjection to the whip. Commenting on the general degeneracy of Roman society, Seneca complained that if a man refrained from having a mistress or an affair with another's wife, then the matrons would label him as "a low sort of man, one possessing a sordid lust, and as a lover of female slaves" (*hunc matronae humilem et sordidae libidinis et ancillariolum vocant, Ben.* 1.9.3-4). The matrons in this example distinguished sexual affairs with slaves from those with free women, describing the former with negative terms such as *humilis, sordidus,* and *ancillariolus.*[32] Plutarch, on the other hand, turned the perceived baseness of female slave sexuality into an advantage, arguing that affairs with slaves protected wives from their husbands' more sordid appetites. He maintained that a wife should view her husband's sexual liaisons with female slaves as respectful gestures, intended to protect her from his drunken debauchery (*paroinia*), licentiousness (*akolasia*), and aggressive/violent advances (*hubris, Mor.* 140B). These authors characterized sexual activity with female slaves as low and debased and, by association, reinforced the degraded status of these unfree individuals.

Even poetic defenses of love affairs with female slaves admit the presence of a perceived stigma of sordidness and commonness associated with these relationships. Writers sometimes attempted to elevate the reputation of female slaves by suggesting the existence of something unique or extraordinary about these common individuals. One approach was to call attention to the exceptional men who chose unfree women as their paramours. In the poem immediately following Ovid's dismissal of slave sexual partners, the reader learns that the author was indeed having an affair with his girlfriend's slave. In response to his own attack, Ovid cited the examples of Achilles and Agamemnon, both of whom loved female slaves. He admits: "I am neither greater than

Agamemnon nor greater than Achilles; why should I think it base (*turpe*) for me, that which was fitting for kings?" (*Am.* 2.8.11–14). Similarly, Horace advised his friend Xanthias not to be ashamed of his love for a female slave (*ne sit ancillae tibi amor pudori*), listing several Greek heroes – Achilles, Ajax, and Agamemnon – who all had relationships with unfree women (*Carm.* 2.4).[33] Horace further praised the character and possible illustrious parentage of Xanthias's lover, suggesting that she may not have been as common as her legal status signified. By associating female slaves with ancient heroes and raising questions about the likelihood of their extraordinary prebondage social status, Ovid and Horace attempted to mitigate the stigma of commonness attached to unfree women due, at least in part, to their sexual availability.

Roman writers also sexualized female slaves when portraying them as integral figures in facilitating their mistresses' illicit love affairs. By acting as confidants and messengers for their owners, female slaves often functioned as the voice of encouragement, pushing their mistresses past their initial hesitation. A clear example appears in a story mentioned in the *Satyrica* of Petronius, where a female slave encourages her widowed mistress to accept the romantic overtures of a soldier. After the widow rebuffs him, the soldier gains the support of her female slave, who then vigorously attempts to overcome the woman's initial reservations.[34] In literary accounts, an *ancilla* often serves as the primary instrument of communication between her mistress and her mistress's lover.[35] Even though these women generally appeared more as passive instruments than as active instigators, their essential role in facilitating these illicit affairs effectively linked the slaves to the scandalous behavior. Writers represented, and effectively classified, female slaves as having mores distinct from those dictating the lifestyles of respectable, free women.

Sexual images and situations dominated representations of female slaves in literature, reinforcing the notion that female slaves, as a category of people, were sexually available and thus of a lower status than free women. In comparison to the respectable Roman woman, whose honor and social standing depended on her chastity outside marriage, female slaves were portrayed as common sexual partners who could be obtained with little effort. Moreover, this representation did not apply only to certain individuals; literary authors habitually depicted the entire rank as potential sexual partners and thus effectively sexualized *all* female slaves regardless of their actual conduct. Indeed, this is a major difference between representations of female and male slave sexuality in Roman literature. Whereas authors portrayed individual young male slaves (*pueri*) as objects of desire much in the same way as they represented individual female slaves, they did not tend to sexualize male slaves as a group. An important contributing factor was the perceived distinction between young boys and adult slaves; in most accounts, as *pueri* grew older they ceased to be objects of desire.[36] Moreover, there was little of the rhetoric stressing the ordinariness of sexual affairs with slave *pueri*, suggesting a banality wrought by accessibility – and thus their distinction from their free counterparts. Even though elite authors eroticized both male and female slaves, sex was explicitly and inextricability linked to the general role of "female slave" in a way that it was not to "male slave."

The sources suggest that the sexual conduct associated with their status rendered female slaves low and disreputable figures with ways of life at odds with those of respectable Roman women. The logical cause and effect relationship between these two concepts was circular; female slaves possessed a degraded status in part because they were sexually accessible individuals, yet it was their low status that made them sexually available. But to understand fully how sexuality affected the perception and standing of female slaves in the context of the honor-shame framework, it is necessary to consider the ambiguous status of slaves, which stemmed from their simultaneous classification as both humans and objects, as both females and entities without gender. Ultimately, the position of female slaves in Roman society in comparison to either freeborn women or male slaves cannot be fully realized without an examination of how slaves' status as property complicated their gendered experience as human beings.

Romans recognized that slaves were biologically identical to free citizens and so never completely denied their basic humanity. Moreover, philosophers and jurists expressed little support for theories of natural slavery and generally considered individual slaves to be capable of the same levels of intellectual and moral thought as free persons, a belief confirmed by the Romans' long-standing practice of incorporating ex-slaves into the citizen community.[37] Slaves undeniably possessed biological sex, which was an essential aspect of their identity that shaped their experiences. The significance of biological sex is perhaps best illustrated by the jurist Julian's attempt to clarify the potential ambiguity caused by Latin grammar:

Qui duos mulos habebat ita legavit: "mulos duos, qui mei erunt cum moriar, heres dato": idem nullos mulos, sed duas mulas reliquerat. Respondit Servius deberi legatum, quia mulorum appellatione etiam mulae continentur, quemadmodum appellatione servorum etiam servae plerumque continentur. Id autem eo veniet, quod semper sexus masculinus etiam femininum sexum continet.

A man who had two mules left a legacy as follows: "Let my heir give two *muli* (male mules) which shall be mine when I die." He left no male mules but two *mulae* (female mules). Servius replied that the legacy was owed, "since *mulae* are included under the term *muli*, in the same way that *servae* (female slaves) are largely included under the term *servi* (male slaves). This comes from the fact that the masculine gender always includes the feminine" (*Dig.* 32.62).

While this opinion reveals the potential for the masculine-normative title *servi* to obscure an individual slave's gender, it also indicates that jurists understood there to have been some important differences between male and female slaves. Here, Servius's qualification about female slaves being "largely" (*plerumque*) included under the term *servi* is significant. Whereas the title *muli* always included female mules, the title *servi* included female slaves only "most of the time." This suggests that the perceived distinction between female and male slaves was greater than that between female and male mules; gender was a more important category for classifying humans than animals.

Surely jurists recognized that such differentiation was essential simply for legal precision and breadth. Since there were both male and female slaves, the law needed to be able to refer clearly to each. Perhaps more importantly, Roman law also reflected popular opinion, which made a real and practical distinction between male and female slaves. Ulpian wrote that if a buyer purchased a female slave thinking that she was male, then the sale was void. Such an error did not have to result from deceit or misinformation; the simple fact that a mistake had been made was enough to nullify the sale (*Dig.* 18.1.11.1).[38]

The different expectations and assumptions influencing the realities of male and female slaves indicated the significant role of gender in shaping slave identity. Roman authors attributed distinct characteristics to male and female slaves, in some cases deriving their beliefs about female slaves from "biological" assumptions about the female sex in general. The best evidence that Roman assumptions about gender shaped the experiences of slaves is in the division of labor in large households. The preferred duties of female slaves resembled the occupations of their free counterparts: indoor domestic tasks, catering and service jobs, and small-scale manufacturing work, especially in textiles.[39] It is clear that both Roman law and popular opinion considered biological sex to be an essential characteristic in defining the nature, the identity, and ultimately the value of slaves.

Such thinking did not preclude lawmakers' classification of slave women as objects who existed to serve and benefit their owners.[40] As property, slaves could be bought, sold, cherished, abused, or destroyed depending on the whims of their owners. In response to, and in support of, this objectification, Roman custom and law systematically dehumanized female slaves by denying them the rights and privileges that defined free women.[41] Slaves lacked a social identity; by law they possessed no kin, no family name, and no place in the community outside the service to their masters.[42] Their degraded status was characterized by their lack of control over their own bodies, suffering physical punishments (especially whippings), torture when giving court evidence, and sexual assault. Slaves not only were social inferiors to free women but were governed by a unique set of laws and societal expectations.

An individual's slave status also had the potential to render gender a less significant category since unfreedom was arguably the most important aspect of slave identity, as constructed by Roman authors and lawmakers. When determining an individual's place in Roman society, the distinction between slave and free was more significant than the distinction between man and woman.[43] The ritual of the Compitalia festival provides an unambiguous example of the obfuscation of slave gender. Hoping to distract hostile Lares by hanging tokens at nearby crossroads, Roman households represented free male members of the *domus* with male dolls, free female members with female dolls, and all slaves with wooden balls, neither gendered nor even anthropomorphic.[44] In this ritual, the sex of a slave was irrelevant compared to the sex of the free members of the household; slaves, both male and female, were defined solely by their unfree status.

Existing in a state of slavery had the potential to obscure a woman's gender, in part because Roman law denied female slaves access to the rights that defined a Roman woman's legal status and her position in the community, most notably the ability to exercise power and control over her own sexual integrity. Because enslaved women had no claim to physical integrity, they had no agency to assure that their behavior resembled the standard of conduct expected of other Roman women. By denying slaves the sexual roles and personal rights that defined free female citizens, Romans not only marked slaves as denigrated and devalued human beings, but also effectively removed them from the category of "women."

Most importantly, the legal status of female slaves placed them outside the honor-shame model that regulated the experiences of Roman women. For the elite male Romans articulating the terms of these principles, female slaves were not included for two related reasons: They were *supposed* to be fulfilling the "dishonorable" or "shameful" sexual duties, and they lacked any recognized self-control and self-interest in their situation. By virtue of the low status associated with slavery, sexual conduct deemed shameful or inappropriate for a respectable woman was acceptable for a female slave. Whereas a free woman might have been dishonored by a sexual encounter because it caused insult or injury to her reputation, a female slave was not shamed (from the perspective of elite men) largely because she was fulfilling an expected duty.[45]

Furthermore, Roman lawmakers and literary authors used the concepts of *pudicitia* and *stuprum* to demarcate the line between slave and free.[46] *Pudicitia* was an attribute of the free woman, and, accordingly, a female slave could not suffer *stuprum* under Roman law.[47] In popular usage, *stuprum* often described the sexual experiences characteristic of a female slave in comparison to the respectable conduct of a free woman. For example, Livy wrote that Verginius feared to see his daughter "seized for *stuprum* like a female slave" (*velut servam ad stuprum rapi*, 3.50.6). As a female slave had no claim to her bodily integrity, and thus lacked the ability – and the right – to protect it, she possessed no recognized self-interest in her status. Roman lawmakers and literary authors did not view slaves as possessing personal honor and self-worth (*dignitas, existimatio*), and so they did not see them as experiencing shame (*verecundia, pudor*).[48] Since there was no expectation that female slaves *should* or even *could* remain chaste, they did not fit into the model of honor and shame governing free women.

The etiological tale of the *ancillarum feriae* calls attention to female slaves' lack of sexual honor in comparison to the expectations governing the lives of free Roman women. According to tradition, in the fourth century BCE, a powerful Latin army advanced on the city of Rome.[49] Weakened by its recent struggle against the Gauls, Rome was unable to challenge the invading soldiers. Recognizing their military advantage, the Latins demanded to receive freeborn Roman maidens for the purpose of marriage, ostensibly to solidify the relationship between the two peoples. The Roman magistrates hesitated to acquiesce, fearing that the Latins planned to use the women as hostages against the city. A female slave named Philotis (or Tutola) suggested a possible solution: she and her fellow slaves would dress in the garments of respectable women and go to the Latin camp in the place of the freeborn girls. That evening, after the invaders fell asleep, the women gathered up the weapons of the invading soldiers and then signaled the Roman army to attack. To commemorate the resounding victory that ensued, the Romans established a festival dedicated to female slaves (*ancillarum feriae*). In this annual celebration, which continued through the classical era, the city's female slaves would run about the city, making playful jokes toward the free people they encountered, and then hold a large mock-battle followed by a feast. All of this was done to honor the special and unique role that the female slaves had played in defeating the Latins.

The doubtful historical accuracy of the tale of how slave women tricked the Latins is far less important than the fact that this story demonstrates the existence of widely shared cultural assumptions about free and enslaved sexual conduct, status, and respectability. The Romans' stratagem only makes sense if one assumes that sending the female slaves to the invading Latins accomplished something that sending free women could not. The city magistrates could not send the free women because such an act would endanger their sexual honor. Even if they were not compelled to consummate their new "marriages," the shame of being possessed by the soldiers – and the possibility of violation – would have dishonored those women who were defined by their chastity.[50] Whereas female slaves would suffer no such ignominy, as they were governed by different expectations and rules of conduct, most notably their inability to avoid physical or sexual abuse.[51] By sending female slaves, who were not expected to remain sexually inviolate, the Romans were able to gain victory over their superior foe and preserve the public *dignitas*.[52] Finally, it is also noteworthy that this story depicts freeborn and slave women as indistinguishable from one another (at least to the eyes of the foreign invaders) outside their clothing – and the status/honor particular garments represented.

The sexualization of female slaves distinguished these women from free individuals, but at the same time subjected them to gendered views on sexual comportment and social standing. Even though the concepts of honor and shame were incompatible with slavery, female slaves were still degraded by their close association with conduct deemed dishonorable and shameful for free women. Consider the famous quote by Trimalchio, who, after describing how he ingratiated himself with his owner through sex, proudly remarks, "That which the master orders is not shameful" (*nec turpe est quod dominus iubet*, Petron. *Sat.* 75.11). As is usual, Trimalchio is technically correct but laughably misses important nuance; servile duties may have been without shame, but they were not without degradation. As women, female slaves could not avoid comparisons with gendered honor-shame expectations. While Romans held slaves to different standards of behavior than respectable free women, they nonetheless constructed these standards from within a framework of gendered assumptions about the relationship between biological sex, sexual conduct, and social status. The sexuality of female slaves marked them as low and degraded figures in comparison to free women. But an examination of legal sources indicates a much more nuanced interpretation of slave sexuality that relied heavily on the gendered assumptions about sexuality and social standing built into the honor-shame model.

THE SEXUAL INTEGRITY OF FEMALE SLAVES IN ROMAN LAW

Although Romans located female slaves outside the honor-shame system that defined the lifestyle of free women, their assumptions about proper and improper feminine sexual conduct affected their perceptions and valuations of slave women. Nowhere more than in legal sources where jurists evaluated the status and worth of female slaves is this subjection to the gendered principles of bodily integrity and sexual behavior more apparent. While Roman lawmakers and jurists confirmed the degraded status and lack of personal honor of female slaves, they also recognized that the sexual experiences of these women contributed to their relative standing and value.

Lawmakers and jurists considered transgressions of an obscene or sexual nature committed against female slaves to be less serious than those committed against free women. The status of the victim was an important variable in Roman law for determining the severity of individual offenses, especially in cases of insult or injury to a person's reputation.[53] When considering the issue of sexual misconduct, the jurist Paul wrote: "Clearly *stuprum* with female slaves is considered less injurious, unless they become worse or through them it affects their mistress" (*PS* 2.26.16).[54] Similarly, if a man verbally accosted women dressed as slaves, Ulpian considered his affront to have been less severe than if the women were wearing the dress of respectable women (*Dig.* 47.10.15.15).[55] Offenses against female slaves, who were the lowest-status women in the Roman world, were lesser transgressions, which reinforced not only slaves' degraded station, but also their sexual accessibility.

Even more significant is that fact that, in certain cases, Roman law treated sexual offenses with or against female slaves as fundamentally different types of legal transgressions than those involving free women. Papinian noted that the *lex Iulia de adulteriis coercendis*, a landmark piece of legislation that asserted illicit sex to be a public concern, did not in fact apply to sexual affairs with slaves.[56]

Inter liberas tantum personas adulterium stuprumve passas lex Iulia locum habet. Quod autem ad servas pertinet, et legis Aquiliae actio facile tenebit et iniuriarum quoque competit nec erit deneganda praetoria quoque actio de servo corrupto: nec propter plures actiones parcendum erit in huiusmodi crimine reo.

The *lex Iulia* is applicable only to free women having experienced adultery or *stuprum*. But as far as female slaves are concerned, an action under the *lex Aquilia* will readily apply and an action for insult is also applicable, nor must the praetorian action for the corruption of a slave be refused; nor ought someone accused of an offense of this kind be spared on account of the various actions available (*Dig.* 48.5.6.pr).

By excluding sexual relations with slaves from the coverage of the *lex Iulia*, Roman lawmakers were not condoning such behavior; on the basis of his interpretation of the law, Papinian understood illicit sex with a slave to have been a different *type* of offense than extramarital sex with a respectable, free woman. While the offenses themselves were similar in form, the legal significance of these acts was fundamentally different because of the slave's status as owned property. As a result, the civil actions available addressed the financial injury done to slave owners and the insult done to their honor. Papinian mentioned three possible legal responses to an illicit sexual affair with a female slave: an *actio legis Aquiliae*, an *actio iniuriarum*, and an *actio servi corrupti*. All of these charges were related, but each emphasized a slightly different aspect of the possible damage done to the female slave and her owner.

Roman lawmakers ruled that an illicit sexual affair could lessen the value of a female slave by causing physical and moral injury. The former was treated under the *lex Aquilia*, which was the standard law addressing damage done to the property of another individual.[57] Per the requirements of the law, the illicit affair must have caused physical damage that resulted in measurable loss in order to warrant an *actio legis Aquiliae*.[58] This legal action would have been especially relevant in cases of rape or sexual assault, where an assailant employed coercive force and caused bodily harm to a female slave. However, the fact that Roman jurists did not limit the action to such cases suggests that they could consider sexual intercourse itself, whether consensual or coercive, to be physical damage and therefore a cause of tangible loss to the owner.[59]

The *actio servi corrupti* provides additional insight into how Roman jurists understood the relationship between a female slave's sexuality and her character. Broadly defined by the praetor's edict as behavior that made a slave worse (*deterior*), *servi corruptio* covered a wide range of misconduct.[60] Jurists conceived of corruption as character damage that either led to direct injury of the slave's owner or affected the value of the slave as an economic instrument.[61] By categorizing sexual encounters as a means by which individuals could corrupt a slave, jurists institutionalized the assumption that a female slave who had sex could be made less useful to her owner by the affair.[62] Indeed, multiple jurists agreed with Papinian that illicit sexual acts committed with a female slave could constitute corruption.[63] Similarly, someone who seduced (*flagitare*) the slave of another, or persuaded a slave "to become a lover" (*amator existere*) would be liable under an *actio servi corrupti*.[64]

There was a clear moral component to these corrupting offenses; the law was not concerned simply with slaves acting without their owner's knowledge, but also acting in an immoral manner.[65] It made no difference whether the slave was initially "good" or "bad"; Ulpian ruled that an individual's actions could make bad slaves even worse by "lending approval" (*laudando*) to their misconduct (*Dig.* 11.3.1.4). With the *actio servi corrupti*, Roman lawmakers concerned themselves with the damage done to a slave's character resulting from such moral corruption, and the slave's ensuing lack of usefulness to her owner. Jurists believed that a female slave who had sex, even if she did not initiate the affair, could sometimes be made worse, and thus less valuable, by the encounter.

Roman jurists maintained that infringing on the sexual integrity of a female slave could also damage her owner's honor, but did not recognize any legal insult to the slave herself. Conduct that injured a person's body or repute could be redressed by means of an *actio iniuriarum*, a legal action in response to insult. Originally conceived as a legal response to physical assault, *iniuria* came to encompass damage to an individual's personal rights or reputation.[66] As Romans believed that conduct insulted not only the recipient of the injurious behavior, but also those who possessed legal authority over the victim, attacks upon slaves could cause injury to their owners.[67] Jurists maintained that sexual acts with a female slave, or even seductive speech, could constitute a delictal insult.

Si quis tam feminam quam masculum, sive ingenuos sive libertinos, impudicos facere adtemptavit, iniuriarum tenebitur. Sed et si servi pudicitia adtemptata sit, iniuriarum locum habet.

If a person attempts to make another unchaste, whether female or male, freeborn or freed, he will be liable for insult. And even if a person should make an attempt upon the *pudicitia* of a slave, he is liable for insult (*Dig.* 47.10.9.4, Ulpian).

Adtemptari pudicitia dicitur, cum id agitur, ut ex pudico impudicus fiat.

A person is said to have made an attempt upon *pudicitia* when something is done so that a chaste person becomes unchaste (*Dig.* 47.10.10, Paul).

Si stuprum serva passa sit, iniuriarum actio dabitur....

If a female slave experienced *stuprum*, an *actio iniuriarum* will be given ... (*Dig.* 47.10.25, Ulpian).

Furthermore, an individual who "verbally accosted" (*appellare*) – later defined as "assailing the *pudicitia* of another by means of seductive speech" (*blanda oratione alterius pudicitiam adtemptare*) – a woman dressed as a slave would also be liable to the *actio iniuriarum*.[68] Having neither legal identity nor any official honor to offend, slaves were incapable of initiating such an action and thus appear as targeted objects in the legal sources – persons who directly experienced the deleterious behavior. In every respect, insult to the slave owner was the primary concern of lawmakers and jurists.

On a basic level, *iniuria* to a slave caused insult to her owner since the injurious act interfered with an individual's control over his possessions. Sexual offenses could further cause direct injury to a slave owner's reputation as the guardian of his household. The *domus* was a focus of honor for Romans; the honor of the *pater familias* depended on his ability to protect his household and the virtue of its inhabitants.[69] In the *pro Caelio*, Cicero declared that one of the restrictions to the sexual license granted to young men was not to invade (*incurrere*) the *domus* and the *familia* of another (42). It is possible to argue that the sexual integrity of female slaves, as members of the household, was also a matter of concern for their owners.[70] An illicit affair with a female slave had the potential to damage the *pater familias's* reputation as the guardian of the household, and thus could warrant a charge of *iniuria*.

The existence of the *actio legis Aquiliae*, the *actio servi corrupti*, and the *actio iniuriarum* confirms that lawmakers and jurists were concerned fundamentally about owners' interest in the sexual integrity of their female slaves rather than the actual affronts suffered by the women themselves.[71] Furthermore, jurists did not explicitly distinguish between cases of rape and consensual sex in the opinions concerning the damage wrought by an individual having illicit sex with a female slave. Such an omission suggests that the woman's intent was not a critical factor in classifying these sexual offenses. However, given the importance of context in determining the exact meaning and extent of injurious behavior, this issue would most likely have factored heavily into individual cases.

Elite Romans expected female slaves to have sex and evaluated the meaning of these acts within a framework of gendered assumptions about sexual conduct. Laws and opinions attributed less value to slaves who were involved in or subject to illicit sexual affairs. Jurists maintained that sexual intercourse might harm a female slave physically and also damage her character. They believed that illicit sexual activity lowered the worth of the slave and effectively made her a worse individual morally, just as would have been the case when considering the status of free women relative to one another.

For all of these legal actions, jurists did not explicitly specify the behaviors that constituted sexual offenses toward slaves, and instead relied on the issue of owners' consent to determine whether or not an offense had occurred. For free women, Roman lawmakers used marriage as the primary means to classify sexual conduct as either appropriate or illicit. Social norms required respectable women to remain chaste outside marriage and thus categorized all forms of extramarital sex as unseemly and possibly illegal. On the other hand, literary authors and legal analysts envisioned female slaves as sexually accessible individuals and expected them to fill the gaps created by the boundaries assigned to respectable free women. And yet, every female slave was not available as a sexual partner to every free Roman male; owners had discretion over the use of their female slaves.[72] Since sexual accessibility relied on an owner's consent, "illicit" sex for a female slave amounted to any affair that was unsanctioned. This is confirmed in the legal evidence, where jurists classified sexual offenses with slaves as the misuse or damage of property. But while the law considered illicit sex in terms of an owner's consent, jurists did not define transgressions using this type of language. Instead, they imagined and described sexual offenses involving female slaves using similar language to that with which they described sexual misconduct involving free women.

The similarity of the terminology used by jurists and lawmakers to define sexual offenses involving female slaves and free women suggests that they considered these transgressions as structurally comparable affronts, despite the differences in legal meaning. As discussed previously, Papinian noted that the *lex Iulia de adulteriis coercendis* did not apply to female slaves, as they could suffer neither adultery (*adulterium*) nor *stuprum*; these crimes involved only free women.[73] However, jurists still explained sexual offenses involving female slaves using the term *stuprum*, despite the lack of legal precision.[74] Papinian, who explicitly included only free women under the crimes of *stuprum* and adultery, implicitly connected female slaves to these crimes; the structure of the opinion suggests that the jurist was envisioning a single type of sexual misdeed and was explaining how the law differed depending on the legal status of the partner. Paul linked the actions of female slaves and free women by amending the language of a preexisting opinion so that the phrases used to describe offenses against free women and slaves were exactly the same.[75] Even a decree forbidding slaves to accuse their *contubernales* of adultery suggests the recognition of behavior akin to adultery in slaves.[76] Similarly, Ulpian described an offense as "making an attempt on the *pudicitia* of a female slave" (*pudicitia adtemptata*, *Dig.* 47.10.9.4) and mentioned owners forcing their slaves into "*impudicitia*" (*Dig.* 1.6.2.pr).[77] Although Roman law treated sexual offenses involving free women and those involving female slaves as subject to different laws – and thus different types of legal issues – jurists were still envisioning similar types of objectionable behavior. Their retention of the language of *pudicitia* and *stuprum* to describe sexual offenses involving female slaves promoted a vision of slave sexuality that resonated with the values of the honor-shame model.

In considering the value of a slave's sexuality to her master, lawmakers and jurists indicated that a female slave's distance from any form of illicit sexual conduct increased her reputation and standing. Roman law indicated that engaging in sexual activity without the consent of her owner consistently devalued a female slave in a way that engaging in sexual affairs with her owner's consent did not. For slave women as well as free women, a diverse range of sexual actions carried associations that could undermine a woman's perceived worth to greater and lesser degrees. Such a belief not only recognized the presence of *pudicitia* in slaves, but also assigned it positive value; Roman law placed more value on a *pudica ancilla* than on an *impudica* one. While the sexual expectations and lack of bodily integrity built into Roman slavery changed the strict meaning of *pudicitia* for female slaves, it is clear that jurists drew upon gendered ideas of sexual conduct that were prevalent in free society.

FEMALE SLAVES AND PROSTITUTION

The best example of how the sexual experiences of a female slave affected her reputation and standing is the slave prostitute, who occupied the lowest station among unfree women. Lawmakers and jurists maintained that there was a significant difference between prostitution and the other sexual duties performed by female slaves. Roman law located this distinction between *ancilla* and prostitute in the indiscriminate conduct of the latter, whose sexual activity was truly public and without boundaries. Jurists developed a definition of "prostitute" that focused on a woman's behavior or lifestyle, more so than the seemingly foundational element of the exchange of sex for money. Consequently, they struggled with creating definitive written regulations to identify and classify these individuals. The core of the definition used in the Augustan marriage legislation (*lex Iulia et Papia*)[78] was the phrase "he or she who openly makes or has made financial gains by his or her body" (*qui quaeve palam corpore quaestum facit fecerit*).[79] Ulpian, interpreting this phrase, wrote:

Palam quaestum facere dicemus non tantum eam, quae in lupanario se prostituit, verum etiam si qua (ut adsolet) in taberna cauponia vel qua alia pudori suo non parcit. (1) Palam autem sic accipimus passim, hoc est sine dilectu: non si qua adulteris vel stupratoribus se committit, sed quae vicem prostitutae sustinet. (2) Item quod cum uno et altero pecunia accepta commiscuit, non videtur palam corpore quaestum facere. (3) Octavenus tamen rectissime ait etiam eam, quae sine quaestu palam se prostituerit, debuisse his connumerari.

We will say that a woman "openly" makes a living not only when she prostitutes herself in a brothel but also if she does so in an inn or a tavern (as is the custom) or if any other woman does not spare her sense of shame. (1) "Openly," then, we take to mean anywhere, that is, without discrimination: not if some woman gives herself to adulterers or those committing *stuprum*, but one who plays the part of a prostitute. (2) Again, because a woman has intercourse with one or two men after accepting money, she does not seem to be "openly making financial gains by her body." (3) Nevertheless, Octavenus quite rightly says that even a woman who has openly prostituted herself without payment should be included in this category (*Dig.* 23.2.43.pr-3).

Ulpian clearly believed that there was a distinct and significant difference between prostitution and other forms of extramarital or illicit sexual activity. He indicated that the key to classifying a prostitute was not simply the exchange of sex for money, deciding that a woman could do so and not be a prostitute. In the same vein, he agreed with the jurist Octavenus, who had ruled that a woman could be a prostitute without accepting payment. These jurists defined a prostitute more by her sexual conduct and lifestyle than the fact that such conduct was purchased.[80] For Ulpian, the key to understanding and categorizing prostitution was the word *palam* – "openly" – which he equated to the word *passim*. *Passim* means not only "anywhere/everywhere" (thus breaking a strict connection between prostitute and brothel), but also "indiscriminately."[81] A prostitute was a woman who had sex indiscriminately – she was a woman who possessed an unbounded sexuality in its truest sense.

It was this unbounded and indiscriminate sexuality that made "prostitute" the definitive low-status social role for a woman in the Roman world. The occupation served as a central determinant for establishing an individual's place in the larger community. "Prostitute" functioned as a juridical status for free women, as those belonging to this category suffered severe civil and legal disabilities even though they still officially may have been Roman citizens.[82] Prostitutes manifestly set themselves apart from female society by customarily adopting the toga instead of the traditional, and respectable, *stola*.[83] This legal and visual separation from other women reinforced the degraded status of the prostitute, which was confirmed by her lack of sexual honor. Authors and lawmakers recognized a difference between prostitutes and other free women who were adulterous or promiscuous, as is clear in Seneca's description of the sexual exploits of Augustus's daughter Julia.

Divus Augustus filiam ultra impudicitiae maledictum impudicam relegavit et flagitia principalis domus in publicum emisit: admissos gregatim adulteros, pererratam nocturnis comissationibus civitatem … cum ex adultera in quaestuariam versa ius omnis licentiae sub ignoto adultero peteret.

The Divine Augustus banished his daughter, who was unchaste beyond the charge of *impudicitia* and revealed the scandals of the imperial house: that she had admitted scores of adulterers, that she had traversed the city in nocturnal revels … and that having turned from an adulteress into a prostitute she sought the right of every indulgence at the hands of an unknown adulterer (*Ben.* 6.32.1).

Although the word that Seneca used for prostitute (*quaestuaria*) implied payment for sexual affairs, it was her willingness to accept random and anonymous partners that defined her transition from adultery to prostitution. Similarly, Quintilian remarked that Cicero's labeling of an unchaste woman (*inpudica*) as a prostitute (*meretrix*) was an example of amplification – using a stronger word or image than was precisely accurate for rhetorical effect (*Inst.* 8.4.1–2).

Roman law also treated prostitution as being different from other forms of sexual activity involving female slaves. Jurists declared that prostituting a female slave held in one's possession as a pledge for a debt (*pignus*) constituted damage to the slave. The law maintained that owners who pledged their slave to another as security for a debt still retained ownership over the slave; the creditor only held the slave in his or her possession, applying any profit from the slave's labor against the amount owed. The debtor had the right to legal action if the creditor damaged the slave in any way. Regarding the prostitution of such a pledged slave, Ulpian wrote:

> In pigneraticio iudicio venit et si res pignori datas male tractavit creditor vel servos debilitavit. ... Quare si prostituit ancillam vel aliud improbatum facere coegit, ilico pignus ancillae solvitur.

> It comes under the action on *pignus* if a creditor mistreats property given as a pledge or weakens slaves.... If, therefore, he prostitutes a female slave or compels her to do something disreputable, the *pignus* of the female slave is discharged immediately (*Dig.* 13.7.24.3).

In this opinion, the jurist ruled that prostitution or other disreputable duties damaged a female slave to such an extent that the pledge was to be immediately dissolved. Furthermore, the debtor still had access to the *actio servi corrupti* and the *actio legis Aquiliae* to recoup funds lost through the injury to his or her property.[84] Lawmakers, who treated the prostitution of an *ancilla* as akin to damaging her, clearly considered the female slave and the slave prostitute to be distinct legal entities.

Authors indicated not only that prostitution was different from other forms of slave sexuality, but also that it imbued both the practicing

slave and her owner with a significant measure of ignominy and disgrace. Dionysius of Halicarnassus highlighted the denigrated status
of slave prostitutes when he criticized the fact that certain individuals
were able to purchase their manumission from funds raised by "base
means" (*ponēros poros*) such as robbery, housebreaking, and prostitution
(*porneia*, 4.24.4). Dionysius identified prostitution as conduct distinct
from socially acceptable or desirable slave duties, classifying it alongside criminal activity.

The degraded status of slave prostitutes is also evident in Roman
law, which provided only minor liability for transgressions or assaults
against these individuals. Jurists differentiated between actions directed
toward a female slave and those toward a female slave prostitute when
evaluating the context of the assault and assigning punishment. Ulpian
wrote that "if someone had verbally accosted respectable young women,
he is understood to have committed a lesser offense if they had been
dressed in slaves' clothing: and a much lesser offense if the women
had been in prostitutes' dress and not that of respectable women"
(*Dig.* 47.10.15.15).[85] While this opinion was primarily about respectable women who dressed inappropriately, it nonetheless indicates the
degraded status of the prostitute compared to that of the female slave.
In addition, lawmakers did not allow owners legal action for theft in
response to the abduction of their slave prostitute.

Qui ancillam non meretricem libidinis causa subripuit, furti actione tenebitur et,
si subpressit, poena legis Fabiae coercetur.

One who abducted a female slave, who is not a prostitute, on account of lust will
be liable on the action for theft and, if he detained her, he is punished with the
penalty of the *lex Fabia* (*Dig.* 47.2.83(82).2, Paul; cf. *PS* 2.31.31).

Verum est, si meretricem alienam ancillam rapuit quis vel celavit, furtum non
esse: nec enim factum quaeritur, sed causa faciendi: causa autem faciendi libido
fuit, non furtum. Et ideo etiam eum, qui fores meretricis effregit libidinis causa,
et fures non ab eo inducti, sed alias ingressi meretricis res egesserunt, furti non
teneri. An tamen vel Fabia teneatur, qui subpressit scortum libidinis causa? Et non
puto teneri, et ita etiam ex facto, cum incidisset, dixi: hic enim turpius facit, quam
qui subripit, sed secum facti ignominiam compensat, certe fur non est.

It is true that if someone abducts or conceals a female prostitute, who is the slave
of another, this is not theft: for one must look at not the action but the reason for

acting, and the reason for acting was lust, not theft. And therefore it is true that even he is not liable for theft, who broke open a prostitute's door on account of lust, and thieves, not having been admitted by him but having entering separately, carried away the prostitute's goods. But should a man who detained a prostitute on account of lust be liable under the *lex Fabia*? I do not think that he is liable, and I said as much when it once happened. He acts more disgracefully than a man who steals, but he balances the ignominy of his deed with himself; certainly he is not a thief (*Dig.* 47.2.39, Ulpian).

Similarly, there was no liability for *iniuria* or the corruption of a slave prostitute, and the legal sources are unclear about the liability for physically injuring or forcibly raping a female prostitute.[86] Responding to a pimp's claim that several young men had inflicted *iniuria* on his slave prostitutes, an adversarial orator remarked that *iniuria* against these slaves was precisely what the pimp sold.[87] Even if Roman lawmakers recognized physical damage done to slave prostitutes, they did not recognize character damage. Unlike other female slaves, prostitutes could not be made worse.

The degrading influence of prostitution endured despite both the understanding that slaves did not control their own sexuality and the close ties between slavery and the robust, even important, Roman sex industry. Both female slaves and prostitutes were sexually accessible individuals, who were associated with common or degraded sexual activity.[88] The logical connection between prostitution and slavery was grounded in a concrete reality, namely, that a significant number of prostitutes were female slaves. Slavery was fundamental to the public sex industry and facilitated the perpetuation of prostitution in the Roman world.[89] There were also elements of coercion, possession, and economic profit common to both prostitution and slavery that helped to fuse the two institutions.[90] A useful example illustrating the connection between slavery and prostitution occurs in Ulpian's comments on the praetor's edict, where the jurist attempted to clarify the phrase "he who keeps a brothel" (*qui lenocinium fecit*):

Ait praetor: "qui lenocinium fecerit". Lenocinium facit qui quaestuaria mancipia habuerit: sed et qui in liberis hunc quaestum exercet, in eadem causa est. Sive autem principaliter hoc negotium gerat sive alterius negotiationis accessione utatur (ut puta si caupo fuit vel stabularius et mancipia talia habuit ministrantia et occasione ministerii quaestum facientia: sive balneator fuerit, velut in quibusdam provinciis fit, in balineis ad custodienda vestimenta conducta habens mancipia hoc genus observantia in officina), lenocinii poena tenebitur.

The praetor says: "One who will have practiced brothel-keeping". He practices brothel-keeping who has had slaves for hire as prostitutes, though one who carries on the trade with free persons is in the same position. He will be liable to the penalty of brothel-keeping whether this is his principal business or whether he uses this as an accessory to another business (for example, if he was the keeper of an inn or tavern and had slaves of this sort working for him who prostituted themselves in the course of their work; or if he was a bath manager having, as it happens in certain provinces, slaves in his baths hired to guard clothing who followed this kind of trade in their workplace) (*Dig.* 3.2.4.2).

Slaves serve as the default type of labor force in this examination of brothel-based prostitution.[91] Furthermore, Ulpian associated prostitution with types of occupational services generally fulfilled by servile labor, implying a close connection between slave and prostitute.

In a gesture that provided theoretical security to some female slaves' statuses, Roman law allowed individuals selling a female slave to attach a restrictive covenant to the sale prohibiting the buyer from ever prostituting the slave.[92] The exact origins of the *ne serva prostituatur* covenant are unclear, but there is unmistakable evidence of its existence during the early Principate.[93] The seller had to notify the buyer of such a restriction at the time of sale, allowing the buyer to assess the conditions fully before purchase. If the slave was sold a second time to a new buyer, the covenant persisted, even if the new buyer was not informed of its existence. Violating the restriction by prostituting the woman led to the original vendor's reacquiring ownership of the slave.[94] In the second century CE, a constitution issued by the emperor Hadrian declared that if, after reacquiring the slave, the original seller proceeded to prostitute her, then the slave was to be freed immediately. Essentially, this meant that once a vendor established a *ne serva prostituatur* covenant, it could not be rescinded, even by the vendor him or herself.[95]

The juristic analysis of the *ne serva prostituatur* covenant reflects an evolving notion that the prostitution of a protected female slave caused insult and injury not only to her original master, but also to the slave herself. Papinian indicated the damage done to both the slave and the former owner:

… Ceterum si ne prostituatur exceptum est, nulla ratio occurrit, cur poena peti et exigi non debeat, cum et ancillam contumelia adfecerit et venditoris affectionem, forte simul et verecundiam laeserit: ….

… But if a provision be made that [a female slave] not be prostituted, no reason exists why a penalty ought not to be sought and exacted, since [the buyer] has insulted both the female slave and the affection of the vendor, and has perhaps injured the vendor's sense of shame as well … (*Dig.* 18.7.6.pr.).

The jurist remarked that prostitution of the protected slave constituted an outrage (*contumelia*, a term central to the classical definition of *iniuria*) that would do harm to both the female slave and the feelings of the vendor, including his sense of shame (*verecundia*).[96] In another opinion, the jurist Paul described the violation of the covenant as an injury (*iniuria*) to the slave, which was removed only by granting the slave her freedom or returning her to her original owner (*Dig.* 18.7.9). Thus, the existence of the *ne serva prostituatur* covenant and the emergent notion of its permanence imply a concession by Roman lawmakers and jurists that female slaves were capable of being injured and insulted by being prostituted, despite their lack of legally recognized honor.

The juridical protection of the *ne serva prostituatur* covenant rested on two principles: the general safeguard of incentives promised to slaves and the significance of promised sexual honor. This covenant effectively limited the buyer's use of his or her property. In Roman slave law, which existed primarily for the benefit of slave owners, there was a clear precedent of restricting individual rights in order to protect the interests of slave owners as a group.[97] *Ne serva prostituatur* clauses would have possessed no value as incentives if Roman law failed to honor them. Yet this explanation does not fully account for the legal structure of these covenants. While jurists displayed a willingness to respect and uphold benefits granted to slaves, such as de facto marriages (*contubernia*) and business allowances (*peculia*), these grants were never irreversible; their existence depended on the continued support of the slave's owner. The inability of the original owner ever to revoke the *ne serva prostituatur* covenant once it was in place suggests that its reward, namely, a lifelong exemption from prostitution, carried additional meaning.

The application of a *ne serva prostituatur* covenant effectively allowed for a sense of sexual honor for female slaves. Jurists who considered cases involving the prostitution of a protected slave expanded the concept of slave injury by further recognizing that female slaves had an interest in redressing wrongs that undermined their personal integrity. Terms used to describe the offense, such as *contumelia* and *iniuria*, drew heavily from the legal language concerning the injury and insult of free persons. Moreover, the law provided a means to alleviate the insult, if only returning the slave to her original owner. The structure of the legal response to violations of the *ne serva prostituatur* covenant resembled actions initiated to redress infringements on the honor of free individuals.[98]

The covenant thus bestowed a measure of sexual honor on a female slave by giving her a sexual integrity protected by law, which would suggest why it was impossible for slave owners to rescind the restriction: Roman lawmakers were reluctant to disregard this honor once imbued. Yet the measure of integrity promised by the *ne serva prostituatur* covenant was much less encompassing than the standards enjoyed by free women. There is no indication that any sort of illicit sex would violate the restriction; only prostitution was prohibited. The existence of such a covenant suggests that Romans perceived there to be a significant difference between the sexual exploitation of female slaves and the sexual duties of slave prostitutes.

There is some evidence that by the second century CE lawmakers and jurists were attempting to curb the introduction of female slaves to the prostitution industry. The *Historia Augusta* credited Hadrian with a law that prohibited the sale of a female slave to a pimp or a procuress (*leno et lanistae*) without just cause (*causa, HA Hadr.* 18.8).[99] Furthermore, there is a noteworthy opinion by Ulpian on the duties of the prefect of the city:

Quod autem dictum est, ut servos de dominis querentes praefectus audiat, sic accipiemus non accusantes dominos (hoc enim nequaquam servo permittendum est nisi ex causis receptis) sed si verecunde expostulent, si saevitiam, si duritiam, si famem, qua eos premant, si obscenitatem, in qua eos compulerint vel compellant, apud praefectum urbi exponant. Hoc quoque officium praefecto urbi a divo Severo datum est, ut mancipia tueatur ne prostituantur.

Moreover, the statement that the prefect should hear slaves issuing complaints against their masters is one we should accept – not slaves accusing their masters (for it is in no way to be permitted for a slave to do this except in specified cases), but if they should make their complaint with due modesty, if they should set forth before the city prefect a case of cruelty or harshness or starvation whereby their masters were oppressing them, or a case of obscenity in performance of which their masters had compelled or were compelling. This duty was also given to the city prefect by the deified Severus, in order that he protect chattels from prostitution (*Dig.* 1.12.1.8).

At face value, the final line of this paragraph seems to indicate that there was a complete ban on slave prostitution, enforced by the city prefect during the reign of Septimius Severus. However, such a ban is not substantiated by the surviving evidence and is even contradicted by the continued existence of *ne serva prostituatur* covenants, which would have been obsolete if a total ban on slave prostitution existed.[100] Regardless, the association between forced obscenity and/or prostitution and acts of cruelty against slaves is striking, reinforcing the notion that such conduct was detrimental to a slave in ways that other forms of sexual service were not.

The example of how Roman lawmakers perceived and defined the status and value of prostitutes complicates any attempt to categorize the standing of slave women solely on the basis of their conformity to their owners' will. While the duties of a female slave may have included frequent sexual intercourse, multiple partners, and tangible rewards, neither were her actions "in the open," nor was she necessarily "making financial gains by her body." The degraded status associated with prostitution continued to exist within the institution of slavery, as Romans distinguished slave prostitutes from other female slaves, despite the classification of both as accessible sexual objects.

THE HOUSEHOLD AND PERCEPTIONS OF SLAVE SEXUALITY

Roman authors evaluated the standing and value of female slaves not so much in regard to the extent of their sexual activity, as in the context under which this activity occurred. In everyday practice neither jurists nor literary writers judged all forms of lawful slave sexual activity as equally suitable or reputable, even if they occurred with an owner's consent. The distinction between sexual behavior contained within the household and conduct outside it remained a key criterion against which elite men judged slave sexuality. It was gendered societal beliefs locating female sex within the household that anchored Romans' perceptions of appropriate slave sexual conduct.

The best evidence of such an association lies in the concern with which Romans perceived female slaves who engaged in sexual affairs outside the household. As was mentioned, prostitutes, who consistently had sex with the consent of their owners but indiscriminately outside their owners' households, possessed the most degraded standing among all female slaves. Non-prostitute female slaves who were sexually active with men from outside the household were viewed with suspicion. In literary sources, most of the sexual affairs between a man and a female slave who did not belong to his household seem to have occurred without the consent of the owner, thus rendering the affair problematic because it challenged the owner's authority over his property. Even in ambiguous texts that romanticized sex between a man and a female slave who was not his own, authors often emphasized the furtive nature of the relationship; these affairs appear almost analogous to adultery in image and tone.[101] In Roman literature, a man who fell in love or became sexually excited with a female slave either purchased the woman for himself or else engaged in activities generally colored as clandestine, violent, or generally objectionable.[102]

There is limited evidence of an owner's condoning a sexual affair between a female slave and man from outside the household, but the context of these examples suggests a general aversion toward such conduct. Nothing in Roman law prevented owners from allowing men sexual access to their female slaves, as they possessed total control over the bodily integrity of their slaves. However, the few literary examples that mention such an arrangement suggest a reluctance to sanction this conduct. Horace advised Lollius that to be a good friend, he should not let "a female slave rouse up his heart" (*non ancilla tuum iecur ulceret ulla*) lest her master delight him with such a "small gift" (*munere … parvo*) or torment him by being unobliging (*Epist.* 1.18.72–75). While Horace counseled Lollius against such an affair because of its potential for damaging a friendship, this statement nonetheless suggests that a slave owner might tolerate a sexual relationship between his female slave and another man. However, the vague meaning of "small gift" complicates this assumption: Was the gift the sexual act or the slave herself?[103] The possibility that by "small gift" Horace may have meant the slave herself would suggest a perceived reluctance to allow a relationship between one's female slave and a man from outside the household, the alternative being to *give* the slave to her admirer.

In a declamation introduced earlier in the chapter, a guest claimed that he had sex with his host's daughter only because he believed that she was an *ancilla* providing wait service for the dinner. Refuting this claim, the owner noted that if the guest truly believed the girl to be a slave, then he could have obtained her by promising her a gift or, if he was bolder (*contumax*), asking her owner for her companionship (*Dec. Min.* 301.17).[104] While the declamation does again indicate that an owner might lend his approval for such an affair, the negative implications of *contumax* may suggest that asking a host's permission was an excessive measure, potentially bold beyond the boundaries of social propriety.

Neither of these examples represents a relationship between a female slave and a man from outside her household in a positive manner, suggesting that in some sense, Roman slave owners considered the practice a violation of social decency.[105] One likely reason why masters did not want their female slaves to have sexual relations outside the household was that they did not want to be associated with pandering or other distasteful forms of impropriety.[106] The ambiguous definition of prostitution and the liabilities of engaging in that practice may have inclined slave owners to place demands upon female slaves that would preserve the household's relative esteem.

In striking contrast to the problematic nature of extrahousehold sexual affairs, literary sources suggest that elite male Romans viewed slave sexuality within the household as comparatively innocuous and mundane.[107] The ordinariness of owners' having sexual relations with their slaves is best evidenced by the silence of sources seeking to defend this practice and the complaints of individuals who depicted themselves as moral reformers outside the status quo. These opponents expressed their distress that casual affairs between owners and their slaves occurred with remarkable frequency and with general acceptance by the community.[108]

Additionally, owners largely permitted their female slaves to have sexual relations with male slaves.[109] Casual sex between female slaves and male inhabitants of the household appears to have been viewed by most elite Romans as a morally neutral activity, especially for the female slave. None of the authors who criticized individuals' having sexual affairs with their slaves considered the possible damage or dishonor done to these women, focusing instead on the moral and/or emotional harm such affairs may have caused the male owner and his wife.[110] Whereas the sexuality of female slaves was degraded in general, there is little indication in the literary works crafted and read by the male elite that the performance of casual sexual duties diminished the standing of individual female slaves, who were merely satisfying the societal expectations for their station.

On the other hand, increased standing and value were attributed to female slaves who achieved more permanent romantic relationships within the household. Roman authors and lawmakers condoned and supported long-term relationships between male owners and their female slaves, so long as they were conducted with respect to standards of social propriety.[111] An owner could express increased esteem for his sexual partner by bestowing the title of concubine (*concubina*) upon her, although legal commentators asserted that women of this status really ought to be manumitted.[112] The idea of the slave *concubina* established an apex of female slave status against which other individuals and relationships could be measured. Here, female slaves were closest to the standing of respectable free women. For example, one surviving funerary monument dedicated to a slave concubine testified to the owner's affection for his "most dutiful" (*piissima*) and "well-deserving" (*benemerens*) concubine. The owner emphasized the worth of his partner and her separation from other female slaves by referring to her as "chaste" (*casta*), an adjective that categorically denied the sexual accessibility that characterized women of her rank (*CIL* 6.21607).[113]

Roman lawmakers also demonstrated increased regard for female slaves who formed quasi-marital relationships with male slaves from their households. Denied the legal right to marry (*conubium*), female slaves could enter into a state of de facto marriage called *contubernium*.[114] While the continuance of this union required the ongoing consent of the slave owner, it nonetheless achieved a measure of durability due to its close association with marriage.[115] In theory, it would have been possible for slaves from different households to establish *contubernium* with both their owners' consent, but there is little evidence to suggest that such unions regularly occurred.[116] Like the concubine, the female *contubernalis* was expected to adjust her sexual activity to conform to the conjugal nature of the relationship.[117] Adherence to the social norms of respectable women imbued the concubine and the *contubernalis* with the positive associations, and a small share in the standing, of the free matrons whose conduct they sought to imitate.[118]

This evidence indicates that the type of partner – either within or beyond the household – and the structure of the relationship influenced how Romans understood the impact of sexual engagement upon a female slave's value and status. Authors assigned increased standing to female slaves who adhered to standards of female conduct resembling those of free women, especially durable, monogamous relationships. For female slaves, it was the confines of the owner's household rather than marriage that provided the boundaries for reputable sexual conduct; as in the case of free women, sex within these boundaries did not have a detrimental effect on a slave's perceived worth. In addition, the more that a female slave emulated the proper sexual conduct of a free woman, the more highly regarded she was.

CONCLUSION

Female slaves could become involved in a wide spectrum of sexual affairs, ranging from long-term, monogamous, quasi-marital relationships to compulsory prostitution in public brothels. As was the case for free women, sexual activity influenced a slave woman's standing, and some slaves had the opportunity to adhere to standards of conduct deemed more respectable than others. Gendered assumptions about sexual conduct, respectability, and social standing assured that sexual activity would be a critical means through which elite male Romans assessed the value of female slaves.

Yet gendered conventions that assured that sexual behavior influenced a woman's standing were complicated by the fact that slave women did not possess the right to control their own sexual integrity and were actually expected to be sexually available. For female slaves, juridical categories of freedom and unfreedom assured that the terms under which these women engaged in sexual behaviors would be more important in determining status than the mere engagement in sexual activity. The boundaries separating licit from illicit sex for female slaves could not be the same as those governing free women given societal expectations regarding the sexual exploitation of slaves. Roman literary authors and jurists effectively eliminated the shame from individual sexual duties imposed on female slaves by classifying them as women without agency, self-interest, and honor; routine sexual exploitation contributed to the degradation of slaves as a rank, but there was little sense that each individual act caused additional denigration or deval- uation, so long as the conduct remained located in the household and occurred with the consent of the owner. In contrast, evidence from Roman law and literature suggests that social norms discouraged slave sexual conduct outside the household, classifying such activity as dis- reputable and disgraceful.

The gendered attitudes toward sexuality and respectability that shaped the honor-shame system also influenced a framework of sexual interpretation and evaluation that was recontextualized for the experi- ences of female slaves. This influence marked female slaves as degraded, identifying them with conduct deemed dishonorable and shameful for free women, but at the same time created standards for assessing slaves' worth based on more or less reputable sexual conduct. Thus, for female slaves, sex within the household could simultaneously be disgraceful and respectable – a situation crucial to understanding Romans' belief that female citizens could be created from female slaves.

2 Gender, Labor, and the Manumission of Female Slaves

The manumission process exemplifies the paradoxical position of female slaves, whom elite Romans envisioned as both marginal and integral, unskilled and specialized, worthless and valuable. Largely dismissed as slaves who "did not work" (*opus non facere*), women nonetheless occupied essential positions in Roman households and had significant success earning their freedom. Constrained by the gendered expectations of slave owners – and indeed the gendered mores of Roman society – women worked primarily in positions that stressed personal attention and service over material production. Concomitantly, this ideology placed increased value on women's work as spousal partners and mothers and, in so doing, perpetuated a model of slavery and manumission that prioritized personal relationships and family life as the key attributes of both female slaves and future citizens. The manumission process institutionalized incentives for female slaves to practice gender roles that they would later be expected to perfect as Roman matrons.

More so than any other part of this book, this chapter will address the real experiences of female slaves. The purpose of this focus on female slaves' lives is twofold. First, I want to demonstrate that elite authors and jurists – those describing, analyzing, and directing Roman slavery – articulated an incomplete portrait of female slaves that trivialized and elided their actual labor. Second, I suggest that this discourse in turn shaped female slaves' actual circumstances. In addition to reinforcing assumptions at the root of the gendered division of labor, elites' conclusions about the work, contributions, and value of female slaves ultimately fostered a distinct and particular manumission pattern for women.

THE WORK AND VALUE OF FEMALE SLAVES

Workspaces were gendered in Roman society, as biological sex largely determined the tasks performed by men and women. The division of labor was rooted in the male/outdoor, female/indoor model prevalent in many agricultural communities. In this model, women were responsible for the maintenance and support of the household whereas men performed the outside physical labor that generated tangible sustenance. In urban settings, the types of work typically gendered as masculine or feminine broadened, yet women remained centered on the household and personal service, and men on income and material production.[1] One important contributing factor to this model was the perceived bodily weakness of women, which encompassed both a physical and an intellectual deficiency.[2] Accordingly, the types of labor classified as "male" acquired more prestige than "female" work. These attitudes toward gender and labor, adopted and perpetuated by the elite strata of Roman society, significantly influenced the assignments that masters imposed on their slaves. While it would have been uncomplicated for owners to ignore these conventions given the marginalized status of female slaves, the surviving sources indicate an overwhelming adherence to these gendered norms.[3]

These same gendered attitudes toward work also contributed to the devaluation and obfuscation of the lives and labor of female slaves. Textual evidence suggests that there were significantly more male slaves than female slaves in Roman society, despite the fact that natural reproduction, the most important source of slaves during the Principate, would have created a more equal sex ratio.[4] Epigraphic sources are similarly skewed; studies of large urban households have found an approximate ratio of one female slave for every two males.[5] Likewise, in agronomic commentaries on rural households, male slaves significantly outnumber females.[6] Surviving sources present a male-dominated image of Roman slavery, which most likely reflects the importance and prestige of their respective duties, rather than a social reality engendered from an uneven ratio of male to female slaves.

This trend is most clearly visible in descriptions of rural settings, where Roman authors largely ignored or devalued the labor of female slaves.[7] Most information on the duties of agricultural slaves is gained from the agronomic writings of Cato, Varro, and Columella, who offered instructions and advice for ideal estate operation. The female slave with the most notable and clearly defined position on a rural estate was the *vilica*, the household manager, who was commonly the wife/partner (*contubernalis*) of the *vilicus*, the slave or freedman placed in charge of an agricultural property.[8] According to the agronomists, the primary responsibility of the *vilica* was to assist her partner in the oversight of the villa, which included supervising the household stores, the production of wool, and the preparation of food.[9] Most likely, the *vilica* was not solely responsible for performing all of these duties, but rather for managing, instructing, and assisting other household slaves engaged in these tasks.

While the agronomists attributed no other specific agricultural jobs to women in their handbooks, there are indications that female slaves other than the *vilica* were present on these farms.[10] The best evidence for a significant female slave presence on rural estates occurs in the legal discussion about farms as testamentary legacies. Testators often bequeathed equipment and supplies in addition to the physical farm (*fundus*). Roman jurists distinguished between a legacy of the *fundus* with *instrumentum* – a farm with the slaves, tools, and supplies necessary for the farm's operation – and the *fundus instructus* – the farm and all the material goods physically located on the property (which included the *instrumentum*).[11] As part of the legal discussion about the exact components of these two categories, jurists made several references to the *contubernales* and children of the male slaves attached to the farm.[12] Cato also suggested a larger presence of female slaves on rural estates when he commented that the *vilica* should not make a habit of visiting neighbors and other women (*vicinae aliaeque mulieres, Agr.* 143). All of these texts indicate that female slaves had a place on the rural villa, if not specific job titles and/or assignments.

Given the presence of female slaves on farms, it seems implausible that owners would not have utilized their labor to some extent. The most probable duties for these women would have been the household tasks under the domain of the *vilica*: textile production, food service, and household cleaning.[13] Furthermore, Columella implied that it was not unusual for female slaves to be working outside the villa in some capacity. He advised that the *vilica* have wool work available for days when a woman could not perform agricultural labor outdoors (*sub dio rusticum opus*) because of inclement weather (12.3.6).[14] It is likely then that female slaves would have participated principally in ancillary support work, such as cooking, cleaning, and the tending of small animals, rather than the primary agricultural labor of the estate.[15]

In urban settings, slave owners tended to assign women to tasks traditionally gendered as feminine. Women worked primarily in "service" jobs (especially food preparation, hospitality, personal care, and prostitution), the sale of foodstuffs, and the manufacture of clothing, jewelry, and perfume.[16] Female slaves in particular appear as weavers, seamstresses, midwives, wet nurses, caregivers for young children, and personal attendants/secretaries for women.[17] In this respect, female slaves were a necessary component of household staffs, as they performed special services that male slaves could not. Outside the household, female slaves most frequently appear working in the fields of prostitution, public entertainment, and textile production.[18] All three were major – and potentially profitable – industries that relied heavily on the labor of female slaves, fulfilling a variety of essential professional roles. As in the case of rural slaves, it is likely that owners used women to staff ancillary or support positions in manufacturing and commerce, yet these jobs rarely, if ever, appear as part of their occupational identity.[19] With the exception of textile production, the "women's work" attributed to female slaves in urban locations generally consisted of personal service rather than material production or financial development.

There are scattered references to female slaves holding more prominent professional positions, but the lack of substantial corroborating evidence makes it difficult to determine the extent to which this was common practice in the Roman economy. Apart from a few references to *lanipendae* (textile supervisors, lit. "wool weighers"), there is no evidence of female slaves working in any type of supervisory position within the household.[20] Ulpian mentioned the possibility of the appointment of an *ancilla* as the manager of a shop (*institor*), indicating that a female slave serving in such a position was certainly conceivable. However, the jurist appears to have been speaking in broad terms in an attempt to clarify the full range of the law rather than noting an example of particular relevancy (*Dig.* 14.3.7).[21]

Most intriguingly, legal sources indicate that it was possible for female slaves to have control over a sum of money (*peculium*) that would allow them to conduct business transactions independently.[22] Regarding the *peculium*, Gaius wrote:

Et ancillarum nomine et filiarum familias in peculio actio datur: maxime si qua sarcinatrix aut textrix erit aut aliquod artificium vulgare exerceat, datur propter eam actio. Depositi quoque et commodati actionem dandam earum nomine Iulianus ait: sed et tributoriam actionem, si peculiari merce sciente patre dominove negotientur, dandam esse. Longe magis non dubitatur, et si in rem versum est, quod iussu patris dominive contractum sit.

An action on the *peculium* is allowed regarding female slaves and daughters-in-power. Especially if a woman is a seamstress or weaver or practices some other common trade, an action is allowed for this reason. Julian says that an action should lie in respect to these women also for deposit and loan: but an *actio tributoria* should be given if they conduct business with the funds in their *peculium* with their father's or owner's knowledge. This is not in doubt especially if something has been turned to his benefit or if it was contracted on the father's or owner's order (*Dig.* 15.1.27.pr).

Gaius implicitly categorizes a female slave in the textile industry as a familiar figure when he cites such an individual as an exemplary type of a woman with *peculium*. Similarly, after discussing the possible penalties against a son's conducting business (*negotia gessisse*) either with a *peculium* or with his father's funds, Ulpian noted that the same was true for a female slave (*Dig.* 3.5.13(14).pr). Here the jurist's use of the gender specific *ancilla* at the end of his opinion about a son might indicate that Ulpian was referring to a specific case involving a female slave.[23] Moreover, jurists' concerns about the performance of *operae* by freedwomen (see Chapter 3) speak to the potential value of work performed by some female slaves. Given the nature of the juridical profession, however, it is difficult to state conclusively whether these examples represent the exceptional or the mundane. Opportunities available for work that allowed a measure of financial independence and influence appear to have been somewhat limited for women, especially in comparison to male slaves' opportunities, even if some few women found employment in these fields.

Undercutting the work actually performed by female slaves, Roman authors devalued the contribution of their labor to the household either by largely ignoring the work or by dismissing their duties as both unskilled and unproductive.[24] Agronomists' focus on male agricultural labor both recorded and reinforced a prevalent belief that female domestic duties were unimportant to the financial success of the household. Perhaps most telling are the estate rubrics formulated by Cato, in which the author outlined the precise types of equipment and personnel necessary to ensure ideal operation of a farm. Here Cato specified the exact number of slaves needed to staff an estate, but only mentioned one woman on his lists: the *vilica* (*Agr.* 10–11). Nor was this elision of female labor confined solely to agricultural writings; authors largely ignored the labor and duties of female slaves in urban households as well.[25] Furthermore, the emphasis on assigning male slaves to staff "female" positions only made sense as a prestige gesture so long as observers were aware of the triviality of "women's work." Not only did Roman assumptions about gendered labor limit female slaves' access to esteemed occupations, but the derisive treatment of their duties in literary sources also reinforced the perception of their work as insignificant.

The general denigration of the category of female labor within elite slaveholding ideology contributed to a persistent characterization of *ancillae* as slaves who did not work. Roman authors often thought of slaves in terms of their occupations.[26] Therefore, a consequence of trivializing the actual labor performed by women was the assessment of female slaves primarily as individuals who did not work. Such a classification would have gained additional support by the fact that there seem to have been more *ancillae* than available work for women in the larger Roman households.[27] The division of slaves into "working" and "not working" categories had some legal foundation. When considering legacies consisting of household stores (*penus*), which included foodstuffs intended to be consumed by the *pater familias*, his family, and the slaves (*familia*) who habitually surrounded them (*quae circa eos esse solet*), Ulpian noted that the jurist Q. Mucius Scaevola believed that the food provided for slaves who did not work (*qui opus non facerent*) should be included. This was apparently a reference to the slaves who personally attended the *pater familias* (*Dig.* 33.9.3.pr, 6).[28] The category of "slaves who did not work" did not only consist of female slaves; nor were all female slaves placed in this category.[29] Nonetheless, because of the limited productive value attributed to most "female" duties, the *ancilla* was the archetypal slave of this classification.[30]

It was the reproductive potential of female slaves, possibly even more than their capacity for productive labor, that was an essential component of their worth. As the imperial expansion of Rome slowed, internal reproduction became an increasingly critical component of the slave supply.[31] Slave owners themselves clearly recognized the value of slave procreation, as reproductive ability (as a product of age) factored into the price of female slaves.[32] Furthermore, the abundance of legal opinions considering the implications of legating or selling the children of female slaves also speaks to the perceived worth of slave reproduction.[33]

Perhaps most illustrative of the value of women's reproductive ability relative to their productive ability is an opinion that considered an edict requiring individuals selling slaves to notify potential buyers of any disease or defect. Ulpian maintained that everyone agreed that the law deemed a pregnant slave to be healthy for the purpose of sale.[34] Given that jurists were principally concerned with defects having the potential to affect a slave's value as an economic instrument, the perceived insignificance of pregnancy is noteworthy. Pregnancy certainly would have limited the actual labor potential of a female slave, but jurists apparently discounted this loss as unimportant and unanimously protected the sale as valid. This prioritization of pregnancy over productive work resonates with the beliefs of Columella, who promised a female slave full exemption from her duties after she had given birth to three children; for the agronomist, the value of three new slaves compensated for any financial loss resulting from the woman's excused work (1.8.19).

Complementing the perceived economic worth placed upon the reproductive ability of female slaves was the value assigned to *vernae*, the slave children born to a female slave within a *familia*.[35] Ancient authors frequently portrayed *vernae* as being more loyal, trustworthy, and productive than slaves purchased from outside the household.[36] Thus, female slaves possessed the ability not only to increase the number of slaves within a household, but also to produce slaves of a superior quality.

Reproductive ability was unarguably an important aspect of the worth of female slaves, but modern scholars have debated the extent to which Romans understood procreation as a *primary* function of female slaves. Scholars have examined one passage in particular as a significant indicator of Roman attitudes regarding the breeding of slaves. Ulpian wrote that "the children and grandchildren of female slaves, although not considered to be fruits (*fructus*), nonetheless do increase the inheritance, since, not without due reason (*quia non temere*), female slaves are obtained in order that they may produce children" (*Dig.* 5.3.27.pr).[37] Interpretations of this passage have rested principally on one's understanding of the *quia* clause. Most scholars have treated the clause as an explanation for why the children of female slaves were not considered *fructus* and thus have read *temere* in a restrictive or qualifying sense.[38] However, Rodger makes a very convincing argument for reading the *quia* as an explanation for why the offspring of female slaves did in fact increase the inheritance given that they were not technically *fructus* – because slave owners, with good reason, purchased female slaves with the intention of having them produce children.[39]

Roman attitudes about the gendered division of labor shaped not only the specific duties performed by individual slaves, but also the type of interactions slaves had with their owners. Even if female slaves technically belonged to a man, their life and work in the household may have fallen under the purview of another. Both literary authors and jurists frequently represented *ancillae* as being in the service of the women and children of the household when considering the duties of female slaves.[40] Scaevola reviewed a case where the testator disinherited his daughter in favor of his wife and son but requested that his wife choose ten *ancillae* for their daughter, to be handed over when the daughter married (*Dig.* 33.5.21). Here, it is notable that a woman was supposed to choose ten female slaves for her daughter. The personal service duties typically assigned to female slaves would have put them in close contact with their mistresses.

While Roman authors largely characterized this work as unskilled and unproductive, they nonetheless recognized its importance given the proximity between slave and master/mistress and the potentially sensitive nature of the duties. Female slaves often worked with their owners' families when members were vulnerable and exposed, circumstances that increased the value of loyal and devoted service. Perhaps the best example of this phenomenon is the slave nurse, whom inscriptions and literary texts commended as a revered and beloved figure with a lifelong emotional bond to her ward. However the nurse might have actually felt toward her master or charge, the successful performance of her duties had the potential to earn a female slave distinction as a beloved and essential household servant, even as the duties themselves were trivialized and denigrated.[41] Being thrust into personal service and child care positions allowed female slaves considerable access to owners and their families and may have facilitated the development of a familiar relationship – one that slave-owning families often characterized as respectful, supportive, and even affectionate.[42]

Both literary and legal sources indicate that a sexual relationship was the principal means for a female slave to gain favor with her male owner. Though coerced into a sexual encounter with a man far more powerful than she, a female slave might nonetheless find in the attention of her master leverage for social advancement.[43] Martial satirically suggested that a female slave could even gain a measure of control over her owner, quipping that the master's lust transforms a woman from *ancilla* to *domina* (6.71). From the owners' perspective, sexual encounters might lead to the formation of a more long-term, affectionate relationship and hence create a pathway toward freedom.

Authors indicate that a master's engagement in sexual affairs with his female slaves could have both positive and negative economic implications for his household. As any children born from such a union were legally slaves, a sexual affair was a means to increase the size of the slave *familia*.[44] Martial mentioned a man who had sex with his female slaves purposely for the production of children (1.84). Alternatively, sexual affairs between master and slave had the potential to limit production and profitability by disrupting the stability of the household. These relationships could upset not only the master's wife, but also the other slaves, either because the master was sleeping with a slave's partner or because he seemed to be elevating one slave into a position of primacy.[45] While economic consequences were certainly possible, the extent to which they created a significant concern for slave owners is unclear.

Roman authors envisioned the purpose and value of female slaves as a whole more in terms of their personal relationships than in the actual labor they provided. As was discussed previously, literary accounts frequently reduced *ancillae* to simple sex objects or personal attendants – and even here authors were generally indifferent to their specific duties, casting them primarily as the personal confidants of their mistresses. Yet despite the trivialization of their labor, female slaves undeniably possessed significant economic value.[46] Their importance as women, wives (in a nonlegal sense), and mothers – individuals who served as the motivators, stabilizers, and producers of slave labor – generally eclipsed their actual value as productive workers in the eyes of the Roman elite. Authors recognized that the presence of female slaves was a useful, and perhaps necessary, component of a stable household.[47] While the agronomists largely ignored female slaves as a source of labor, they did mention these women as potential rewards and a support network for male slaves. The writers even described the *vilica*, whose duties were emphasized as important in their own right, as a reward for the *vilicus*.[48] Varro argued that allowing estate overseers (*praefecti*) to have fellow slaves as conjugal partners made them "stronger and more attached to the farm" (*firmiores ac coniunctiores fundo*), and it was on account of these relationships that slave families from Epirus were both very esteemed and highly valued (*Rust.* 1.17.5).[49] These writers reasoned that the prospect of a partner or wife was an effective reward for male slaves, a reward that could encourage loyal and productive service. Furthermore, allowing slaves to create families effectively increased the value of male servants and facilitated the production of new chattel.[50]

The juridical discussion on legating farms implies that "wife" and "mother" functioned almost as occupational titles for female slaves. Recognizing that farms employed a variety of slaves, jurists needed to distinguish between those included in legacies of *fundus* with *instrumentum* and those in legacies of *fundus instructus*. There appears to have been some disagreement about whether the *contubernales* of male slaves attached to the farm were included in the *instrumentum* or only in *fundus instructus*.[51] The jurist Paul classified the "wives" of those who work (*uxores eorum qui operantur*) as part of the *instrumentum* (PS 3.6.38). In comparison, Trebatius included the "wife" of the *vilicus* in the *instrumentum* with the caveat "only if she assists her husband in some duty"

(*si modo aliquo officio virum adiuvet, Dig.* 33.7.12.5, Ulpian).[52] Ulpian
agreed that the "wives" (*uxores*) and children of male agricultural slaves
should be included in legacies of *fundus* with *instrumentum*, but not
because they contributed to the working of the farm (i.e., constituted
part of the actual *instrumentum*). Instead, the jurist included them among
the implements used by the slaves who worked the farm (*instrumenti
instrumentum*) because he believed that a testator would not have wanted
to impose a harsh separation (*dura separatio*) upon slave families (*Dig.*
33.7.12.6–7). The *instrumenti instrumentum* included slaves whose work
did not contribute directly to the operation of the farm, but instead
provided the resources necessary for the slaves who did work directly
on the land: the kitchen staff, wool workers, stone masons, millers, and
others. What is important is that the *instrumenti instrumentum* did actual
work on the farm in the eyes of the jurists. Adding family members to
this list of occupational titles implies both that slave owners understood
"wife" and "mother" to have been the primary duties of certain female
slaves and that the presence of these female slaves in some way supported the agricultural staff and thus benefited the household.[53]

THE DECISION TO MANUMIT

What were especially notable about the Roman practice of manumission
were the large number of slaves manumitted and the young age at which
many of them were freed.[54] As a society, Romans embraced manumission
as an integral aspect of the slave system. However, manumission was
never a foregone conclusion for slaves; freedom was granted solely at the
whim of the owner.[55] The slave's status as an owned possession always
made the decision to manumit economic in nature, especially given the
financial resources dedicated to the procurement and maintenance of this
labor force. By definition manumission was the deliberate devolution of
one's property.[56] Sources suggest that some owners developed affectionate
relations with certain slaves and offered manumission as a reward for con-
scientious and devoted service.[57] Concurrently, this decision could be an
expression of economic rationalism. The promise of future manumission
was an incentive for slaves to work hard and remain loyal to the interests of their masters.[58] Owners might demand financial compensation in

exchange for freeing a slave, thereby creating funds to purchase replacement personnel. Since female slaves as a group lacked both a perceived productive value and real opportunities to acquire extensive resources through their labor, they must have had to rely more heavily on their personal relationships to improve their odds of manumission.[59]

Arguably the most important factor influencing the decision to manumit was the personal relationship between a master and slave. Owners drove the manumission process, as they decided if and when to release an individual from servitude. Here, the gendered division of labor that located female slaves predominantly in personal service positions within urban households increased their visibility to their owners and possibly their opportunities to gain their freedom.[60] It is certainly reasonable to assume that a slave known to his or her master had a better chance at earning manumission than one who was unknown. Accordingly, slaves performing agricultural tasks in rural locations almost certainly had a smaller chance of being freed than urban slaves because they generally had less contact with their masters.[61] Owners were also more likely to notice and esteem not only the achievements of the individuals who held more prestigious positions, but also the work of those slaves performing valued personal care and support.[62]

The surviving sources highlight sexual relationships with male owners as a principal intimate bond contributing to the manumission of female slaves. Authors mention several cases where female slaves received their freedom, and sometimes even an additional payment, as a reward for their sexual relationship. Appian described how a certain Fulvius, fleeing the proscriptions of the civil war, ran to the house of his freedwoman, whom he had provided with freedom and a dowry because she had been his mistress (BC 4.24).[63] Similarly, Valerius Maximus related the story of the wife of Scipio Africanus, who, after the death of her husband, freed his slave mistress and gave her in marriage to a freedman (6.7.1). Both anecdotes suggest that owners granted manumission as a reward for the affection, devotion, and loyalty that these women showed while involved in sexual relationships.

In cases where owners freed their female slaves in order to marry them themselves, manumission functioned both as a reward and as the foundation for a new partnership. The inscriptional evidence for patrons married to their freedwomen is considerable, suggesting that manumissions "for the sake of marriage" (*causa matrimonii*) were reasonably common.[64] An owner's affectionate feelings toward a female slave might have mitigated any financial concerns about the economics of manumission. For example, a funerary altar established for a deceased girl by her parents suggests an owner's willingness to manumit a female slave without charge in order to form a family.

> Dis Manibus
> Iuniae M(arci) f(iliae) Proculae vix(it) ann(is) VIII m(ensibus) XI d(iebus) V miseros
> patrem et matrem in luctu reliquid fecit M(arcus) Iuniu[s]
> Euphrosynus sibi et [[.......]]e tu sine filiae et parentium in u[no ossa]
> requ(i)escant quidquid nobis feceris idem tibi speres mihi crede tu tibi testis [eris]
> To the divine shades of Iunia Procula, daughter of Marcus, who lived eight years, eleven months, and five days. She left her wretched father and mother in grief. Marcus Iunius Euphrosynus made (this altar) for himself and for [name deleted]. Allow the bones of the daughter and parents to rest in one place. Whatever you have done for us, may you hope for the same for yourself. Believe me, you will be a witness to yourself.

On the reserve side of the altar, the following curse was inscribed:

> Hic stigmata aeterna Acte libertae scripta sunt vene/nariae
> et perfidae dolosae duri pectoris clavom et restem
> sparteam ut sibi collum alliget et picem candentem
> pectus malum commurat suum manumissa gratis
> secuta adulterum patronum circumscripsit et
> ministros ancillam et puerum lecto iacenti
> patrono abduxit ut animo desponderet solus
> relictus spoliatus senex e[t] Hymno ⌐e⌐ ade(m) sti(g)m(a)ta
> secutis
> Zosimum.
> Here the eternal marks of infamy have been written for the freedwoman Acte, a poisoner, and a treacherous, deceitful, and hard-hearted woman. (I bring) a nail and a rope made of broom so that she may bind her own neck, and boiling-hot pitch to burn her evil heart. Manumitted free of charge, she cheated her patron, following an adulterer, and she stole away his servants – a slave girl and a boy – while her

patron was lying in bed, so that he despaired, an old man left alone and despoiled. And the same marks of infamy to Hymnus, and to those who followed Zosimus (*CIL* 6.20905).[65]

Judith Evans Grubbs assumes that the author of the curse is M. Iunius Euphrosynus, and that Acte was his wife and the mother of the deceased Iunia Procula, whose name was deleted from the original memorial. She reads the explicit mention of *gratis* manumission, the existence of a family unit, and Acte's "evident youth" as evidence that the female slave had been freed for the purpose of marriage.[66] If Evans Grubbs's assumptions about the family and its history are correct, it makes explicit inclusion of *gratis* in the curse inscription an interesting addition. Assuming that it was common for owners to free future wives without cost, it is notable that dedicators rarely noted this circumstance in inscriptions.[67] Placing emphasis on the *gratis* nature of Acte's manumission communicated two points. Not only did it signify that manumission was a reward, earned by the slave's dedicated service to her master, but, perhaps more importantly, it implied the freedwoman's continued obligation, an obligation that she failed to honor (hence *patron circumscripsit*).[68]

Personal service clearly provided some female slaves with opportunities to gain a master's confidence. This was particularly important considering that female slaves' household employment patterns were not conducive to earning supplementary personal funds to defray the cost of their manumission. Roman slave owners sometimes permitted slaves to use funds – either those provided by a third party or perhaps those accumulated in a *peculium* – to buy their freedom, which allowed owners to recoup their financial loss by purchasing new slaves as replacement labor.[69] Given the references to female slaves with *peculia* in the legal sources, it seems likely that at least some *ancillae* were able to accumulate a measure of savings. However, since female slaves had limited access to the more respectable, lucrative professions, it would have been more difficult for them personally to amass the funds necessary to purchase their manumission without suffering additional stigmatization.[70]

Prostitution and entertainment were two occupations that provided female slaves with some ability to acquire outside revenue through their own labor. Slave prostitutes, especially those serving wealthy clients, may have been able to save the necessary funds to purchase their freedom – at least from the perspective of literary authors. A poem from the *Priapea* describes a slave prostitute who was able to purchase her freedom from her own funds (40, *de quaestu … suo*). Dionysius of Halicarnassus also suggests the potential for profit in this profession by mentioning prostitutes in his list of disreputable and unworthy slaves who were able to buy their own freedom (4.24.4).[71] Similarly, stage acting and other forms of public entertaining might allow female slaves to acquire sufficient personal attention and financial resources to facilitate their manumission.[72] However, using these professions as a springboard to freedom was potentially problematic. While arguably providing female slaves with a realistic financial opportunity to purchase manumission with their own funds, working as prostitutes or actresses could degrade their standing and limit their opportunity to attain full citizenship.[73]

The financial limitations of most female slaves are implied in several case examples from Roman law, which describe women receiving outside support to cover their manumission costs. In an opinion considering the case of a female slave who was to be freed if she gave ten thousand *sesterces* to her owner, the jurist established a scenario where the sum was ultimately paid by another person (*Dig.* 1.5.15, Tryphoninus).[74] Similarly, the jurist Gaius discussed a case where a female slave obtained her manumission essentially by receiving financial assistance from an outside party and undertook repayment after she earned her freedom (*Dig.* 16.1.13.pr).[75] I have yet to find a clear example of a female slave who purchased her freedom solely with her own *peculium*; in the surviving sources the cost of the manumission was consistently paid with the assistance of another person.[76] These opinions do not indicate that female slaves never purchased their own manumission, nor that slave owners believed them to be incapable of doing so. Rather they imply that jurists envisioned financial support as an integral aspect of women's manumission expenses. While the evidence is extremely limited, it nonetheless suggests an expectation among Roman jurists that female slaves would most likely receive outside assistance to cover the costs of their manumission.[77]

But money was not the only currency female slaves could use. Some authors suggested that female slaves could "purchase" their manumission through their reproductive capacity, earning their freedom after giving birth to a predetermined number of children. The most famous proponent of this practice was Columella, who remarked that he often manumitted female slaves who produced more than three children (1.8.19).[78] Similar examples appear in the *Digest*, where jurists considered cases of manumission that were conditional upon a female slave's giving birth to three children.[79] Accordingly, the prospect of manumission served as an incentive to encourage procreation among female slaves. Columella pointed to the economic benefits of this practice, noting that slave owners who adhered to his instruction would increase their patrimony (1.8.19).[80] Roman authors and legal analysts understood procreation as a unique and fundamental attribute contributing to the economic value of female slaves; as such, in their opinion female slaves could barter their reproductive ability in exchange for their freedom.

Relationships and partnerships formed with other slaves may have also facilitated a woman's ability to overcome financial obstacles to manumission. Given the economic disabilities suffered by women in slavery, *contubernium* and other personal relationships were central to the success of female manumission strategies.[81] Certainly a male partner or family member, who had access to a more lucrative profession, would have been a vital financial resource. A female slave could also have benefited from her partner's bond with their owner, who might be persuaded to make her freedom a reward for her partner's service. For example, Scaevola referred to a will that read, "To all my freedmen, those whom I have manumitted while alive and those whom I have either manumitted in this will or shall manumit in the future, I bequeath their "wives" (*contubernales*), sons, and daughters" (*Dig.* 32.41.2).[82] Such a testamentary bequest suggests that male slaves could earn the freedom of their families through their own loyalty and labor.

As a category of individuals, female slaves must have relied more on their personal relationships with their owners and fellow slaves than on their material production in order to achieve manumission. The same gendered attitudes that denied women access to the more prestigious and lucrative professions also thrust them into personal service positions, which facilitated the development of a closer, and perhaps more intimate, relationship between master and slave. Furthermore, the trivialization of women's work may have helped to enable a woman's manumission in two ways. Since owners considered women's work to be less valuable, they may have been less reluctant to part with a female slave, especially after she had passed her prime childbearing years. The trivialization of labor may have also created a gender imbalance within urban households – a locus for manumission in general – thereby increasing the chances of a female slave's forming a long-term partnership with a male member of the household, either slave or free. While extremely fragmentary and limited, there is some evidence to suggest that Romans manumitted more – or at the very least a greater percentage of – female slaves than male slaves, a proportion that may indicate the effectiveness of these personal connections.[83] Thus, it seems reasonable that the manumission of female slaves was founded on the performance of traditional feminine roles, such as wife, mother, and caregiver, more than on material or financial production.

MANUMISSION AND FEMALE CITIZENSHIP

While slave owners possessed sole discretion over whether or not to free their female slaves, this decision was made in the context of a broader conversation among lawmakers, jurists, historians, and other elite male Romans about how owners should make this decision, particularly how they should determine which female slaves deserved to be freed. The private interests of slave owners did not exist in a vacuum completely removed from social concerns. At the core of the larger community discussion on manumission was the issue that freed slaves would become citizens themselves. Recognizing the autonomous role of the slave owner in granting slaves not only freedom, but also citizenship, authors and lawmakers subtly encouraged owners to act in the best interests of the community. The social norms and laws promulgated in these sources did not dictate the actions of slave owners and had only limited ability to influence the individual master's decision to manumit. Nonetheless, the vision of citizen manumission expressed in these sources indicates how Roman elites believed manumission should ideally function as a citizen building process.

There were three formal modes of manumission that would grant a slave both legal freedom and Roman citizenship, all of which appear to have originated very early in the Republic. Two of these forms – manumission *vindicta* and manumission *testamento* – were available to female slaves. Manumission *vindicta* required an owner to manumit a slave in the presence of a magistrate, who then certified the slave's freedom by touching her with his official rod.[84] Manumission *testamento* allowed slave owners to provide for the freedom of their slaves in their will; manumission would occur upon the execution of the document.[85] Both of these formal modes of manumission granted female slaves not only their freedom, but also full Roman citizenship, with rights nearly equal to those of freeborn women.[86]

In addition to these modes of formal manumission, slave owners could manumit their slaves informally, where freedom was not accompanied by citizenship or even full legal rights. The two primary methods of informal manumission appear to have been manumission *per epistulam* (by letter) and manumission *inter amicos* (among/as friends).[87] In each case, it was simply the owner's decision to manumit that ended the female slave's servitude.

During the Republic, informally manumitted women obtained no official citizenship and only limited legal rights along with their freedom. Most importantly, Roman law still considered their possessions to be part of the property of their ex-owner (held by freedwomen as *peculium*) and any children born after informal manumission still to have been slaves.[88] These legal limitations effectively confined freedwomen within a mitigated form of servitude; the jurist Gaius noted that during this time Roman law regarded informally freed individuals as slaves (*olim servi viderentur esse*, 1.22).[89] For ex-slaves, the primary benefit of informal manumission in the Republic appears to have been that their owners could no longer compel them to work full-time.[90]

In the early Principate, the *lex Iunia* reformed the practice of informal manumission by creating a new legal category for individuals freed in this manner. As Junian Latins, individuals manumitted informally still maintained a precarious existence between slavery and freedom. However, the law now clearly demarcated their position and created means for Junian Latins to attain full citizen rights.[91] Owners most likely freed slaves informally when they wanted to maintain an additional measure of control over their freedpersons or when they were unable to fulfill the necessary conditions for formal manumission completely.[92]

Roman authors closely linked the general concepts of manumission and citizenship to loyal and meritorious service, both to slave owners and to the state.[93] Lawmakers and jurists conceived of manumission not simply as the grant of freedom, but also as the creation of a Roman citizen.[94] This principle was also built into the structure of the process, given the necessary participation of the state in the formal modes of manumission.[95] Authors idealized slaves' service to Rome as a principal element of manumission, associating such service both with general theories of manumission and with the origins of specific practices. Thus, a slave deserved citizenship, which necessitated freedom, because he or she acted in the manner of a citizen by directly assisting the state. Cicero connected the ideas of meritorious public service, manumission, and citizenship, writing that "we see slaves, whose rights, fortunes, and condition is the lowest of all, having deserved well by the state, very often presented with liberty – that is to say citizenship" (*Balb.* 24).[96] Similarly, one popular account attributed the origins of manumission *vindicta* to the actions of the slave Vindicius, who received freedom and citizenship after informing the consuls about a conspiracy against the newly formed Republic (Livy 2.4–5). These idealistic depictions of slaves receiving freedom in exchange for their direct service to the state reinforced the perceived connection between manumission and Roman citizenship.[97]

Ancient authors expanded this connection between direct public service and manumission, understanding both fidelity to one's master and the institution of manumission itself as civic benefits. When considering the origins of Roman manumission, Dionysius of Halicarnassus explained the criteria for freedom primarily in terms of loyal service to one's owner:

So that neither Tullius, who established his custom, nor those who received and maintained it thought they were doing anything dishonorable and detrimental to the public interest, if those who had lost both their country and their liberty in war and had proved loyal to those who had enslaved them, or to those who had purchased them from these, had both those blessings restored to them by their masters. Most of these slaves obtained their liberty as a free gift because of meritorious conduct, and this was the best kind of discharge from their masters; but a few paid a ransom raised by lawful and honest labour (*Ant. Rom.* 4.24.3–4, Loeb translation).

Dionysius offered a very idealistic vision of citizen manumission, where any female slave could earn her freedom and place in the community by providing good and loyal service to her master – although what this constituted remained unspoken.[98]

Authors validated the entire institution of manumission as a public good because it acted as a mechanism to produce new citizens. Outside commentators such as Philip V of Macedon and Dionysius both believed that manumission's primary function was to produce new citizens in order to increase the strength of Rome.[99] Pliny articulated a similar sentiment upon receiving word of the manumission of a large number of slaves in his hometown. He responded that this news produced particular joy because he hoped that his homeland would grow in all ways, especially in the number of citizens, which was the surest distinction for towns (*Ep.* 7.32).[100] Accordingly, it was possible to construe the act of manumission itself as an intrinsic civic good. Plautus even went so far as to depict manumission as an act of virtuous citizenship. After setting free one of his courtesans, the comic pimp Dordalus remarks: "Surely am I not an upright and agreeable citizen, who today made great Athens even greater and increased her size by one female citizen?" (*Per.* 474–475).[101]

Citizen manumission was not simply an archaic practice that remained as a static element of Roman society; the community and its leadership consistently debated the terms of this institution. Even though individuals challenged the specific details of this process throughout the Republic and early Principate, especially as the influence of freedpersons increased, the Roman people never overturned the practice of citizen manumission.[102] Although authors rarely mentioned freedwomen and female slaves in this discussion of manumission, women clearly fit into this vision as wives and mothers. Family life and reproduction were central to Romans' understanding of manumission as a civic benefit; without women, such a model of reproduction and growth could not have functioned. Thus, even though Plautus intended for Dordalus to be read somewhat as a fool and a blowhard, his pride in the production of a new female citizen has a measure of substance.

While the roots of both the legal and the perceived ethical connection between manumission and citizenship lie in the Republic, this issue received increased attention and emphasis during the reign of

Augustus. Following the tumultuous and destructive civil wars of the first century BCE, Augustus attempted to stabilize Roman society (and strengthen his own political authority) by promoting a moral reform program intended to reinvigorate and bolster the citizen body. While ostensibly a return to traditional values, the "Augustan ideology" promoted by the emperor in many ways represented a new ethos premised on the ideas of individual virtue and social responsibility.[103] Two critical focal points, discussed and regulated in both literature and law, were feminine virtue and manumission. The Augustan ideology not only asserted that both were critical to the preservation of the citizen body, but, in the process, also effectively characterized them as interrelated issues. As was discussed in the previous chapter, the Roman elite viewed sexual integrity as essential to the definition of a female citizen and, as such, essential to the preservation of the state.[104] The Augustan focus on citizen manumission – evidence of which can be seen in the examples by Livy and Dionysius discussed previously – would reinforce many of these same values.

In concert with the Augustan ideology, authors and lawmakers argued that the personal element of manumission, namely, the self-interested desires of the slave owner, could interfere with the larger, citizen-building motives of the institution. Dionysius spoke to possible faults in his defense of the origins of manumission, maintaining that greed and depravity had made this system unsatisfactory for contemporary Roman society (*Ant. Rom.* 4.24.4–8). He criticized the fact that some slaves earned money for their freedom by performing base activities such as robbery, theft, and prostitution (4). He also complained about unscrupulous slave owners, who chose to free unsuitable candidates as a reward for criminal activity or in order to achieve their own self-serving ends. For Dionysius, the problem was that slave owners were putting their own selfish interests ahead of the welfare of the state. The author's solution was not to halt the practice, however, but rather to have magistrates perform a direct inquiry into the character of individuals designated for manumission (7).

Tacitus recorded a senatorial debate from 56 CE about the misconduct of freedpersons that depicted informal manumission as a form of probationary freedom, intended to ensure that only worthy individuals received citizenship.

Non frustra maiores, cum dignitatem ordinum dividerent, libertatem in communi posuisse. Quin et manu mittendi duas species institutas, ut relinqueretur paenitentiae aut novo beneficio locus. Quos vindicta patronus non liberaverit, velut vinclo servitutis attineri. Dispiceret quisque merita tardeque concederet, quod datum non adimeretur.

Not without reason did our ancestors grant freedom to all, when they were arranging the status of the orders. And furthermore two kinds of manumission were established so that a place was left for regret or new favor. Those whom a patron did not free *vindicta*, were held as if in the chains of slavery. Each man should examine the merits (of a slave) and give away slowly that which may not be removed once given (*Ann.* 13.27).

This speech, attributed to a senatorial faction sympathetic to ex-slaves, responded to opponents who wished to grant patrons the universal right to reenslave insolent or ungrateful freedpersons. The speaker contextualizes the issue as a matter of citizenship and admonishes slave owners to manumit only deserving individuals. This senatorial opinion and the critique of Dionysius were clearly premised on the idealistic belief that the act of creating good citizens was, and should continue to be, a central component of Roman manumission.

Responding to many of the same problems mentioned by Dionysius, Augustus supported a series of legislative reforms intended to protect the integrity of the Roman *populus* by restricting the number of slaves manumitted. The *lex Fufia Caninia* (2 BCE) attempted to limit the total number of slaves freed by restricting the amount of people able to be manumitted by a single will.[105] The *lex Aelia Sentia*, enacted in 4 CE, likewise attempted to reduce the total number of slaves freed by requiring the owner to be older than the age of twenty and the slave older than thirty in order to qualify for formal manumission.[106] In cases where one or both of the individuals did not meet the age criterion, informal manumission was the only option.

However, lawmakers were willing to make an exception to this rule, and thus ensure full citizenship, for slaves manumitted with "good reason" (*iusta causa*). Jurists understood *iusta causa* primarily in terms of close, personal relationships, especially those formed during the owner's childhood. Specific examples mentioned by legal analysts include a slave who was a blood relative, a foster-child (*alumnus*), a foster-sibling (*conlactaneus*), a foster-parent (*educator*), a nurse (*nutrix*), or an educational

assistant (*paedagogus* or *capsarius*). Jurists additionally included the creation of two future relationships as proper grounds: manumitting a
slave in order to make him a financial agent (*procurator*) or manumitting
a female slave in order to marry her (*causa matrimonii*).[107] Furthermore,
it was essential that individuals actually complete these obligations;
according to a decree of the senate, a slave owner had to swear an oath to
marry his slave within six months of manumission before the exception
was approved.[108] In all cases, the law required owners seeking an exception to the age limits to appear before a specially convened committee
made up of five senators and five *equites*.[109]

The desire to protect the integrity of the citizen body is most evident in the creation of the *dediticii* by the *lex Aelia Sentia*. This new
category of freedpersons consisted of those individuals whose conduct
during slavery was so reprehensible that it prohibited them from receiving Roman citizenship or even living within one hundred miles of the
city of Rome.[110]

Both the *lex Fufia Caninia* and the *lex Aelia Sentia* focused on the
conduct of owners rather than that of slaves, attempting to mitigate the
abuse of manumission for personal gain.[111] As profit and exploitation
were central aims motivating manumission, Roman lawmakers did not
seek to impinge on slave owners' general right to manumit or somehow
to restrict manumission only to wholly altruistic reasons. Instead they
attempted to limit the net total of freedpersons being incorporated into
the citizen community, hoping that this would also curtail the infusion
of undesirable individuals.[112]

Finally, the *lex Iunia* (17 BCE?) formalized the process of informal
manumission by creating both a legal status for individuals freed in
this manner (Junian Latinity) and a process by which they might earn
full freedom and citizenship.[113] This law associated the status of informally freed slaves with that of free individuals who had migrated to
the Latin colonies and thus achieved "Latin" rights. Junian Latins possessed most of the property and personal rights of citizens but lacked
testamentary power, with the result that all of their possessions still
reverted to their ex-owners (as if *peculium*) upon their death.[114] Perhaps
most interestingly, the *lex Iunia* effectively separated citizenship
from freedom, creating a rank of free individuals who lacked citizen
status.[115]

Roman law nonetheless provided several mechanisms for Junian Latins to earn full citizenship rights. Most notable was the process entitled the *anniculi probatio* (evidence of a one-year-old child), whereby a Junian Latin married in front of seven witnesses expressly for the purpose of producing children and, after having a child who reached the age of one, went before a magistrate to prove these facts.[116] Later legislation allowed Junian Latins to gain full citizenship by performing a specific act of civic service: serving in the *vigiles* for a set period, constructing a ship and importing grain to Rome, building a house in the city of Rome (after the Neronian fire), or operating a mill in the city of Rome.[117] The *Tituli ex corpore Ulpiani* also mentions that a female Junian Latin could gain citizenship by giving birth to three children (3.1).[118]

By prioritizing marriage and reproduction as grounds for manumission and citizenship, historians and lawmakers in the early Principate not only rewarded the female slaves fulfilling these roles, but also asserted that these activities had value and were citizenlike. The *lex Aelia Sentia* thereby validated the typical female slave existence, which emphasized personal bonds over economic production. Similarly, the regulations governing the status of Junian Latins and the process of the *anniculi probatio* accentuated the standard female social roles of wife and mother. The later legislation creating new opportunities for Junian Latins to advance in status both reemphasized the notion of citizenship as a reward for direct service to the state and effectively associated family and childbirth with this concept. Recall the criticisms of Dionysius, who included prostitution among the list of criminal activities that actively damaged the resources of citizens and the state. By association, Dionysius changed the meaning of prostitution from something base into something injurious – a view closely in line with the vision of moral citizenship promulgated by Augustus. Prostitution was harmful not simply because it had moral implications, but also because it diverted resources from the production of citizens.

Roman lawmakers in the early Principate promoted a vision of citizen manumission conducive to the lifestyles of female slaves because of its emphasis on personal relationships. Furthermore, the Augustan legislation solidified a vision of citizen manumission premised on loyalty and probity in the scope of a slave's daily life and reintegrated these duties with state service. Not only did Roman law create a set of standards conducive to manumitting female slaves, but it also characterized the duties of female slaves as being citizen-worthy. Consider again Columella's explanation for the supervisory duties assigned to the *vilica* (12.pref.8–10). Originally performed by free women, these duties only fell to *vilicae* after the former began to neglect their responsibilities and to live lives of idleness and luxury. So the good *vilica* – a female servant singled out by the author for praise – was noteworthy essentially because she fulfilled the traditional work of the Roman matron.[119]

CONCLUSION

There were two primary avenues for slaves to gain the resources and esteem that would encourage their masters to consider manumission: productive financial success and devoted personal service. Having limited access to the more lucrative professions, female slaves possessed fewer tangible benefits to offer their owners in exchange for their freedom; they had fewer opportunities to acquire funds to compensate for the inherent cost of their manumission. Roman attitudes about gender, work, and slavery compelled female slaves to rely upon their personal relationships – either with their masters or with male slaves – to earn their freedom, at least more so than their male counterparts.

The gender norms structuring slavery and manumission both increased female slaves' opportunity to gain freedom and facilitated their inclusion within the citizen community. Slaves' desire to form families, which owners encouraged out of their own self-interest, would have amplified the demand for women serving as partners/wives and mothers. This enhanced the ability of female slaves to achieve freedom by increasing their perceived economic value and by strengthening their relationships with other slaves, who would have been able to facilitate the manumission of these women. Furthermore, by generally adhering to a vision of slavery that reflected established gender norms regarding women's life and labor, Roman slave owners provided for female slaves' integration into the citizen community. Women's work, while ignored or trivialized, nonetheless identified female slaves as similar to free Roman women, in comparison to the masculine duties undertaken by "less civilized" women. Finally, Roman lawmakers reinforced the value of the lifestyle and labor of female slaves by emphasizing marriage and childbirth as foundational elements in their developing structure of citizen manumission.

3 The Patron-Freedwoman Relationship in Roman Law

Roman lawmakers and jurists established a framework for the post-manumission relationship between freedpersons and their ex-owners, delineating the rights and responsibilities of each party. Romans understood this affiliation as a form of patronage – a relationship based upon the reciprocal exchange of goods and services between individuals of unequal status.[1] The specific duties of patron and freedwoman had been dictated largely by custom in the early Republic, but were increasingly formalized and regulated under classical law.[2] Freedwomen owed their former owners gratitude, respect, and economic compensation, which they demonstrated by attitude, testamentary bequests, and tangible services. In return, patrons were expected to provide financial assistance and general support to their ex-slaves.

The most important difference between the patron-freedwoman relationship and other forms of patronage was its compulsory, rather than voluntary, nature. As a requisite to manumission, Roman lawmakers *required* freedwomen to remain in a legally defined position of obligation and deference for their entire lives. Patrons could excuse themselves from certain responsibilities, but they too could never completely extricate themselves from this relationship. As a result, manumission created a persistent and lasting bond between patron and freedwoman.

Some historians have interpreted the expectations of lifelong deference and service built into the patron-freedperson relationship as a repressive mechanism for socially degrading ex-slaves. Accordingly, they conflate "patron" with "upper-class" and represent freedpersons as a separate, socially distinct group, defined by their continued submission and service to their social betters.[3] However, this view is difficult to sustain when one considers that by the late Republic it was quite common for freedpersons to be patrons themselves. Freedpersons existed at every socioeconomic level in Roman society. While the patron-freedperson relationship was certainly hierarchical and a public manifestation of an individual's servile background, it would be erroneous to assert that the *primary* purpose of these legally defined responsibilities was the social subjugation of an entire category of people.

More recent scholarship has focused on elements of socialization and social control built into the patron-freedperson relationship. Andrew Wallace-Hadrill argues that Romans designed this obligatory relationship to help integrate freedpersons into wider society. He concludes, "As a citizen, the ex-slave is a full member of Roman society; yet his membership is in some sense conditional, mediated through his patron who continues as a sort of sponsor."[4] Expanding upon these ideas, Jane Gardner reasons that the ongoing connection with a citizen *familia* was an essential mechanism for social integration for ex-slaves because it gave these new citizens "some points of attachment within the existing society."[5] For Wallace-Hadrill and Gardner, the legal relationship between patron and freedperson was significant on a societal level not merely for the work that it accomplished, but more importantly for its manifestation of an essential bond between the two individuals. This chapter contributes to this line of scholarship by exploring the patron-freedwoman relationship in Roman law, and how social and economic concerns shaped specific rights and responsibilities – the constitutive components of these "points of attachment."

Even though the patron-freedwoman relationship would have manifested itself in a variety of forms in practice, the legally defined structure of general rights and responsibilities can provide modern scholars with important information about elite Romans' conceptions of female honor, respectability, and citizenship. Lawmakers and jurists struggled with two critical and often conflicting issues when considering the specific terms of this relationship: patrons' right to benefit from the manumission of their slaves and freedwomen's capacity to achieve the respectability and social honor required of female citizens. Romans steadfastly believed that individuals who chose to manumit their slaves deserved some compensation for their loss of property and labor.[6] Given that Roman law permitted patrons to exploit their freedpersons, it was essential for lawmakers to establish boundaries in order to maintain a separation between freedwomen and female slaves. It is unsurprising then that two central issues for jurists were a freedwoman's sexual integrity and her ability to form marriages, which were defining aspects of the iconic Roman woman – the *matrona*.[7] In establishing the legal guidelines for the ongoing relationship between patrons and their ex-slaves, jurists attempted to craft a framework of rights and responsibilities that would not impair a freedwoman's capacity to establish herself as a respectable Roman matron.

FREEDWOMEN'S OBLIGATIONS TO PATRONS: GENDERED FORMS OF *OBSEQUIUM* AND *OPERAE*

Prior to the second century BCE, most freedwomen's daily lives may have been very similar to those they had experienced as slaves.[8] A recently manumitted woman would have likely continued living with her patron and performing the same type of open-ended service for his household. Modern scholars have noted how the domestic, agricultural economy of early Italy likely compelled freedpersons to remain in "a kind of dependent symbiosis" with their patrons, performing the same duties they had completed while in bondage.[9] The most useful source for discerning the types of duties imposed on freedwomen prior to the late Republic is commentary found in the *Digest*:

Hoc edictum a praetore propositum est honoris, quem liberti patronis habere debent, moderandi gratia. Namque ut Servius scribit, antea soliti fuerunt a libertis durissimas res exigere, scilicet ad remunerandum tam grande beneficium, quod in libertos confertur, cum ex servitute ad civitatem Romanam perducuntur. (1) Et quidem primus praetor Rutilius edixit se amplius non daturum patrono quam operarum et societatis actionem, videlicet si hoc pepigisset, ut, nisi ei obsequium praestaret libertus, in societatem admitteretur patronus. (2) Posteriores praetores certae partis bonorum possessionem pollicebantur: videlicet enim imago societatis induxit eiusdem partis praestationem, ut, quod vivus solebat societatis nomine praestare, id post mortem praestaret.

This edict has been put forward by the praetor for the purpose of regulating the respect that freedpersons ought to have for their patrons. For, as Servius writes, in former times [patrons] were accustomed to make very harsh demands on their freedpersons, naturally for the purpose of repaying the enormous benefit conferred on freedpersons when they are brought out of slavery to Roman citizenship. (1) And indeed Rutilius was the first praetor to proclaim that he would not give a patron more than an action for services and partnership, namely, if he had pledged, so that if a freedperson did not show respect to his patron, the patron would be admitted to partnership [in his goods]. (2) Later praetors promised patrons *bonorum possessio* of a fixed part [of the freedperson's property]; for clearly the idea of partnership led to an offer of the same share with the result that what the freedperson was accustomed to offer in the name of partnership while alive, he or she gave after his or her death (*Dig.* 38.2.1, Ulpian).

This passage suggests that at one time patrons could have imposed stringent obligations on their freedpersons, maintaining a considerable degree of control over both their labor and their finances, but that this condition was subject to later revision.[10] There does not appear to have been an attempt to regulate legally the behavior of freedpersons vis-à-vis their patrons, but rather an underlying belief that *fides* imposed a moral obligation of respect and dutifulness on ex-slaves.[11]

Lawmakers in the late Republic and early Empire developed a more precise body of legal regulations and penalties governing the patron-freedperson relationship. Around the year 118 BCE, the praetor Rutilius introduced an edict ostensibly designed to lessen the labor and financial burden levied on freedpersons by allowing patrons to exact only services specified in agreements contracted at the time of manumission.[12] While the extent to which this edict actually reduced the amount of labor performed by freedpersons is debatable, given that there was little to stop patrons from contracting for considerable obligations, it reinforced an important distinction between slave and freed. Instead of the constant and perpetual service required of slaves, freedpersons were liable only for specific duties established by pledge after manumission. By the end of the Republic, jurists had placed even more limitations on the types of labor and financial services that patrons could require from their freedpersons, most notably by invalidating the *societas*, an agreement where a patron received a portion of a freedperson's income.[13] Lawmakers transformed freedpersons' financial obligations to their ex-masters from open-ended service and attendance to a discrete set of duties and contracted labor. The format of these obligations came to resemble the work of free persons rather than the service of slaves.

Modern scholars generally classify the obligations of freedpersons in the classical era into two main categories: *obsequium* (general respect) and *operae* (labor and services).[14] *Obsequium* is a blanket term used primarily by modern scholars to describe a wide range of prohibitions and duties designed to ensure freedpersons' proper treatment of their patrons.[15] While there is some dispute over strict definitions, all agree that during the Principate, Roman law required freedpersons to demonstrate a general attitude of respect, gratitude, and loyalty to their ex-masters.[16] Jurists concentrated primarily on the litigious restrictions and financial responsibilities of freedpersons when describing the details of such behavior. Freedpersons could not levy criminal charges or any legal action that might discredit their ex-masters.[17] Furthermore, the law forbade freedpersons to give evidence against their patrons, either of their own volition or under the compulsion of the court.[18] *Obsequium* also required freedpersons to support their ex-masters in times of need, which included providing financial assistance and serving as a guardian for a patron's children.[19] In the surviving legal sources, there is only one example that explicitly mentions a woman's conduct. Papinian decided that a freedwoman was not ungrateful (*ingrata*) if she practiced her profession (*arte sua ... utitur*) against the wishes of her female patron (*Dig.* 37.15.11).[20] Within the different manifestations of *obsequium* described in the legal sources, the ideas of reverence and gratitude are foundational qualities for the expected behavior of freedpersons toward their patrons.

After the establishment of the *lex Aelia Sentia* in 4 CE, patrons had the ability to bring formal legal action against freedpersons who violated the prescribed standards of respectful conduct. In addition to failing to adhere to the requirements outlined, insults, physical attacks, and failure to support patrons in times of need were actions worthy of legal proceedings for ingratitude.[21] Depending on the offense, punishment could have included financial reparations in the form of cash or extra services, physical castigation, and temporary exile. Even reenslavement was an option for serious violations or repeat offenders.[22] The threat of legal action helped to enforce standards of respectful behavior for freedpersons in their relationships with their ex-masters.

There was also a reciprocal element to *obsequium*, in that Romans expected patrons to demonstrate proper behavior toward their former slaves. The jurists mentioned two specific requirements imposed on patrons. Patrons needed to provide appropriate support for freedpersons in times of need. The *lex Aelia Sentia* cancelled contracted obligations owed by the freedperson if a patron failed to provide maintenance (*aluere*).[23] Perhaps most importantly, Roman law forbade patrons to treat their freedpersons as slaves.[24] The surviving legal sources do not explain the nuances of such a prohibition, but one example condemned patrons who chastised their freedpersons with whips or rods – the archetypal punishment for slaves (*Dig.* 47.10.7.2, Ulpian).[25] In these rulings, lawmakers expected patrons to respect the new status that they had bestowed upon their ex-slaves, and to help them succeed as citizens.

Given the expectations of deference and service, the demands of *obsequium* could potentially injure a freedwoman's status and reputation. While Roman law normally prohibited freedwomen to initiate legal action against their patrons, it allowed them access to the *actio iniuriarum* (legal action for insult) in order to redress severe damage to their honor. As was discussed in Chapter 1, the charge of *iniuria* originally had covered only physical assaults, but by the late Republic it encompassed interference with personal rights and verbal insults, which caused injury by lowering the estimation of the victim in the eyes of others.[26] Roman law further held that individuals suffered injury not only from transgressions against them, but also from offenses toward a spouse or those in their *potestas*.[27] There was not a standard or discrete list of acts that caused *iniuria*; the existence of *iniuria* was contingent upon factors such as the relative status of the parties and the nature of their relationship.

In the case of freedpersons and their ex-masters, Ulpian ruled that only the most serious of affronts by patrons (*si atrox sit iniuria*), such treating their freedperson in the manner of a slave, warranted legal attention.[28]

Praeterea illo spectat dici certum de iniuria, quam passus quis sit, ut ex qualitate iniuriae sciamus, an in patronum liberto reddendum sit iniuriarum iudicium. Etenim meminisse oportebit liberto adversus patronum non quidem semper, verum interdum iniuriarum dari iudicium, si atrox sit iniuria quam passus sit, puta, si servilis. Ceterum levem cohercitionem utique patrono adversus libertum dabimus nec patietur eum praetor querentem, quasi iniuriam passus sit, nisi atrocitas eum moverit: nec enim ferre praetor debet heri servum, hodie liberum conquerentem, quod dominus ei convicium dixerit vel quod leviter pulsaverit vel emendaverit. Sed si flagris, si verberibus, si vulneravit non mediocriter: aequissimum erit praetorem ei subvenire.

Furthermore, it is relevant that the insult that someone suffered be specified, so that we may know from the nature of the insult whether an action for insult should be granted to a freedperson against his or her patron. For it is necessary to remember that an action for insult is not always given to a freedperson against his or her patron but only at times when the insult which he or she suffered was heinous, for example if he or she was treated as a slave. We will absolutely allow a patron the limited punishment of his or her freedperson, and the praetor will not allow a freedperson to make a formal complaint that insult was suffered unless the heinousness [of the insult] moves him; for the praetor ought not to tolerate a former slave, now a freedperson, complaining because his or her master verbally abused him or her, or because the master moderately chastised or corrected him or her. But if the chastisement was done with lashes or rods, or if the patron seriously wounded the freedperson, it is eminently right that the praetor support the freedperson (*Dig.* 47.10.7.2, Ulpian).

Formal accusations were not easy to make, as freedpersons required the approval of the praetor to initiate any legal action against their patrons.[29] The unstated correlative to this opinion on *iniuria* was that Romans permitted patrons to treat their freedpersons in ways that might be injurious to others because of the unique nature of their relationship.

The issue of *iniuria* became more complicated when a married freedwoman was involved.

Quamquam adversus patronum liberto iniuriarum actio non detur, verum marito libertae nomine cum patrono actio competit: maritus enim uxore sua iniuriam passa suo nomine iniuriarum agere videtur. Quod et Marcellus admittit. Ego autem apud eum notavi non de omni iniuria hoc esse dicendum me putare: levis enim coercitio etiam in nuptam vel convici non impudici dictio cur patrono denegetur? Si autem conliberto nupta esset, diceremus omnino iniuriarum marito adversus patronum cessare actionem, et ita multi sentiunt. Ex quibus apparet libertos nostros non tantum eas iniurias adversus nos iniuriarum actione exequi non posse, quaecumque fiunt ipsis, sed ne eas quidem, quae eis fiunt, quos eorum interest iniuriam non pati.

Although the action for insult is not given to a freedperson against his or her patron, the husband of a freedwoman can have an action in respect to her against her patron: for when a wife suffers insult, her husband is regarded as bringing an action for insult in his own name. Marcellus admits this. But I have made note on him that I do not think that this must be prescribed concerning every insult; for why should a patron be denied the mild chastisement or verbal reproach – so long as it is not lewd – of even a married woman? But if she is married to a freedman of the same patron, then we should admit that an action for insult is absolutely unavailable to the husband against the patron. And many feel this way. From all this it is clear that our freedpersons are unable to avenge against us with an action for insult, not only insults which they themselves endure, but also insults endured by people in whom our freedpersons have an interest in their not suffering insult (*Dig.* 47.10.11.7, Ulpian).

Under Roman law a husband could suffer *iniuria* from insults directed at his wife and therefore was allowed to initiate proceedings in his own name. So, according to Marcellus, a freedwoman's husband could take legal action on the basis that he suffered personal insult from a patron's conduct toward his freedwoman. In such cases, the husband initiated legal proceedings in his own name, not in the name of his wife.[30] However, if a freedwoman's husband was also a freedman of her patron, he could not bring an action for insult, falling under the same legal restrictions as his wife. Marcellus's decision was a simple extension of the general rule regarding freedpersons and the *actio iniuriarum*: There was nothing to prohibit a husband from initiating legal action against an individual who was not his patron, even though the standards of *obsequium* prevented his wife from initiating her own action against the same person.

Ulpian, in turn, attempted to qualify the opinion of Marcellus by reasserting patrons' *right* to berate their freedwomen verbally and physically punish them.[31] He believed that patrons should be able to employ mild chastisement (*levis coercitio*) or verbal abuse (*convici dictio*) against their freedwomen, provided that it was not lewd (*non impudici, Dig.* 47.10.11.7). Both of these behaviors would be unacceptable if directed at freeborn citizen women. *Coercitio* could imply physical punishment, an aspect that seems emphasized by the word's oppositional placement to "verbal abuse" (*convici dictio*).[32] In a preceding passage (*Dig.* 47.10.7.2, quoted earlier), Ulpian described appropriate *coercitio* as mildly striking or verbally correcting (*leviter pulsaverit vel emendaverit*) an individual. *Convicium* was a specific legal term, defined by the jurists as shouting that was against good manners and aimed at someone's disgrace or unpopularity (*quae bonis moribus improbatur quaeque ad infamiam vel invidiam alicuius spectare*, *Dig.* 47.10.15.5–6, Ulpian quoting the praetor's edict and Labeo). Furthermore, this abuse must have been loud (*vociferatione*) and public (*in coetu*).[33] Ulpian agreed with earlier jurists that *convicium* was clearly *iniuria* (47.10.15.3; cf. Gaius 3.220), but not in the case of a patron correcting his or her freedwoman. However, the jurist qualified his statement by explicitly declaring lewd (*impudicus*) language as wholly unacceptable behavior in every respect. According to Ulpian, Roman law guaranteed patrons' license to address their freedwomen in ways that could be construed as offensive and demeaning if directed at other citizen women. But it strictly prohibited conduct that threatened freedwomen's sexual honor.

The format of Ulpian's opinion suggests that he considered the *actio iniuriarum* to be of particular relevance to women. In addition to the main statement quoted previously, the jurist added that a freedman's wife could also bring action in her own name in response to insults toward her husband (*Dig.* 47.10.11.8).[34] However, in legal opinions that concerned freedpersons of both sexes, jurists generally subsumed freedwomen under the masculine-neutral term *liberti*. It is significant, then, that Ulpian used the husband of a freedwoman as the principal actor in his example, including the wives of freedmen in the follow-up statement.[35] The structure of this opinion implies that even though the law technically applied to spouses of either sex, this particular question of *iniuria* was primarily associated with freedwomen and their husbands. It is also important that in both the opinion considering married freedwomen (*Dig.* 47.10.11.7) and the opinion considering freedpersons in general (*Dig.* 47.10.7.2), Ulpian mentioned verbal abuse (*convicium*) as acceptable conduct for patrons. Only in the passage considering married freedwomen did he feel the need to prohibit lewd discourse explicitly. Again, this ruling would have technically applied to freedpersons of both sexes; the explicit mention in the opinion considering married freedwomen highlighted a particular concern.

The legal analysis of the relationship between *obsequium* and *iniuria* suggests two conclusions. First, despite the fact that patrons possessed license to address their freedwomen in ways that could be construed as offensive and demeaning if directed at other women, conduct that transgressed, or even blurred, the line between freedwoman and female slave was strictly prohibited. Second, at least one jurist believed that a patron's conduct meant something different when it involved a married freedwoman, not so much because it could adversely affect the woman's honor, but rather because it could injure the status of her spouse. Jurists protected patrons' authority so long as it did not infringe on a new citizen's right to respectability or the honor of her husband.

Obsequium itself was not necessarily an attempt to restrict or infringe upon the status of freedwomen, as it was an intrinsic aspect of relationships between individuals of unequal power. It is certainly significant that family members were subject to comparable rules of *obsequium*. This is not to say that patrons would have treated their freedwomen and their female relatives in the same manner, or would have expected the same displays of reverence. Rather, it is evident that lawmakers and jurists envisioned the obligations of freedpersons and the obligations of kin to be structurally similar. Roman social norms required children to express reverence and gratitude to their parents and imposed similar legal restrictions. Furthermore, jurists did not construe potentially insulting or injurious behavior between family members as meeting the standards of *iniuria*. Ulpian declared that, in cases of *convicium*, an action for insult would neither be given for or against heirs (*Dig.* 47.10.15.15). As in the case of patrons and freedpersons, the law allowed parents to treat their children in a manner unacceptable for other Roman citizens. Given the parallel to relationships between kin, it seems likely, then, that *obsequium*, and the potentially insulting conduct it condoned, was not designed to degrade freedwomen as members of the Roman community, but instead signified their close – and hierarchical – affiliation with their patrons.

Jurists had similar concerns about the satisfaction of *operae* and its potential effect upon a freedwoman's reputation. *Operae* were tangible services that freedpersons commonly performed for their ex-masters after manumission. Literally, *operae* were a specific number of days' work (*diurnum officium*) that freedpersons promised to provide to their patrons as recompense for their freedom.[36] By the classical period, this labor was neither automatically owed nor limitless, but rather a "voluntary" contractual obligation.[37] While *operae* were not necessarily part of the manumission process, jurists considered them a common and "natural" obligation.[38] They divided *operae* into two loosely defined categories: trade services (*operae fabriles*) and official duties (*operae officiales*).[39] Patrons could require freedpersons to offer *operae fabriles* in the trade (*artificium*) that they had taken up after manumission so long as the services were honorable and without risk to life. The law also obligated patrons to consider a freedperson's age, status, heath, needs, and way of life when determining the type and extent of the labor. Contracted services that infringed on any of these considerations were not to be rendered.[40] The jurists did not define *operae officiales* in any detail, but the surviving evidence suggests that the duty included some form of personal attendance and service.[41]

Jurists understood the goal of *operae* primarily to be serving one's former owner rather than producing profit. Roman law recognized an individual's right to obtain recompense from the manumission of a slave, and *operae* created a structured means for patrons to financially exploit their freedpersons. However, jurists eschewed a purely capitalistic view of *operae*, limiting patrons' ability to hire out the labor of their freedpersons to third parties.[42] This suggests that, from the perspective of Roman law, providing service to one's ex-master was an essential component of this requirement.

There are no examples of distinctive female *operae* in the ancient sources, but it seems most likely that freedwomen also provided services in the form of professional labor and personal duties. Support for the former is found in a legal opinion of Callistratus, who forbade patrons to demand *operae* in the form of sexual duties from a freedwoman who was a practicing prostitute (*Dig.* 38.1.38.pr). In this example, the jurist essentially prohibited a patron to acquire a freedwoman's professional labor as contracted services. Such a restriction was necessary only if patrons were accustomed to receiving the professional labor of freedwomen as *operae*. Therefore, it follows that feminine *operae* could have taken the form of any type of nonsexual professional labor common among women in Roman society.

The opinion of Callistratus lends insight to types of forbidden *operae* and the separation between free and servile labor. The case of a patron demanding sexual favors as *operae* served as an example of services that were forbidden because their performance caused the disgrace (*turpitudo*) of the freedwoman.[43] If performing these services disgraced a professional prostitute, then they certainly must have disgraced other freedwomen as well. However, as the freedwoman in this example was earning her living as a prostitute, there is no reason to assume that her patron could not solicit her as a paying client. Furthermore, there was nothing to stop a patron and freedwomen from engaging in sexual affairs on their own. Male slave owners had nearly unrestricted sexual access to their female slaves, and continued relationships between patrons and their freedwomen were common and even encouraged. It seems, then, that the main concern of Callistratus was not the performance of the sexual act itself, but rather the imposed obligation to provide sex. To establish freedwomen as female citizens with honor, it was necessary for jurists to distinguish the patron from the master.[44] While Roman law protected an ex-owner's right to demand labor in exchange for manumission, jurists limited the scope of these services in order to preserve personal integrity and social propriety.[45]

In addition to classifying certain types of services as improper, Roman law indicated several situations where the performance of *operae* in general would be unseemly for a freedwoman. In his commentary on the Augustan marriages laws (the *lex Iulia et Papia*), Paul noted that when a freedwoman turned fifty, she was no longer obligated (*non cogitur*) to perform *operae* for her patron (*Dig.* 38.1.35.pr). Paul's opinion gives little insight to the reasoning behind this ruling, which does not appear to have had a male parallel.[46]

The jurist Hermogenian further ruled that if a male patron or his male descendants gave consent to the marriage of a freedwoman, they were no longer owed services.[47]

Sicut patronus, ita etiam patroni filius et nepos et pronepos, qui libertae nuptiis consensit, operarum exactionem amittit: nam haec, cuius matrimonio consensit, in officio mariti esse debet. (1) Si autem nuptiae, quibus patronus consensit, nullas habeant vires, operas exigere patronus non prohibetur. (2) Patronae, item filiae et nepti et pronepti patroni, quae libertae nuptiis consensit, operarum exactio non denegatur, quia his nec ab ea quae nupta est indecore praestantur.

Just as a male patron, so too his son, grandson, and great-grandson, if they have consented to the marriage of a freedwoman, lose the exaction of services: for the woman to whose marriage a male patron has consented ought to be in the service of her husband. (1) If, however, the marriage to which the male patron has consented has no validity, the patron is not prevented from exacting services. (2) The exaction of services is not denied a female patron or likewise the daughter, granddaughter, or great-granddaughter of a patron who has consented to the marriage of a freedwoman, because the performance of services for these individuals is not unseemly for a married freedwoman (*Dig.* 38.1.48).

The primary justification for this ruling was that a married freedwoman should be in the service (*officium*) of her husband rather than her patron. This was not merely an issue of time conflict, in the sense that a woman would not have the ability to satisfy her duties as both a wife and a freedwoman.[48] Jurists had no reservations about married freedwomen fulfilling promised *operae* for female patrons, and there is no indication that the types of services performed for female patrons were in any way different from those owed to male patrons. The issue was not the tangible set of duties associated with the roles of wife and freedwoman, but instead the condition of owing service to two different men: husband and patron. Moreover, it was specifically the performance of *operae* that was potentially problematic, rather than the complete set of obligations that freedwomen owed to their patrons.[49]

Later in the passage, Hermogenian suggests that the performance of *operae* for a male patron by a married freedwoman could be unseemly (*indecore*) for both of them. Obviously gender mattered in this ruling, as the male patron–freedwoman relationship was problematic in a way that the female patron–freedwoman relationship was not. Given this, the most logical assumption is that the perceived unseemliness derived from some infringement on the freedwoman's sexual honor.[50] Indeed, jurists indicated that the obligation to provide *operae* to one's patron conflicted with the status of being a wife.[51] Being in a current state of marriage was central to the cancellation of *operae*, as most jurists believed that male patrons could renew their demand for services if a freedwoman ceased to be married, or if the marriage became void.[52] Furthermore, patrons were able to seek financial compensation for *operae* owed before a freedwomen's marriage, but not the completion of the services themselves.[53] Such a decision suggests that the issue lay in the actual performance of *operae* rather than the material liabilities of this service, such as the loss of time or capital. The obligation to perform *operae* was problematic because it kept a married woman in the service of a man other than her husband. It warrants repeating that jurists were not willing to curtail the rights of patrons by universally eliminating all services upon a freedwoman's marriage, but only when a male patron lent his consent to the union.[54]

Finally, Romans released a freedwoman from the obligation of *operae* if she attained a social status (*dignitas*) where it was not appropriate for her (*inconveniens*) to perform such services.[55] The jurist did not elaborate on the details of such a *dignitas*, most likely leaving the matter open to interpretation in individual cases. Wolfgang Waldstein believes that the most likely cause for a woman's rise in *dignitas* was a high-status marriage.[56] If so, then the automatic cancellation of services for women who married men of high rank suggests that Roman jurists were primarily concerned with how the performance of *operae* affected the status of a freedwoman's husband rather than that of the freedwoman herself.

Performing obligatory labor for one's former owner reenacted the master-slave relationship in a way that the other responsibilities of freedwomen did not. However, the jurists' unwillingness to cancel *operae* for all freedwomen – or even all married freedwomen – suggests that any status loss resulting from the performance of these services was not an insurmountable challenge to a woman's honor. The obligation to provide *operae* only appears to have become unavoidably injurious when the freedwoman achieved a certain level of *dignitas*, at which point Roman law ended the contract *ipso iure*. Clearly, there was some concern about a married woman's submission to a male authority other than her husband. But so long as the services themselves were not disreputable, jurists were unwilling to deny patrons completely the right to exploit their female ex-slaves.

There was some tension between the structured, legally defined service of a freedwoman to her former master and her ability to function as a respectable Roman matron. Romans expected all freedwomen to continue to demonstrate reverence to their ex-owners. The law mandated the terms of this respectful behavior, which jurists conceptualized both as a general attitude and as a set of required and prohibited actions.

Policymakers devised these guidelines to ensure that patrons would not suffer ingratitude from their ex-slaves, but in doing so they also sanctioned patrons' right to treat their freedwomen in a manner inappropriate for other citizens. Furthermore, Roman law allowed patrons to demand professional and personal labor from their freedwomen as recompense for their freedom. Jurists recognized that these expectations of deference and service could blur the line between freed and slave and therefore attempted to protect a freedwoman's ability to maintain a level of honor and respectability required of female citizens.

GUARDIANSHIP (*TUTELA*) AND INHERITANCE RIGHTS (*BONA*)

From the time of the Twelve Tables, Roman law placed freedwomen into the guardianship (*tutela legitima*) of their male patrons after manumission.[57] Roman lawmakers established the *tutela mulierum* ostensibly to protect a woman's economic interests and to safeguard a family's wealth for its agnatic descendants.[58] Accordingly, *tutores* oversaw a woman's financial and legal affairs; doing so did not necessarily involve direct administration, but generally consisted of lending approval (*auctoritatis interpositio*) to certain transactions that could potentially diminish the woman's estate. These transactions included entering into marriage *cum manu*, promising a dowry, alienating *res mancipi*, formally manumitting slaves, and creating a will.[59] In most cases, a *tutor legitimus* was the nearest male agnate, whom Roman law appointed as guardian when no other testamentary provisions had been made. Because of the close family relationship, Romans considered a *tutor legitimus* to have more of a personal stake in the financial affairs of his wards than other types of guardians. As a result, unlike other types of guardians, a *tutor legitimus* could not be compelled by law to lend his approval to desired transactions.[60] Thus, naming male patrons as *tutores legitimi* of their former female slaves not only gave them significant influence over their freedwomen's financial conduct, but also highlighted their perceived personal stake in these affairs.

Roman law protected a patron's possession of the *tutela legitima*, even to the point where the efficacy of the office was severely diminished.

There was no way for a freedwoman to extricate herself from her ex-master's guardianship completely other than by his death. And upon the death of a patron, *tutela legitima* automatically passed to his male descendants.[61] Guardianship could be passed from a patron to his underage son, despite the fact that the son could not legally impose his own authorization (requiring a *tutor* himself) and therefore was unable to fulfill his legal responsibilities.[62] Moreover, a freedwoman could not petition for a new *tutor* to replace an absent patron.[63] Gaius noted that in these situations, a freedwoman could apply to a magistrate to obtain another guardian temporarily in order to satisfy a specific, time-sensitive objective, such as collecting an inheritance or assembling a dowry for marriage. However, he stressed that this was an interim measure and that the right of guardianship remained preserved for the male patron or his son (1.176–181). Only when a patron died without any male issue could a freedwoman apply to the magistrates for a new permanent guardian.[64] The fact that Roman law protected a patron's right to serve as *tutor*, even when he could not satisfy the basic requirements of the position, unambiguously indicates the significance of this patronal right.[65]

According to later jurists, the Twelve Tables also guaranteed a patron's ability to inherit the entire estate of a deceased freedperson if there were no will and no direct heirs (*sui heredes*).[66] The law treated a freedperson's estate exactly like that of a freeborn citizen and did not accord the patron any special privilege or entitlement to inherit.[67] Instead, the earliest Roman lawmakers identified the patron as the final individual in an established line of agnatic succession, and as a result, the existence of either a will or *sui heredes* meant that a patron received nothing. According to Gaius, this decision to make patrons heirs also provided the legal foundation for conferring upon them *tutela* over their freedpersons (1.165).[68] Since the Twelve Tables made agnates heirs and granted guardianship to them in cases of intestacy and the absence of *sui heredes* as a general rule, the older jurists (*veteres*) assumed that the code also meant to grant guardianship to patrons when it named them heirs.

While the Twelve Tables did little to guarantee that a patron would gain a share of a freedman's estate, it effectively positioned a male patron to inherit from a deceased freedwoman. According to Roman law, a woman did not possess *sui heredes*, and therefore, a patron would automatically be the first in line to succeed to the estate of an intestate freedwoman. Furthermore, since a woman required the official approval of her *tutor* to create a will, a male patron could legally dismiss any document that did not name him as an heir. It appears that jurists considered exercising this testamentary authority a reasonable and appropriate action. Gaius wrote that, during this era, a male patron could not suffer *iniuria* in such an inheritance case because it was his own fault if a freedwoman's will failed to name him as an heir (3.43). The implication is that male patrons deserved to receive a share of their freedwomen's estates, and that exerting their influence as *tutores* was an appropriate means to achieve this. Yet at the same time, the complete power that male patrons possessed over the estates of their freedwomen arose not because they had any special patronal authority, but rather because Roman law devalued the legal relationship between a mother and her children and severely restricted a woman's ability to create a will in general.

During the late Republic, the praetor's edict recognized the unique position of patrons by granting them greater inheritance rights against the claims of heirs who were not biological descendants of freedpersons.[69] The edict guaranteed male patrons or their male descendants one-half of a freedperson's estate if the freedperson died intestate or left a will naming only heirs other than natural children.[70] This decision indicates a developing opinion among Roman lawmakers that patrons should be *entitled* to a share of their freedpersons' estates. Gaius wrote that the praetor's edict cured an injustice (*iniquitas*) by allowing patrons to inherit ahead of adoptive children or wives *in manu* (3.40–41). It is likely that this entitlement was in part understood as financial compensation for loss incurred by freeing one's slaves.[71] From a strictly legal standpoint, this new regulation did little to affect situations involving freedwomen, since they still lacked *sui heredes* and the agency to validate their own wills. Yet it is reasonable to assume that the sense of patronal entitlement conveyed in this edict lent even stronger moral authority to male patrons who used their guardianship of freedwomen to shape testamentary distribution.

The next significant piece of legislation, the *lex Papia Poppaea* (9 CE), further extended the inheritance rights of patrons by giving them an automatic share of large estates owned by their freedpersons and bolstering the testamentary claims of female patrons. This law guaranteed patrons a share of a freedperson's estate worth more than 100,000 *sesterces*, regardless of the presence of a will or natural heirs. Only freedpersons who had three or more biological children could exclude their patrons from inheriting.[72] The *lex Papia* also increased the rights of female patrons, giving them a stronger claim to the estates of testate freedwomen.[73] Roman law not only continued to increase the ability of patrons to obtain a share of their freedpersons' estates, but also increasingly distinguished patrons as entities apart from familial successors – as individuals who deserved to inherit on the basis of their decision to manumit a slave.

The *lex Papia* also provided the means for freedwomen to escape the near-total control that patrons had held over their financial management from the time of the Twelve Tables. The law released freedwomen with four children from *tutela mulierum*, giving them the right to create wills under their own *auctoritas* and thus exclude their patron from inheriting the entire estate.[74] This concession to freedwomen was not a statement about their particular situation insomuch as it expressed the wider goals of the Augustan social legislation, which lawmakers designed to encourage the production of legitimate children.[75] At the same time, this law highlighted the significance of the patron-freedwoman relationship by only requiring freedwomen to have three children to escape guardianship of an individual other than a patron.[76] Lawmakers were reluctant to exclude patrons altogether, and the *lex Papia* still guaranteed patrons a share of their wealthy freedwomen's estates proportional to the number of surviving children.[77] It was not until the *senatus consultum Orphitianum* of 178 CE that the children of a freedwoman received the right of intestate succession ahead of their mother's patron.[78]

Lawmakers in the Principate continued to ensure that patrons retained solid control over the economic affairs of their freedwomen, which was a striking deviation from a more general tendency among jurists to dilute the potency of *tutela mulierum* constraining the transactions of freeborn women. By this time, jurists had clearly recognized that women were capable of managing their own financial concerns.[79] Gaius noted that Romans commonly attributed the existence of the *tutela* to the light-mindedness (*animi levitas*) of women but remarked that this belief was unsubstantiated. He firmly asserted that he found no reason why women who had reached the age of maturity needed to be in guardianship (1.190; cf. 1.144).[80] Women in *tutela* could compel any guardian other than a *tutor legitimus* to lend his approval to transactions by applying to the magistrate.[81] Furthermore, a *lex Claudia* (generally attributed to the emperor Claudius) abolished the agnatic guardianship of women, ostensibly because of the declining influence of agnatic relatives and the weakening of the *tutela* in general, and effectively ended *tutela legitima* in all cases except those involving freedwomen; the law continued to classify male patrons as the *tutores legitimi* of their female ex-slaves, protecting their influence and control over their freedwomen's finances.[82] Despite changing views toward women and the role of *tutela mulierum*, Roman lawmakers ensured that patrons would still possess a measure of economic control over their freedwomen. While the economic interests of the guardian had always influenced the institution of the *tutela*, the situation in the early Principate represents a conscious effort by jurists to protect patrons' economic interests vis-à-vis their freedwomen.[83]

The evolving nature of both patrons' role in the guardianship of freedwomen and their rights as inheritors indicates the desire of Roman lawmakers to protect patrons' ability to continue to profit from their ex-slaves. In the early Republic, lawmakers inserted patrons into the existing system governing the affairs of women by categorizing them as de facto agnatic relatives. Since freedwomen lacked agnatic relatives under Roman law, patrons were the first in line to administer and inherit freedwomen's estates. What changed over time was not the control that patrons wielded over freedwomen's property, but rather the basis upon which they exercised these rights. By the late Republic, jurists increasingly indicated that former owners should be entitled to a share of their freedpersons' estates as *patrons* rather than as substitute agnates. To a large extent, jurists understood this privilege as recompense for individuals' willingness to manumit their slaves.

While the transforming terms on which patrons exercised their rights to freedwomen's property did little to affect the already limited financial and testamentary abilities of freedwomen, they reinforced the legitimacy of patrons' administration. During the Principate, the perceived entitlement of patrons remained in place, and jurists even codified beliefs of patronal entitlement by explicitly protecting patrons' control of freedwomen's affairs and their right to share in the estates of the deceased. Here, freedwomen's rights to property began to lag noticeably behind those of freeborn women; when the Augustan legislation curbed the authority of the agnates and the power of the *tutela* over kinswomen began to weaken, freedwomen benefited substantially less from this transition than their freeborn counterparts. This growing separation between the economic rights of freed and freeborn female citizens should not be read as an attempt to marginalize freedwomen, but rather as an indication of Roman lawmakers' desire to protect the exploitative nature of patrons' relationship with their ex-slaves.

MARRIAGE AND CONSENTS TO MARRIAGE

The issue of marriage consent pertained to freedwomen and their male patrons more than their counterparts because of two factors: Freedwomen were also under the *tutela* of their male patrons, and it was more common for freedwomen to marry their male patrons than for freedmen to marry female patrons.[84] The marriage of a freedwoman was an important concern for lawmakers because it could significantly alter her economic relationship with her patron. Marriage could lead to the cancellation of *operae* and the birth of legal heirs, which would decrease the share of funds available to patrons after her death.

Acting as *tutores* for their female ex-slaves, male patrons possessed a degree of influence, both official and informal, over the marital affairs of freedwomen. Most notably, women in *tutela* required their guardian's approval to enter into marriage *cum manu* because of the transfer of authority and property rights involved. A freedwoman's marriage *cum manu* would require leaving the *tutela* of her patron and entering the *potestas* of her husband.[85] In these instances, Roman law required the official approval of male patrons/*tutores* for the unions to be valid. Even in cases where Roman law did not require the official consent of *tutores* to sanction a marriage, the general authority of the *tutela* gave them informal influence over freedwomen's marital affairs. Marriages *sine manu*, which became the default form of matrimony by the imperial era, did not require the official consent of *tutores*.[86] However, the personal and financial relationship between a freedwoman and her *tutor*, which would continue through her marriage, could have conceivably given male patrons the necessary leverage to influence individual marital plans.[87]

At the same time, Roman law forbade male patrons to deprive freedwomen of the right to marry in general. Legislation created during the reign of Augustus expressly barred patrons from denying freedwomen the right to contract valid marriages. The *lex Iulia de maritandis ordinibus* (18 BCE) released a freedwoman forced to swear an oath not to marry from her vow if she desired to contract a proper marriage (*nuptias ... recte*).[88] In his commentary on the *lex Aelia Sentia*, Paul stated that patrons could not compel their newly manumitted freedwomen to swear oaths (*adigere iureiurando*) never to marry (*Dig.* 37.14.6.pr).[89] Furthermore, the jurists believed that any stipulations placed on freedwomen limiting their ability to marry, such as requiring a set amount of time before marrying or establishing categories of eligible spousal candidates, also violated the spirit of this law.[90] Patrons who compelled freedpersons to swear an illegal oath lost their patronal authority over these individuals, including the right to succeed upon intestacy.[91] Roman lawmakers and jurists prioritized marriage as a right of newly freed ex-slaves, even to the point that they were willing to curtail patrons' personal authority and economic rights that they otherwise aggressively guarded.

The assumption underlying these laws was that some patrons might attempt to impede the marriages of their freedwomen in order to preserve the financial benefits they received from their ex-slaves. An example from the *Satyrica* alludes to the financial stakes of a freedwoman's marital status. During his famous dinner, Trimalchio listens to an *actuarius* read out the day's financial accounts, which include the divorce of one of his freedwomen as an individual entry (53).[92] Unmarried freedwomen could neither escape their obligation to provide *operae* nor produce legal heirs, who would reduce patrons' shares in estates.[93] The *lex Aelia Sentia* substantiates the existence of the latter goal, as it expressly forbade patrons who knowingly forced such an oath to succeed to the estate of an intestate freedwoman.[94] The law suggested that the patron no longer would have access to the funds he sought by preventing the birth of legitimate heirs.

The loss of promised *operae* was another possible consequence of a freedwoman's marriage, but the issue is complicated by the question of patronal consent. As was mentioned previously, Hermogenian declared that male patrons who consented to the marriage of a freedwoman (*qui libertae nuptiis consensit*) lost the right to exact *operae* (*Dig.* 38.1.48.pr). The verb *consentire* implied an active act of granting approval rather than an absence of censure.[95] Furthermore, this consent does not seem to have been a routine formality. Ulpian remarked that if a patron was an *impubes*, his consent must be ratified by his *tutor* in order to be valid (*Dig.* 38.1.13.4).[96] While a patron certainly could voice his or her disapproval of a freedwoman's marital plans, the exact meaning and implications of granting "consent" are not clear. There is no indication in any of the legal sources that a patron's consent was necessary to validate a freedwoman's marriage.[97] Most likely, the marriage was valid, but the freedwoman was still obligated to perform any *operae* owed to her patron.[98] Paul pursued this idea to its logical extreme, ruling that if a freedwoman had two patrons and married with the consent of one, the other retained the right to her services (*Dig.* 38.1.28.pr). Even though there was some tension between the roles of wife and freedwoman, jurists were reluctant to cancel services outright, prioritizing the need for patronal sanction.[99]

The main assumption underlying the issue of patronal consent was that marriage was an essential aspect of being a free Roman woman. Although Roman law allowed slave owners to set strict terms of conduct for both before and *after* manumission, jurists explicitly denied manumitters the right to stipulate oaths for nonmarriage. While patrons had the ability to refuse to lend their consent to a particular union, they could not actually prevent their freedwomen from marrying. Furthermore, jurists did not grant freedwomen any choice in this matter. It is certainly reasonable to presume that some female slaves would have voluntarily given up their ability to marry if the alternative meant remaining in a state of perpetual servitude. Instead, jurists presented slave owners with two choices: allow freedwomen the right to marry or else continue to keep them in bondage. This ruling suggests that Roman jurists firmly associated female citizenship with possessing the capacity to marry.

There was an important exception here: A male patron possessed more control over a freedwoman's marital abilities if he was the one marrying her or if he had been married to her in the past. Roman law not only permitted male patrons and freedwomen to marry, but also endorsed such unions by granting exemptions to the manumission age minimums established by the *lex Aelia Sentia*.[100] Jurists even upheld the right of male patrons to compel freedwomen to swear oaths (*adigere iureiurando*) to marry them as a condition of their freedom so long as they actually intended to wed.[101] In these cases where a woman was manumitted for the purpose of marriage (*matrimonii causa*), she would have been returned to slavery if she did not fulfill her obligation within six months or if she became the wife or concubine of another man.[102] Although, after manumission, a patron could not coerce his freedwoman to marry him against her will, it was well within his power to establish a situation where marriage was the only alternative to slavery.[103]

Roman law had little power actually to compel individuals to marry or to halt separations, but it could prevent freedwomen from forming new marriages without the consent of their patrons. Any freedwoman who had married her patron needed his consent to divorce and to marry again.[104] In his commentary on the *lex Iulia et Papia*, Ulpian quoted the law as reading, "Let there be no power of creating divorce for a freedwoman who is married to her patron" (*divortii faciendi potestas libertae quae nupta est patrono, ne esto, Dig.* 24.2.11.pr). However, the jurist noted that this law could not actually undo a separation or divorce, since the dissolution of marriage was a matter of *ius civile*.[105] Rather, this law prevented freedwomen from marrying other individuals if their patrons did not lend approval (*invito patrono*).[106]

The fear of manipulation and abuse – namely, that a female slave would promise marriage in exchange for manumission, only to leave her patron-husband at the first opportunity – clearly guided jurists' opinions on this subject. Those patrons who were not involved in a manumission decision, such as individuals fulfilling a *fideicommissum*, had no need for protection because the female slave's freedom had already been resolved. Marcellus remarked that such a manumitter did not deserve the rights of a patron because he merely conferred to the freedwoman a benefit that was already owed (*Dig.* 23.2.50.pr).[107] Jurists also insinuated that a freedwoman's obligation to her patron strengthened his control over the marriage. For example, several jurists had considered whether or not a freedwoman could dissolve her marriage with a patron who was being held in captivity. Normally, a marriage was dissolved if a husband was captured in battle. However, in the case of a freedwoman whose patron/

husband was taken, some jurists believed that marriage persisted because of the respect (*reverentia*) the freedwoman owed her patron.[108]

The legal privileges bestowed upon respectable concubinage indicate an idealization of unions between patrons and their freedwomen, which may also explain why lawmakers and jurists protected the limited patronal rights to consent to marriage. Roman law treated concubinage as a conjugal relationship akin to marriage, both characterized by monogamy, cohabitation, and intent to form a union. From the perspective of the jurists, concubinage was a legitimate and respectable institution, one that allowed partners deemed inappropriate for marriage because of inequalities in their social status to form an honorable relationship.[109] The Augustan legislation on marriage and adultery complicated jurists' understanding of "respectable concubinage" by classifying as *stuprum* any extramarital sexual affair with a freeborn woman or freedwoman who was not a prostitute, procuress, or actress. As a result, jurists needed to reconcile the gap between the preferred concubine for elite males – a respectable woman who lacked the *dignitas* to warrant marriage – and the category of women exempted from *stuprum*; in doing so, jurists examined three categories of women as potential concubines: a freeborn woman, the freedwoman of another man, and one's own freedwoman.[110] While there appears to have been significant debate over whether or not concubinage with a freeborn woman or the freedwoman of another man conflicted with the Augustan law of *stuprum*, even the most conservative jurists agreed that concubinage with one's own freedwoman was an honorable relationship.

Moreover, jurists referenced concubinage between a male patron and his freedwoman as the preeminent example of a respectable union. Ulpian used this case to illustrate when a woman retained the title *matrona* after entering into concubinage (*Dig.* 48.5.14(13).pr). Similarly, the jurist Marcellus held that a concubine possessed the honorable status of *mater familias* only if she was a freedwoman living with her patron (*Dig.* 23.2.41.1).[111] As in marriage, a freedwoman in concubinage with her patron was exempted from the performance of *operae*.[112] Finally, a famous opinion by Ulpian reads:

Quae in concubinatu est, ab invito patrono poterit discedere et alteri se aut in matrimonium aut in concubinatum dare? Ego quidem probo in concubina adimendum

ei conubium, si patronum invitum deserat, quippe cum honestius sit patrono lib-
ertam concubinam quam matrem familias habere.

Can a woman who is living in concubinage leave her patron without his consent
and enter into marriage or concubinage with another man? Indeed I think that
a concubine should be deprived of the right of marriage if she leaves her patron
without his consent, under the circumstances when it is naturally more respectable for a patron to have his freedwoman as a concubine than as a wife (*Dig.*
25.7.1.pr).[113]

In this opinion, Ulpian argues that a patron should have the same
rights of consent to marriage over a concubine as over a wife. This
opinion is a logical extension of the rules governing the patron-
freedwoman relationship, treating concubinage – a more respectable
conjugal option in cases where partners possessed unequal social status – as akin to marriage. Perhaps more importantly, Ulpian's decision ultimately prioritized concubinage – a position of less social
status – over that of wife, which is significant given the importance
that jurists placed on the ability of freedwomen to marry. Jurists
elevated concubinage between a patron and his freedwoman, closely
associating it with marriage. Furthermore, their analysis suggests a
general idealization of conjugal unions between patrons and their
freedwomen.

CONCLUSION

Roman lawmakers established an exploitative relationship between
patrons and their ex-slaves that nonetheless allowed freedwomen to
maintain the honor and respectability required of female citizens. It is
difficult, if not impossible, to ascertain the effectiveness of these regulations and their success in protecting the rights of these new female citizens. Yet this legal relationship is important because it established an
ideal model for exactly how manumitted slaves could achieve the status
and respectability required of female citizens.

There were two clear goals driving laws and legal opinions. First,
lawmakers and jurists believed that patrons were entitled to certain
benefits because they voluntarily chose to manumit their slaves. Second,

they needed to protect freedwomen from status loss and degradation in order to ensure that they could achieve their newfound social standing. These two goals could easily come into conflict. Given that Roman law permitted patrons to exploit their freedpersons, it was essential for lawmakers and jurists to establish boundaries to separate freedwomen from female slaves.

The legal rules that limited patrons' authority over their freedwomen are important because they inform modern scholars about Roman attitudes on female respectability and its role in defining citizen status. Despite their limited involvement in the actual process of granting freedom or determining which slaves were to be freed, Roman lawmakers imposed a set of rights and responsibilities on both patrons and freedwomen that framed social understanding of the meaning of both manumission and citizenship. Perhaps even more interesting than the fact that Romans believed that female slaves could become respectable female citizens was that this transition occurred within a continued hierarchical – and, one could even argue, servile – relationship with their ex-masters. The legal evidence suggests a prevalent belief in the integrity and importance of this connection; the ongoing relationship between female slave/freedwoman and master/patron was a real bond with significant social meaning. Like the master-slave relationship, the patron-freedwoman relationship was fundamentally characterized by the latter's obligation, deference, and service. However, jurists changed the meaning of this relationship, even though it retained a similar form, by changing the specific rules governing interaction and obligation.

Providing compensation for patrons was a primary goal of forming such a compulsory and enduring relationship. Roman lawmakers and jurists recognized that patrons had voluntarily forfeited their property by choosing to manumit their slaves. The obligations imposed on freedpersons placed these individuals in a position of limited economic servitude, where they owed cash or labor services to their ex-masters. In addition to financial gains, enforced clientage could serve both personal vanity and political aims by increasing the size of a patron's retinue.[114] The personal benefits underlying compulsory patronage are unquestionably important, but the considerable legal effort given to defining the structure of this relationship also suggests a larger social purpose behind such an intricate and persistent bond.[115]

Most importantly, patrons provided necessary "points of attachment" that allowed freedwomen access to the citizen community. Roman lawmakers clearly envisioned the patron-freedwoman relationship in the structure and form of a quasi-familial bond. This was most evident in the names of freedpersons, who received the *nomen gentilicium* of their ex-masters upon manumission. The types of rights and responsibilities possessed by patrons and their freedwomen resemble in many ways the relationships among family members. The duties of *obsequium*, the role of the *tutor*, and the limited influence over a woman's marital abilities were all fundamental and defining aspects of connections among kin. This is not to say that Romans actually considered the patron-freedwoman relationship to be on a par with relationships of actual kin; there would have been many key differences. However, it is significant that Roman lawmakers chose to structure the patron-freedwoman relationship in such a manner.

Integrating freedwomen into the citizen community involved patrons not only providing a social link, but also refraining from degrading conduct. Behavior that blurred the line between freedwoman and slave – such as sexual obligations, servile punishments, and oaths not to marry – was strictly prohibited. Conduct of this type placed freedwomen in a state incompatible with female citizenship. Other potentially problematic issues, such as the tension between *operae* and duty to one's husband, became more complicated as jurists attempted to mediate the rights of patrons, the reputation of freedwomen, and the honor of their husbands. Even though there would have been many different nuances to patron-freedwoman relationships in practice, the legally defined structure of general rights and responsibilities illustrates how Romans' conceptions of female honor and respectability shaped manumission as a citizen-building process.

4 The Patron-Freedwoman Relationship in Funerary Inscriptions

Manumission functioned as an unparalleled moment of transformation, fundamentally altering a woman's identity and place in the Roman world by legally converting her from property to citizen. While manumission recontextualized a freedwoman's social status, many aspects of her slave experience nonetheless persisted into her new life. The social relationships formed as a slave continued to shape the lived experience of freedwomen well after they obtained their freedom. Freedwomen often remained within the same familial, societal, and occupational networks which they had participated during slavery. Roman law institutionalized this social continuity not only by mandating an ongoing relationship between freedwomen and their ex-owners, but also by promoting and valorizing bonds formed during servitude.[1] This chapter will explore how freedwomen themselves drew upon their personal history as slaves and their new status as ex-slaves in funerary epitaphs to explain and legitimize their identity as free Roman women and their enduring social networks. It will focus on freedwomen's relationship with their patrons as a particularly powerful means of communicating information about individual worth and social standing.

Epigraphic evidence is the best means for investigating both the lived experience of freedwomen and how they viewed their place in Roman society. Through inscriptions – largely funerary epitaphs – modern scholars have been able to discern not only the societal and familial relationships of freedwomen, but also the specific occupations and social roles these individuals held.[2] Romans erected funerary monuments to commemorate the dead and preserve their memory, an important aspect of which was to communicate an individual's economic, social, or legal status.[3] Beyond the specific words chosen to commemorate an individual, the funerary monument itself – both its physical form and its very existence – would have conveyed important messages about kin, personal relationships, and legal status. In addition to visual images selected for the monument, the layout of burials in multiperson tombs would have indicated relationships and hierarchies.

While this evidence has been an invaluable source for filling in the silences of the more elite-centric literary texts, it still offers an incomplete view of freedwomen's place in, and vision of, Roman society. This is in part due to the limited information revealed by the inscriptions and the fragmentary nature of the sources; even when intact, funerary epitaphs usually contained only sparse details about the lives of the deceased. This incompleteness also stems from the textual decisions made by inscription writers, who chose to commemorate specific aspects of their lives and omit others.[4] Writers deliberately selected the recorded information to represent their experiences and those of their relatives and associates. In addition to budgetary and space concerns, which limited the substance of the texts, funerary inscriptions were subject to a general standardization of form and language. Commemorators frequently drew from a stock list of phrases and personal epithets to describe both the deceased and the burial space.[5]

There was still space for creating nuanced and personal epitaphs and, even within prescribed societal expectations regarding commemoration, inscription writers chose how the deceased would be described. They decided what, if any, personal qualities and social relationships to mention on the monument and chose the specific language to describe these qualities and relationships. Finally, when reading funerary epitaphs, historians must also consider their construction as either private memorials to be viewed solely by family members or more public documents, created to relay a particular image of the deceased to both an intimate and an unfamiliar audience.[6] Thus, there is the difficult question of the expected audience of the text, whether they were family, friends, or strangers – and how this might have shaped the language and presentation of the inscription.

This decision-making process was especially important to individuals occupying common commemorative categories that were not mutually constitutive, such as freedwomen, who participated in both familial and servile relationships. It is a safe assumption that inscription writers, while operating within both social convention and personal means, were nonetheless deliberate about the language and imagery that they chose to represent the deceased.[7] Although the silences built into epigraphic sources are difficult to overcome, funerary epitaphs can illuminate how freedwomen understood their place in Roman society.

This chapter will explore indicators of legal status included in these monuments, looking primarily at representations of the relationship between freedwomen and their patrons. Status markers, whether formal libertination or status-specific titles, both served as an indicator of individual identity and located individuals within particular social networks. Examining specific inscriptions may suggest the emotional range of the patron-freedwoman relationship, and, perhaps more importantly, how patrons, and especially freedwomen, understood how women's personal histories as slaves influenced and communicated their present status. Rather than obliterating vestiges of their life in servitude, freedwomen drew upon these roles and relationships to define their new place in Roman society. They recontextualized these servile relationships – freedwomen referred to their ex-owners as "patron," not "master" – but there was not a wholesale attempt to ignore this past life

In order to gather the evidence necessary to identify attitudes toward the patron-freedwoman relationship and the information these titles communicated to the readers of epitaphs, this chapter draws primarily upon evidence from the nearly forty thousand Latin inscriptions from the city of Rome cataloged in the *Corpus Inscriptionum Latinarum*, volume 6 (*CIL* 6). In this survey of funerary epitaphs, I have been less concerned with identifying all possible freedpersons. Instead, I have concentrated on those who explicitly – and deliberately, I would argue – claim status as ex-slaves. While using appropriate examples from any inscription referring to a freedwoman, the bulk of the evidence presented in this chapter focuses on inscriptions that clearly indicate the overt commemoration of a patron-freedwoman relationship. I have identified such relationships primarily by the writer's inclusion of the title "patron," but in some cases such a relationship can be identified by the use of the title "freedwoman" (e.g., *liberta et coniunx*). Rather than focusing on aggregate numbers (except in the case of *patronus/liberta et coniunx* dedications),[8] I have surveyed the sample to find exemplary inscriptions that provide qualitative insight into the motives of writers. In particular, I have closely examined inscriptions that include information beyond the name of the deceased and his/her relationship to the dedicator. In some cases these inscriptions include personal epithets, professional titles, or references to individuals other than the dedicator and deceased. Furthermore, I have focused on inscriptions that contain related form and content. Such inscriptions most likely were from the same monument and thus suggest the multiple ways that dedicators chose to represent the same social relationship.

FUNERARY INSCRIPTIONS AND LEGAL STATUS

Understanding the social status of freedwomen and how they viewed their place in Roman society depends primarily on the interpretation of status markers on funerary inscriptions. Status indication, whether formal or informal, functioned on two distinct yet related levels; not only was it part of a freedwoman's personal identity, but it also explained and rationalized her social relationships with other individuals. Together, these functions served to locate a freedwoman in the citizen community and to identify her wider social networks. There were two types of markers that quickly and unmistakably identified a woman as an ex-slave: the inclusion of formal libertination and the presence of a status-specific title, such as patron or *collibertus*, in the inscription. Structurally, the existence of these two types of status indicators is easily explained. As all freedpersons officially lacked fathers under Roman law, libertination replaced filiation, which was traditionally included with the names of citizens inscribed on funerary monuments. Similarly, status-specific titles represented personal relationships customarily deemed worthy of commemoration. The frequent use of libertination and status-specific titles clearly indicates a perceived place for "freed" status indicators in the Roman epigraphic habit.

Deciphering the meaning of status indicators is complicated by the large number of individuals appearing in inscriptions with the *nomen gentilicium* of a free citizen, but without any indication of their legal status – the *incerti*. Interpretations of how individuals chose to use (or not use) status indicators have largely relied on assumptions made about this group of *incerti*. Conclusions about the ratio of freeborn individuals to freedpersons contained within the *incerti* have led to differing views on the use of status indicators. Some scholars have understood this category as consisting primarily of freedpersons unwilling to declare their inferior legal status publicly.[9] Accordingly, the *incerti* became evidence for a stigma attached to freed status – a stigma from which many freedpersons hoped to escape. Such a conclusion cannot help but make relationships characterized by status-specific titles such as "patron" and "freedwoman" seem more obligatory and less personal.

Alternatively, scholars who have noted that inscriptions with status indicators were more common for freedpersons than freeborn individuals have argued that ex-slaves embraced these markers as a means of asserting their newly obtained freedom and citizenship.[10] Along with the *nomen gentilicium*, the title of "freedwoman" not only confirmed an escape from slavery, but also indicated a woman's standing as a free member of the citizen community.[11] Accordingly, scholars have noted how freedpersons placed particular emphasis on the vestigial icons of citizenship and portraits of family members in their funerary monuments in order to celebrate their new legal and social status.[12]

Recognizing that status indicators had both negative and positive connotations, it is clear that their inclusion was a matter of choice. The large number of individuals without status indicators – approximately 30 percent of those commemorated and 15 percent of dedicators – would suggest that this was not an essential element to defining one's place in society.[13] Accordingly, scholars have broadened the scope of their inquiries on the specific work done by employing status indicators in funerary inscriptions. Recent scholarship has shifted the focus of the inquiry from individual identity to societal networks, examining how indications of freed status communicated information about an individual's social relationships.[14]

The varied use of status indicators, whether formal libertination or mention of a servile relationship, patently demonstrates that the issue cannot simply be about asserting or hiding one's status as a freedperson. Certainly such concerns would have influenced individual inscription writers, yet these concerns would have been part of a larger decision about commemoration. Freed status indicators were expressions of both an individual's identity and his or her place in wider social networks and, as such, were used in different ways by different individuals. The following epitaphs indicate the flexible use of libertination and other status indicators.

> P(ublius) Congius P(ubli) l(ibertus) Alexand(er)
> P(ublius) Congius P(ubli) l(ibertus) Valatius
> Iulia C(ai) l(iberta) Aletia (16066).[15]

> Publius Congius Alexander, freedman of Publius
> Publius Congius Valatius, freedman of Publius
> Iulia Aletia, freedwoman of Gaius (16066).

> D(is) M(anibus)
> L(ucio) Iulio
> Abascanto
> Redempta lib(erta)
> patrono
> bene merenti (19793).

> To the divine shades. The freedwoman Redempta (made this monument) for Lucius Iulius Abascantus, her well-deserving patron (19793).

In the first example, libertination seems to function primarily as a marker of individual identity. The two freedmen share the same *nomen gentilicium* and libertination, which suggests some sort of personal connection between them. While the inclusion of the freedwoman Iulia Aletia's libertination demonstrated her equivalent legal status and preserved the formatting aesthetic of the inscription, it communicated nothing about her possible relationship with the freedmen listed – and buried – alongside her.

In the second inscription, the dedicator, Iulia Redempta, described herself as a freedwoman but omitted her *nomen gentilicium*, an omission that suggests that her use of a status indicator was more about defining a social relationship than about establishing her personal identity. Since the epitaph provided the full name of the patron, a reader could easily determine Redempta's full name. Yet it seems likely that if asserting her standing as a free citizen was the primary motive for including the superfluous title of *liberta*, she would have also included her *nomen gentilicium*.[16] This example demonstrates that emphasizing the status of "freedwoman" could have been a statement about the relationship between dedicator and dedicatee rather than an individual's legal status.

L(ucio) Arleno L(uci) l(iberto) Philogeni patrono

L(ucius) Arlenus L(uci) l(ibertus)	L(ucius) Arlenus L(uci) l(ibertus)
Demetrius	Heraclida
L(ucius) Arlenus L(uci) l(ibertus)	L(ucius) Arlenus L(uci) l(ibertus)
Artemidorus	Pamphilus
Arlena Rufa	Arlena Iucunda
coniunx	coniunx
L(ucius) Arlenus LL(uciorum) l(ibertus)	Arlena Saturnina
Helenus	

sibi et suis fecerunt (12331)

For our patron Lucius Arlenus Philogenus, freedman of Lucius,
Lucius Arlenus Demetrius, freedman of Lucius,
Lucius Arlenus Artemidorus, freedman of Lucius,
Arlena Rufa, wife,
Lucius Arlenus Helenus, freedman of Lucius and Lucius,
Lucius Arlenus Heraclida, freedman of Lucius,
Lucius Arlenus Pamphilus, freedman of Lucius,
Arlena Iucunda, wife,
Arlena Saturnina,
made (this monument) for themselves and their families (12331).

Hic siti sunt

L(ucius) Arlenus L(uci)	Arlena L(uci) l(iberta)	L(ucius) Arlenus L(uci)
l(ibertus)		l(ibertus)
Demetrius	Rufa	Artemidorus
nat(ione) Cilix	coniunx	nat(ione) Paphlago
negotiat(or) sagar(ius)		mercator sagarius

Helenus et Nice liberti d(ederunt) (9675 = *ILS* 7577).
Here lies:
Lucius Arlenus Demetrius, freedman of Lucius, a native of Cilicia, a dealer of cloaks
Arlena Rufa, freedwoman of Lucius, wife

> Lucius Arlenus Artemidorus, freedman of Lucius, a native of Paphlagonia,
>   a dealer of cloaks
> Their freedpersons, Helenus and Nice provided (this monument for them)
>   (9675 = *ILS* 7577).

These examples, which were discovered at the same site, indicate that the omission of status indicators was not simply the result of shame about one's legal status. In the first inscription, the shared *nomen gentilicium* of women and the inclusion of their names in the nominative case on a monument dedicated to a single patron suggest that they belonged to the same *familia* as all of the other commemorated individuals, even though they were not represented with formal libertination as all the men were. Libertination works to define the relationship between patron and freedmen, which was most likely economic given the gendered use of the marker. Furthermore, the title *coniunx* was associated with two of the three women. This title, which was a clear indictor of their perceived social role, seems to exist in parallel with the libertination associated with the men; it explains their relationship to the commemorated group.[17] Interestingly, the second inscription, which contained more detailed information about two of the men, explicitly stated the libertination of Arlena Rufa in addition to her position as "wife."

An often discussed inscription that effectively illustrates the connection between status markers and social networks is a group commemoration of a community of dyers.

> V(ivit) D(ecimus) Veturius D(ecimi) l(ibertus) Diog(enes)
> (obiit) D(ecimus) (vacat) D(ecimi) l(ibertus) Nicepor
> v(ivit) Veturia D(ecimi) l(iberta) Fedra
> de sua pecunia faciund(um) coir(avit)
> sibi et patrono et conlibert(o)
> et liberto
> Nicepor conlibertus
> vixit mecum annos XX
> purpuraria Marianeis
> viv(it) D(ecimus) Veturius D(ecimi) (mulieris) l(ibertus) Philarcur(us)
> (37820 = *ILLRP* 809).[18]

Decimus Veturius Diogenes, freedman of Decimus, (living), and Decimus Nicepor, freedman of Decimus, (deceased). Veturia Fedra, freedwoman of

Decimus, (living) had (this monument) made with her own money, for herself, her patron, her fellow freed slave, and her freedman. Nicepor, my fellow freed slave, lived with me for 20 years, a purple-dyer from the Marian
district. Decimus Veturius Philacurus, freedman of Veturia Fedra, (living)
(37820 = *ILLRP* 809).

In this funerary inscription, Veturia Fedra commemorated several pur-
ple-dyers all connected through patronal links, including her conjugal
partner, Decimus Veturius Nicepor.[19] Scholars have argued that Fedra
emphasized the status indicators of patron and freedperson to memorialize the work bond shared by all of these individuals, to the point
that she characterized her partner as a *collibertus* rather than as a "husband."[20] For Veturia Fedra and the other individuals commemorated
on this monument, explicit indications of their legal status communicated a specific social relationship to their audience, illustrating a direct
occupational link.

Interpretations of an individual's decision to include specific status
indicators and the information communicated by these titles must also
consider the context and intended audience of the inscription. While
these factors are difficult, and usually impossible, to ascertain, tomb 87
from the Isola Sacra cemetery ("The Tomb of the Varii") provides useful
insight into the question of how familiarity with an audience may have
shaped the formality of the text.[21] Built in the style of a house tomb, this
monument included the following inscription over the doorway to the
forecourt and repeated again over the doorway to the burial chamber:[22]

P(ublius) Varius Ampelus
et Varia Ennuchis
fecerunt sibi et
Variae P(ubli) f(iliae) Servandae patronae
et libert(is) libertabus posterisq(ue) eorum
ita ne in hoc monimento sarcophagum
in feratur h(oc) m(onumentum) h(eredem) f(amiliae) ex(terae)
non s(equetur)
in fronte p(edes) xs in agro p(edes) xxxiii (Thylander A 268).

Publius Varius Ampelus and Varia Ennuchis made (this monument) for
themselves and for Varia Servanda, daughter of Publius, their patron, and

for their freedmen and freedwomen, and their descendants, on the condition that no sarcophagus be interred in this tomb. This monument will not
follow to an heir outside of the *familia*. This (funerary plot) measures 10½
feet wide and 33 feet long (Thylander A 268).

Although there were several burials inside the chamber, only one
inscription has been found (a marble plaque inscribed in a font different
from that of the exterior ones):

D(is) M(anibus)
Variae P(ubli) f(iliae) Ser/vandae
Ampelus et
Ennychis
liberti d(e) s(ua) p(ecunia) (Thylander A 270).

To the divine shades of Varia Servanda, daughter of Publius. Ampelus and
Ennychis, her freedpersons, (made this monument) from their own money
(Thylander A 270).

The exterior inscriptions indicate that Publius Varius Ampelus and
Varia Ennuchis built the monument for themselves; their female patron,
Varia Servanda; and their unnamed freedpersons. The dedicators provide their own *nomina* in full, as well as that of their patron (although
they chose to omit their own libertination).[23] However, in the interior
inscription, Ampelus and Ennuchis declined to use their full *nomina*.
This certainly suggests that the dedicators intended the outer inscription to provide information for a more unfamiliar public audience.
Conversely, the space inside the tomb was most likely reserved only for
members of the *familia*.[24] Ampelus and Ennuchis's use of their single,
personal names in the interior epitaph may have been intended to evoke
their time as slaves, but it also conveyed a degree of intimacy between
them and their patron. In this respect, the addition of the notation *de
sua pecunia* ("from their own money") is also noteworthy. This may have
been a simple reflection of funding sources, in that the larger monument was provided for by the estate of the deceased, whereas Ampelus
and Ennuchis paid for the smaller, interior epitaph out of their own
personal funds. Alternatively, a statement such as this used exclusively
in a more private context may again suggest the intimate bond between

patron and freedpersons, representing the act of commemoration more as a personal wish than simply as a patronal obligation.[25]

The following inscription also suggests a perceived sense of the audience's familiarity with the deceased:

> Iulia Erotis femina optima hic sitast
> nullum dolorem ad inferos mecum tuli
> viro et patrono placui et decessi prior
> C(aius) Iulius Blastus   C(aius) Iulius
> C(aius) Iulius Celadus   divi Aug(usti) l(ibertus)
>   Messius (5254).

> Iulia Erotis, the best woman, lies here. I brought no pain with me to the underworld. I was pleasing to my husband and my patron, and I died before (him/them). Gaius Julius Blastus. Gaius Julius Celadus. Gaius Julius Messius, freedman of the divine Augustus (5254).

In this epitaph from a columbarium, written in iambic senarii, the freedwoman Iulia Erotis described herself as pleasing to her husband and patron, but it is unclear whether she is referring to one or two individuals. On the one hand, in most inscriptions, the phrase *vir* (or similar) *et patronus* is used to describe a single individual. However, with two different names following her statement, one may also logically assume that Blastus was her husband and Celadus her patron.[26] Ultimately, this inscription displays a lack of precision in identifying individuals' links to the deceased compared to other examples. Given its location in a columbarium, it is likely that this inscription was intended primarily for family members who had previous knowledge of the relationship and could easily identify husband and patron.[27] Dedicators chose to use status indicators in epitaphs to communicate different types of information, influenced not only by the individuals being commemorated, but also by the context and intended audience of the monument.

THE PATRON-FREEDWOMAN RELATIONSHIP

It is not uncommon to see the patron-freedperson bond commemorated among the surviving funerary inscriptions that name the dedicator and dedicatee.[28] Given the exploitative nature of the patron-freedperson relationship, one way of understanding this pattern might be to categorize (or even dismiss) it as a routine expression of duty and fidelity. Yet an examination of several epitaphs illuminates the emotive and social possibilities of relationships contained within the titles of "patron" and "freedwoman." For some patrons and even some freedwomen, the relationship was a significant bond worthy of emphasis.

The legal conception of the patron-freedwoman relationship actively obfuscated the intimate personal bond that could possibly exist between these two individuals. Roman lawmakers defined the relationship as inherently hierarchical and exploitative, undoubtedly invoking the dynamic between master and slave.[29] There were certainly different types of master-slave relationships in the Roman world, which would account for patron-freedwoman relationships that were more or less affectionate and thus the varied styles of commemoration. Furthermore, the title "patron" could have encompassed a range of different types of individuals. Given the laws regulating the processes of manumission and patronage, the "patron" could have been the individual who had controlled and subjugated the woman as a slave or someone who had just recently purchased her for the express purpose of setting her free, possibly even a fellow slave, a relative, or an acquaintance.[30] The absence of any additional embellishment did not necessarily preclude the existence of such a bond, even though some epitaphs elaborated on the prior relationship between patron and freedwoman. The patron was the slave's owner at the moment of manumission, but one should not automatically conflate the title "patron" with the social role of the master.

In the case of most funerary inscriptions, the only thing known for certain about the "patron" is that this was the person who ultimately manumitted the woman. But this fact is not insignificant. Focusing on the patron as manumitter rather than slave owner may be a useful context for analyzing funerary inscriptions involving freedwomen. It is clear that the title, as it appears in epigraphic evidence, could and did mean something more than the position outlined in Roman law.

Epitaphs involving patrons and freedwomen are well represented among the sample of inscriptions collected in *CIL* 6. In most of these funerary inscriptions, the dedicator described the connection between

the two individuals solely in terms of the patronal relationship, with no
explicit indication of any other bond between the two. For example:

> D(is) M(anibus) Deciae
> Tryphaenae
> Fecit
> C(aius) Decius Faustus
> libertae
> bene merenti (16794).

> To the divine shades of Decia Tryphaena. Gaius Decius Faustus made (this
> monument) for his well-deserving freedwoman (16794).

> L(ucius) Stlaccius Phileros
> Stlaccia L(uci) l(iberta) Moschis
> patrono suo fecit (26868).

> Lucius Stlaccius Phileros. Stlaccia Moschis, freedwoman of Lucius, made
> (this monument) for her patron (26868).

These inscriptions are rather standard examples of monuments involving patrons and their freedwomen. There does not appear to be a
preference in using the term "patron" or "freedwoman" to describe
the relationship; following general trends among epitaphs, the
appropriate title was usually associated with the individual being
commemorated.

While it is difficult to pinpoint the exact reasons why one individual
chose to commemorate another, it is clear that this was not an arbitrary
custom, but rather one grounded in social and legal traditions. Roman
law primarily associated the obligation of burial and commemoration
with that of heirship to the point that Ulpian warned against automatically assuming that the individual overseeing the burial was also
the heir.[31] There are a few examples where an epitaph explicitly refers
to a freedwoman as her patron's heir, such as the first inscription that
follows:[32]

> L(ucius) Seius Pilero(s)
> Vener(ia) L(uci) l(iberta)
> Seia (h)eres v(iva)

emit duas
ol(l)as sib(i) et patr(ono) (26115).[33]

Lucius Seius Pileros. Seia Veneria, freedwoman and heir of Lucius, (living) purchased these two funerary urns, one for herself and one for her patron (26115).

Dis Manibus
Pontia Calliope
L(ucio) Pontio Erasto
patrono suo fecit
bene merenti
vixit an(nos) LXXXV
permissu collibertorum (24739).

To the divine shades. Pontia Calliope made (this monument) with the permission of her co-freedpersons for Lucius Pontius Erastus, her well-deserving patron, who lived for 85 years (24739).

While there is no explicit mention of an heir in the second example, the phrase *permissu collibertorum* ("by the authority of her co-freedpersons") may suggest that Lucius Pontius Erastus named several of his freedpersons as inheritors, who then delegated responsibility for the commemoration to one of their number.[34] The association between burial and the duties of inheritors suggests that Romans perceived the patron-freedwoman relationship as being of the type that could result in heirship.[35] Despite the legal focus on heirship as the primary impetus for commemoration, the epigraphic evidence indicates that individuals also chose to memorialize others out of a sense of affection, devotion, or respect. Freedwomen occasionally recorded that they had established the monument to their patron *libens* ("freely").[36] Such a remark implied both a perceived obligation for freedpersons to commemorate their patrons, and a desire to distinguish oneself as someone who acted out of affection in addition to duty.

Perhaps the best indication of the significance of the patron-freedwoman relationship is its structural similarity to familial relationships in the epigraphic record. The most important parallel was the very act of commemoration itself. By establishing a funerary monument,

freedwomen and patrons were engaging in an activity that was predominantly performed by family members. Patron-freedwoman
inscriptions were textually nearly identical to those involving kin,
drawing from the same stock language and epithets.[37] Even the use
of libertination in place of filiation identified the patron as a figure
analogous to the father, at least in terms of social identity.[38] And like
family members, patrons and freedwomen often shared the same burial
space. This practice certainly originated in the traditional household
burials of the Republic that also included members of the *familia* and
continued in the form of the impersonal *libertis libertabusque posterisque
eorum* formula included by many patrons. However, there are many
personalized inscriptions that explicitly mention both individuals
by name, emphasizing a more intimate sharing of burial space. Both
freedwomen and patrons act as the "creators" of such monuments, suggesting a more egalitarian approach to commemoration and burial.[39]
The epigraphic evidence suggests that nonelite Romans understood
the patron-freedwoman relationship as being similar to familial relationships in form and function.

While the patron-freedwoman relationship could contain two individuals bound by mutual feelings of love, respect, or devotion, some
inscriptions suggest that the idea of the relationship itself could convey
such emotions. Several epitaphs suggest the presence of a romantic or
conjugal relationship between patron and freedwoman, without using
the actual titles of such a relationship.

> D(is) M(anibus)
> Q(uinto) Valerio Mitreio fecit
> Valeria Hermeris patron
> benemerenti sibi et suis
> libertis libertabusque
> posterisque meorum
> vixit annis cum ea XXIII (28063).

> To the divine shades. Valeria Hermeris made (this monument) for Quintus
> Valerius Mitreius, her well-deserving patron who lived with her for 23 years,
> and for herself, and for her freedmen and freedwomen, and descendants
> (28063).

D(is) M(anibus)
C(aio) Venatidio
Sabino patro/no
dulcissimo
et pientissimo
bene merenti fecit
Venatidia
Helpis libertis liber/tabusq(ue)
p(osteris)q(ue) e(orum) (28439).

To the divine shades. Venatidia Helpis made (this monument) for Gaius
Venatidius Sabinus, her most gracious, devoted, and well-deserving patron,
and for their freedmen, freedwomen, and descendants (28439).

The first example is a dedication from Valeria Hermeris to her patron,
Quintus Valerius Mitreius, who, Hermeris recorded, had lived with her for
twenty-three years. Such declarations of years lived together were common
in epitaphs commemorating individuals in conjugal (or conjugal-like) relationships.[40] The lack of a conjugal title may simply indicate that Hermeris
and Mitreius never formalized their relationship. However, this does not
explain why they did not either use a quasi-marital title or co-opt a formal
title, as many individuals without *conubium* appear to have done. Instead,
Hermeris chose to represent and commemorate their relationship primarily in terms of patron and freedwoman. In the second example, Venatidia
Helpis used the adjectives *dulcissimus* and *pientissimus* to describe her patron.
While these were stock epithets commonly found in funerary inscriptions,
they were almost never used to commemorate patrons. Dedicators traditionally used *dulcissimus* to indicate close, intimate relationships, often
emphasizing the erotic aspect of conjugal life, and *pientissimus* was used
primarily between family members.[41] While the epithets chosen by Helpis
suggest the presence of a more intimate or romantic relationship, she too
eschews the use of any marital or quasi-marital title in the epitaph.

There are other indications of a romantic or conjugal bond between
a freedwoman and her patron. Perhaps the best example is the
following:

Diis(*sic*) Manibus
Ti(beri) Claudi Dionysi

fecit Claudia Prepontis
patrono bene merenti
et sibi (15003).

To the divine shades of Tiberius Claudius Dionysius. Claudia Prepontis made
(this monument) for her well-deserving patron, and for herself (15003).

Dis Manibus Ti(beri) Claudi Dionysi
fecit Claudia Prepontis patrono
bene merenti sibi et suis
posterisq(u)e eorum (15004).

To the divine shades of Tiberius Claudius Dionysius. Claudia Prepontis
made (this monument) for her well-deserving patron, and for herself, and
for their descendants (15004).

The first inscription is located on a funerary altar, created by Claudia
Prepontis for herself and her patron, Tiberius Claudius Dionysius.
What is notable about this rather banal text is that the altar also contained a portrait of a man and woman clasping right hands (*dextrarum
iunctio*).[42] *Dextrarum iunctio* was a typical pose of married individuals
and would suggest that Prepontis and Dionysius enjoyed a similar
relationship.[43] The second inscription is from a cippus that most likely
served as a companion piece to the altar. The cippus also includes a
portrait of a man and woman sharing a couch, another possible indication of the intimacy shared by patron and freedwoman. The addition
of the phrase *et suis posterisque eorum* to the text suggests that Prepontis
and Dionysius had children, further intimating the presence of a family unit.[44] While the visual imagery of the two monuments arguably
made any textual reference to the (quasi-) marital relationship between
Prepontis and Dionysius superfluous, it is nonetheless notable that
Prepontis chose to define their relationship principally by using the
title "patron."

Several epitaphs mention freedwoman, patron, and children and may
represent the commemoration of a family unit.[45]

Vipsania Hilara
liberta
M(arco) Vipsanio Ilisso patron(o)

Vipsaniae Chari f(iliae) (29009).

Vipsania Hilara, freedwoman, (made this monument) for Vipsanius Ilissus, her patron, and for Vipsania Charis, their (her? his?) daughter (29009).

D(is) M(anibus)
Claudius
Damas
fecit libertae
bene merenti
Claudiae Helpid(i)
et fili(i)s duobus
firmis (14991).

To the divine shades. Claudius Damas made (this monument) for his well-deserving freedwoman, Claudia Helpis, and their (his? her?) two strong sons (14991).

Baebia Trophime
monimentum(*sic*) fecit sibi et
L(ucio) Baebio Pisto patrono
suo bene merenti et
L(ucio) Baebio Pisto et Baebiae Phoebe
filiis suiis(*sic*) et
Phoebo liberto suo et ceteris
libertis libertabusque suiis(*sic*)
posterisque eorum praeter
Epitynchanum et Fortem
in fronte p(edes) XIIII in agro p(edes) XIIII (13498).

Baebia Trophime made this monument for herself, and for Lucius Baebius Pistus, her well-deserving patron, and for their (her?) children, Lucius Baebius Pistus and Baebia Phoebe, and for Phoebus their (her?) freedman, and the rest of their freedmen and freedwomen, and their descendants, except for Epitynchanus and Fortis. (This funerary plot) is 14 feet long and 14 feet wide (13498).

The personnel mentioned in the first two epitaphs – man, woman, child(ren) – would suggest a family unit, but of course there is no decisive testimony. In the third inscription, Baebia Trophime commemorated her patron Lucius Baebius Pistus, her two children, one named freedman, and most of her other freedpersons. The fact that Pistus was buried in what is quite obviously a family tomb and that one of Trophime's children shares his name may indicate that Pistus had a conjugal relationship with Trophime.[46]

All of these examples suggest that the idea of the patron-freedwoman relationship could convey a sense of intimacy compatible with a marital relationship. In each epitaph there is some evidence pointing toward the presence of a marital(-like) relationship between the freedwoman and her patron, yet textually these references are subordinate to titles indicating legal status, on which the dedicators relied to express the primary structure of their bond. As elements of public documents, these inscriptions suggest a common and familiar perception of emotional substance within the patron-freedwoman relationship. Such a perception would also have influenced readings of inscriptions involving patrons and freedwomen that did not include additional signs of intimacy and affection. Ultimately, there is no way to discern accurately whether or not a conjugal relationship, or even actual affection, existed within simple epitaphs commemorating patrons and their freedwomen. Yet these funerary inscriptions indicate that some dedicators believed that the idea of the patron-freedwoman relationship *could* convey an appropriate sense of fondness and intimacy.

PATRONS AND HUSBANDS

It is evident from the epigraphic evidence that the patron-freedwoman relationship persisted after the woman's marriage to another man. There was a definite concern among Roman lawmakers and jurists about how a woman's relationships with her patron and her husband would coexist.[47] Despite this concern, a freedwoman's devotion or duty to her patron continued – and was worthy of commemoration – even when she married another man. For example:

> D(is) M(anibus) s(acrum)
> Iulia Eutychia

Iulio Privato

patrono et

C(aio) Reio Celeri filio

pientissimis bene

merentibus fecit

cum Baebio Iunio

marito

sib(i) et suis et

posterisque eorum (20449).

To the divine shades. Iulia Eutychia made (this monument) for Iulius
Privatus, her patron, and Gaius Reius Celer, her son, both very devoted
and well-deserving. (She made this) with Baebius Iunius, her husband, for
herself, her family, and her descendants (20449).

This inscription highlights the personal bond tied to the establishment
of a funerary monument. The principal dedicatory bond is that of Iulia
Eutychia; her patron, Iulius Privatus; and her child, Gaius Reius Celer.
Her husband, Baebius Iunius, who appears to have been Eutychia's second husband (given Celer's *nomen gentilicium*) and to have had no formal
connection to her patron or her child, was relegated to a subordinate
position in the text, in terms of both the location and the grammatical
case of his name. Even though Baebius contributed to the establishment of the monument, this epitaph was about Eutychia and her relationship with her patron and her son.

The multiple commemorative responsibilities of the freedwoman are
perhaps best illustrated in a relatively unusual case where a freedwoman
memorialized both her patron and her husband in the same epitaph. In
CIL 6, I have found only eighteen examples of this kind of commemoration (see Table 4.1).[48] While this sample is too small to draw statisti-
cal conclusions, two trends are potentially interesting. In 83 percent of
these inscriptions (N = 15), the freedwoman commemorates the patron
before her husband. Given the significance of spousal commemorations
in funerary inscriptions, the primary textual position of the patrons
highlights the perceived importance of this bond.[49] The small number
of examples in this sample may reflect the perceived tension between a
woman's roles as wife and freedwoman, and thus represent an unwillingness to commemorate both patron and husband in the same epitaph.[50]
Second, in 67 percent of the inscriptions (N = 12), the husband has a

Table 4.1 *Order of Commemoration in Epitaphs Dedicated to Both a Patron and a Husband*

Husband Precedes Patron	Patron Precedes Husband	Total
3	15	18
17%	83%	100%

Table 4.2 *Nomen Gentilicium of Commemorated Husbands in Epitaphs Dedicated to Both a Patron and a Husband*

Same as Wife[51]	Different from Wife	Total
6	12	18
33%	67%	100%

different *nomen gentilicium* than his wife and her patron, and thus (apparently) no direct servile connection (see Table 4.2). The lack of married freedpersons with the same patron – a category that certainly must have existed in significant numbers – may suggest a preferred style of commemoration that obscured conjugal bonds in favor of patronal links.

While these inscriptions emphasized patrons' status by their foremost position on the monuments, there was varied emphasis placed on the family. Some commemorators seem to highlight their relationship with their husbands by including an emotional epithet with their names and not their patrons', yet nearly as many attach epithets to their patrons and not their husbands.[52]

Two epitaphs demonstrate the varied priority that could be placed on the conjugal family. In each case, the freedwoman mentioned her patron first on the monument, and her husband also appears to have had a connection with her patron.

> Diis(*sic*) Manibus
> M(arco) Iunio Perso patrono
> et M(arco) Iunio Satyro
> et M(arco) Iunio Iusto
> et Iuniae Piae
> fecit

Iunia Venusta coniugi suo
et fili(i)s dulcissimis
una cum Pharnace lib(erto) (20819).

To the divine shades. For Marcus Iunius Persus, her patron, and for Marcus Iunius Satyrus, her husband, and for Marcus Iunius Iustus and Iunia Pia, her sweetest children, Iunia Venusta made (this monument). (She made this) alone along with Pharnaces, her freedman (20819).

This epitaph is located on a funerary altar below four portraits: an old man alone in the apex, and a male adult flanked by a male and a female child in the center pane of the monument, just above the inscribed text. The most likely interpretation of the visual images is that the portrait in the apex represented Marcus Iunius Persus, the patron, and the family portrait in the center depicted the husband and children of Iunia Venusta.[53] Given the foregrounded title of patron attributed to Persus and shared *nomen gentilicium* of all the commemorated individuals, it is probable that wife, husband, and children were all freedpersons who had belonged to the same *familia*. The monument seems to have memorialized the larger social unit of patron and freedpersons, prominently locating the patron at the head of the unit both visually and textually.[54] At the same time, this monument also distinguished Venusta's nuclear family as its own unit of commemoration. The altar separates patron and nuclear family into distinct visual components, and the image of the family, while located lower in the monument, was arguably more prominent given its proximity to the text and size of the individual portraits, all of which appear larger than the portrait of the patron.

The text of the inscription itself also highlighted the nuclear family as a distinct unit. After listing the names of all the commemorated individuals together, Venusta grouped her husband and cherished children together by title as the recipients of her dedication. While indicating the eminent status of Persus and honoring his role as patron, the dedicator shifted focus to the nuclear family as the prominent unit being commemorated on this monument.

[Camer]ia L(uci) l(iberta) Iarine fecit
[L(ucio)] [Cam]erio L(uci) l(iberto) Thrasoni patron

[et] L(ucio) Camerio L(uci) l(iberto) Alexandro

patrono eius et

[L(ucio) C]amerio Onesimo lib(erto) et

[vi]ro suo posterisque omnibus

[vest]iariis tenuariis de vico Tusc(ulano) (37826).

Cameria Iarine, freedwoman of Lucius, made (this monument) for Lucius Camerius Thraso, freedman of Lucius, her patron, and for Lucius Camerius Alexandrus, freedman of Lucius, his patron, and for Lucius Camerius Onesimus, her freedman and husband, and all of their descendants. All were makers of fine clothing located on Tuscan Street (37826).

This inscription also detailed a freedwoman commemorating both her husband and patron, but in this case, the woman deemphasized her conjugal relationship in favor of the occupational bond shared by patrons and freedpersons. The "multigenerational" nature of this commemoration, which indicated four generations of named freedpersons, emphasized the business relationship shared by patron and freedperson.[55] Cameria Iarine noted that her freedman Onesimus was also her husband (*vir*), but this seems almost inconsequential to the larger purpose of the epitaph. All of these examples indicate the strength and persistence of the patron-freedwoman relationship and how it intersected with familial commemoration.

The epigraphic record indicates that the patron-freedwoman bond was still worthy of note, even when both individuals were also married to one another, a point that suggests that, for some, commemorating this link was more than simply an act of affection or devotion. The best evidence for the work done by one's identity as a patron or a freedwoman is the numerous epitaphs that commemorate an individual as "patron and husband" or "freedwoman and wife" (see Table 4.3). I have found eighty-two inscriptions in *CIL* 6 that title a dedicator or dedicatee as "patron and husband."[56] Furthermore, these inscriptions emphasize the significance of the patronal bond and the honorific status of the patron by listing this title before "husband" in 87 percent of the epitaphs (N = 71). Similarly, out of ninety inscriptions that describe an individual as a "freedwoman" and a "wife," 84 percent (N = 76) use the title freedwoman before that of wife.[57] These examples are particularly

Table 4.3 *Order of Commemoration in "Patron and Husband" and "Freedwoman and Wife" Epitaphs*

"Husband" Precedes "Patron"	"Patron" Precedes "Husband"	Total
11	71	82
13%	87%	100%

"Wife" Precedes "Freedwoman"	"Freedwoman" Precedes "Wife"	Total
14	76	90
16%	84%	100%

illuminating because one might expect the servile bond to be subsumed within the conjugal relationship rather than emphasized.[58]

Dedicators used the titles of "patron" and "freedwoman" to reference a particular relationship between the two individuals that was distinct from, but not necessarily at odds with, their conjugal bond.

> D(is) M(anibus)
> Baebiae Polli
> coniugi et lib(e)rt(a)e
> Q(uintus) Albius Zoes
> co(n)iux et patronus (13491).

> To the divine shades. Quintus Albius Zoes, husband and patron, (made this monument) for Baebia Pollis, wife and freedwoman (13491).

> Dis Manibus
> Quinctiae M(arci) l(ibertae)
> Chaerusae
> libertae isdem coniugi
> suae benemeritae posu(it)
> M(arcus) Quinctius
> Thiopompus
> patronus (25319).

> To the divine shades. Marcus Quinctius Thiopompus, patron, erected (this monument) for Quinctia Chaerusa, freedwoman of Marcus, his well-deserving freedwoman and at the same time wife (25319).

Table 4.4 *Use of "Freedwoman" in "Patron and Husband" Epitaphs*

"Freedwoman"	Omit "Freedwoman"	Total
7	75	82
9%	91%	100%

Table 4.5 *Use of "Patron" in "Freedwoman and Wife" Epitaphs*

"Patron"	Omit "Patron"	Total
11	79	90
12%	88%	100%

In the first epitaph, Quintus Albius Zoes used the titles *coniunx*, *liberta*, and *patronus* to explain the relationship between him and Baebia Pollis in detail. The parallel structure adopted by the author of the inscription appears to have been an emphatic attempt to identify and clarify the precise relationship between these two individuals, possibly stressed because Pollis did not share the same *nomen gentilicium* as her patron-husband.[59] In the second inscription, the repetition of patronal titles reinforced the importance of this bond and the significance of these social roles to the dedicator. Inscription writers infrequently used both titles of patron and freedwoman, usually relying on only one title to indicate the existence of such a relationship (see Tables 4.4 and 4.5). Of patron-husband inscriptions 91 percent do not use the title freedwoman as well, and 88 percent of the freedwoman-wife inscriptions do not mention the title patron. The dedicator usually explained the relationship by establishing the identity of one individual relative to the other.[60] There does not appear to have been a significant preference for using either "patron" or "freedwoman" to describe the relationship. Instead, the inclination was to attach the appropriate label to the individual being commemorated.[61]

The context of the inscription and the intended audience would have also shaped when and how dedicators mobilized this relationship. For example, consider the following inscriptions, which were located on the opposite sides of a funerary monument:

Side A

D(is) M(anibus)

Cl(audius) Apelles fecit et
Cl(audia) Primitiba libertis libertab/usq(ue)
et familiae utrisq(u)e poster(is)q(ue)
eorum praeter Eutycho libert(o)
malae merito de se si quis
hoc mono(men)tum(!) vendere aut
abalenare volet inferet
aerario p(opuli) R(omani) HS X m(ilia) n(ummum) aut is
qui emerit
in f(ronte) p(edes) IX in ag(ro) p(edes) XII.

Side B
D(is) M(anibus)
Cl(audius) Apelles fecit sibi et
Cl(audiae) Primitivae coniugi idem lib(ertae)
cum qua vix(it) sine querella ann(is)
XXXII mensibus III ipsa vix(it) ann(is)
XXXXV si quis hanc aram vendere
aut abalenare volet inferet aera/rio
p(opuli) R(omani) HS XX m(ilia) n(ummum) aut is qui emerit
in f(ronte) p(edes) X in ag(ro) p(edes) VIIII (14930).

Side A
To the divine shades. Claudius Apelles and Claudia Primitiba made (this monument) for their freedmen and freedwomen, and for any members of their *familia*, and their descendants, except for the freedman Eutychus, who has behaved poorly towards them. If anyone should wish to sell or to transfer possession of this tomb, let him, or the one who is buying, pay 10,000 sesterces to the treasury of the Roman people. (This funerary plot) measures 9 feet wide, 12 feet long.

Side B
To the divine shades. Claudius Apelles made (this monument) for himself, and for Claudia Primitiva, his wife and freedwoman, with whom he lived without complaint for 32 years and 3 months. She lived for 45 years. If anyone wishes to sell or to transfer possession of this altar, let him, or the one who is buying, pay 20,000 sesterces to the treasury of the Roman people. (This funerary plot) measures 10 feet wide and 9 feet long (14930).

While these two inscriptions are similar in form, they are in fact marking separate burial sites and fulfilling different functions.[62] The inscription on side A describes a plot nine feet by twelve feet whereas the inscription on side B describes a plot ten feet by nine feet. Side A was a dedication from Claudius Apelles and Claudia Primitiva to their unnamed freedpersons and other members of their *familia*, whereas on side B, Apelles commemorated only Primitiva. Thus, it is most likely that side A marked the burial site for ex-slaves and members of the household, and side B marked the burial site for Apelles and Primitiva themselves. On side B, Apelles described Primitiva as his "wife" and "freedwoman," but the epitaph on side A gives no indication of their relationship. Clearly these titles were not necessary in the first inscription, because the epitaph commemorated the relationship between Apelles and Primitiva and their household; this epitaph was about the household, whose relationship to the dedicators was indicated by *libertis libertabusque*. The relationship between Apelles and Primitiva was implied by their joint dedication as heads of house, but did not need to be explicitly mentioned because it was irrelevant for the purposes of the commemoration. Side B, however, was about the couple and the terms of their relationship, making the descriptor *coniunx idem liberta* more pertinent.

Moreover, there was a second monument from Apelles and Primitiva commemorating the imperial freedman Chrysaor, whom they describe as their most dutiful son:

> D(is) M(anibus)
> Chrysaori Aug(usti) lib(erto) adiutori
> a commentari(i)s ornamentorum
> filio piissimo qui vixit ann(os) XXVII
> m(enses) VIIII fecerunt
> Cl(audius) Apelles et Cl(audia) Primitiva parent(es)
> et sibi
> in f(ronte) p(edes) X in ag(ro) p(edes) VIIII (8951 = *ILS* 1783).

> To the Divine Shades. Claudius Apelles and Claudia Primitiva, parents, made (this monument) for the imperial freedman Chrysaor, the assistant to the official in charge of costumes, a most dutiful son who lived 27 years, 9 months, and for themselves. (This funerary plot) measures 10 feet wide and 9 feet long (8951 = *ILS* 1783).

Given that the size of the plot recorded in this inscription matches the dimensions of the plot mentioned on side B of the first monument, it is likely that this memorial was situated close to the other. Much like the inscription on side A, this epitaph did not call attention to the relationship between Apelles and Primitiva. Rather, it highlighted their role as parents and their relationship with their son. These monuments effectively illustrate that Roman funerary commemoration was not always about providing all the information, but the information deemed necessary for the appropriate context.

Given the importance of spousal commemorations in Roman society and the perceived intimacy and love underlying the conjugal relationship, the deliberate reference to the patron-freedwoman link must have communicated unique information as part of the dedication. Consider the following epitaphs:

> Liberta et coniunx Petronia cara patrono
> Thallusa hoc tumulo condita luce caret
> quae bis vicenos complerat lucibus annos
> erepta est subito coniugis e gremio
> hanc sic adsidue deflet Petronius ut iam
> deficiant oculos lumina cara suos
> desine per terras infernas tendere ad arces
> fata animam dederant fata eademq(ue) negant (24049).

The freedwoman and wife, Petronia Thallusa, dear to her patron, having been buried in this tomb, lacks the light of life. She, who filled up forty years with her brightness, was suddenly snatched from the lap of her husband. And so Petronius mourns her constantly with the result that precious sight is no longer available to his eyes. Finish pressing on through the lower regions to the heavens. The same fates that had given life, have also ended it (24049).

> Dis Manibus
> C(aius) Cassius Verecundus
> fecit sibi et Cassiae Damalidi
> libertae carissimae et bene mer(enti)
> idem coniugi et
> C(aio) Cassio Cotyno et Cassiae Mos/chidi

parentibus suis isdem patron(is)
libertis C(ai) Cassi Longini et libertis suis
libertabusque posterisque eorum (14529).

To the divine shades. Gaius Cassius Verecundus made (this monument) for
himself and for Cassia Damalis, his very dear and well-deserving freedwoman and at the same time wife, and for Gaius Cassius Cotynus and
Cassia Moschis, freedpersons of Gaius Cassius Longinus, his parents and
patrons, and for his own freedmen and freedwomen, and their descendants
(14529).

The first inscription is a very emotional epitaph written in elegiac cou-
plets seemingly intended to convey a sense of deep grief and loss. It is
unsurprising that a husband would feel such sadness in response to the
death of his wife. Furthermore, if both uses of *coniunx* were removed
from the epitaph, most readers would postulate an intimate, loving,
(and even marriage-like) bond between patron and freedwoman. And
still Petronius felt compelled to identify Thallusa as his freedwoman,
and even reinforced this characterization by immediately describing
her as *cara patrono* ("dear to her patron"). The overall departure from
the more standardized funerary texts suggests a degree of personaliza-
tion and thus underlines the deliberateness of the inclusion of the status
indicators of "freedwoman" and "patron." In the second inscription,
Gaius Cassius Verecundus emphasized his wife's role as a freedwoman
by attaching the epithets *carissima* and *bene merens* to *liberta* rather
than placing them in their more traditional location following both
titles.[63] In effect, this epitaph seems to have commemorated Cassia
Damalis principally as freedwoman, one who also happened to be her
patron's wife.

The addition of the title "patron" or "freedwoman" to a spousal commemoration evoked an idealization of marriages between patrons and their
freedwomen. As was explained in the previous chapter, legal sources indicate a preference for freedwomen marrying their own patrons, even to the
point that jurists believed that it was better for a freedwoman to live as a
concubine with her patron than as the wife of another man. Describing an
individual as a spouse and patron/freedwoman evoked this ideal and thus
attached additional moral legitimacy to the union. Not only did these
status indicators illustrate the depth and length of the relationship, but

they also highlighted the virtue of both persons: the freedwoman as an upright and devoted individual worthy of manumission, and the patron as a virtuous individual who granted freedom to those who were worthy. The following inscription seems to reference both of these qualities.

> Dis Manibus
> Claudiae Stepteni vix(it)
> annis LXXII fecit Ti(berius)
> Claudius Aug(usti) l(ibertus) Nympho/dotus
> patronus et contub/ernalis
> co(n)iugi suae kar/issimae
> bene meritae de se
> cum qua vix(it) ann(os) XLVI sibi et suis
> posterisque eorum (15598).

> To the divine shades. Tiberius Claudius Nymphodotus, the freedman of (Claudius) Augustus, patron and *contubernalis*, made (this monument) for Claudia Stepte, who lived for 72 years, his very dear wife, well-deserving of him, with whom he lived for 46 years, and for himself, and for their descendants (15598).

Here, the freedman Tiberius Claudius Nymphodotus, describing himself as "patron and *contubernalis*," commemorated his wife, Claudia Stepte. Nymphodotus was clearly interested in delineating the time the two had spent together, referencing their premarital relationship as *contubernales* and the number of years they had lived together. This seems to make the addition of the title *patronus* superfluous in terms defining their relationship, but by pairing the titles, Nymphodotus emphasized his role in Stepte's obtaining her freedom. The titles *patronus* and *contubernalis* helped to explain and legitimize their conjugal relationship.[64]

Emphasizing the continuity of the conjugal relationship from slavery to marriage may have also had sexual implications, possibly evoking the idea of the *univira*. Literary authors and inscription writers often idealized a woman who died having only had a single husband.[65] While the language associated with the *univira* emphasized the dedication, devotion, and service of the woman, there is some implicit evidence to suggest the significance that the *univira* only had sexual relations with one partner. Perhaps the best evidence for such a connection is Livy's reference to the creation of the shrine to the Plebeian *Pudicitia* (10.23). The historian noted that "no woman possessed the right to make a sacrifice [at the shrine] unless she was a matron of attested *pudicitia* and had been married to only one husband."[66] Given the general expectation that female slaves would perform sexual duties within their households, asserting that a freedwoman's husband was also her patron may have implied that the woman had not had sexual relations with another man, much like the *univira*. Furthermore, associating patron and husband effectively recontextualized the woman's servile sexual duty by associating it with her conjugal relationship.

The following monument also indicates an important connection between the patronal and the marital relationship.

> Side A
> D(is) M(anibus)
> Ti(berius) Claudius
> Primitibus
> Claudia Blaste
> co(niunx)
> Claudia Secundina
> fi(lia) be(ne) me(renti) fe(cerunt)
> li(bertis) li(bertabus) po(sterisque) eo(rum).
>
> Side B
> D(is) M(anibus)
> Ti(berio) Claudio Primitivo
> Claudia Blaste patro/no
> et coniugi bene
> merenti et Claudia
> Secundina patri
> fecerunt et A(ulo) Here/nnuleio
> Epytunch/ano
> coniugi Claudia
> Blaste fecit suis liber/tis
> libertabusque pos/terisque
> eorum (34890).

Side A

To the divine shades. Tiberius Claudius Primitibus. Claudia Blaste, his wife, and Claudia Secundina, his daughter, made this (monument) for him, well-deserving, and for their freedmen and freedwomen, and their descendants.

Side B

To the divine shades. Tiberius Claudius Primitivus. Claudia Blaste made (this monument) for her well-deserving patron and husband, Claudia Secundina for her father. Claudia Blaste also made (this monument) for Aulus Herennuleius Epytunchanus, her husband, and for their freedmen and freedwomen, and their descendants (34890).

In this example, Tiberius Claudius Primitivus (Primitibus) was commemorated by his wife, Claudia Blaste, and his daughter, Claudia Secundina. The funerary monument has similar inscriptions on both sides, but with a few important distinctions. The most significant difference for the purposes of this chapter is that, on side A, Blaste referred to Primitivus only as her "husband," whereas on side B he was "patron and husband." I see two possible explanations for the existence of these two similar epitaphs on the same monument. The first is that they simply represent a minor case of textual editing and correction: amending Primitibus to Primitivus, changing *filia* to *patri* to preserve parallel structure, writing out the numerous abbreviations, and adding desired text that was accidentally excluded. In this case, the omission of *patrono* may have merely been an oversight that was corrected in the new version. What is perhaps more likely is that side B was not simply a corrected version of side A, but rather an updated version. The addition of a new dedication from Claudia Blaste to her "husband," Aulus Herennuleius Epytunchanus, suggests that Blaste had remarried after the death of Primitivus. If this was true, the addition of the title patron served to distinguish Primitivus from his successor, commemorating the unique bond that he and Blaste had shared. It seems, then, that married couples continued to emphasize the patron-freedwoman relationship as a means to define and validate their conjugal relationship.

CONCLUSION

Popular prejudices against freedpersons and the obligatory, exploitative legal relationship between patrons and their ex-slaves assured that
freedpersons' standing was degraded because of their servile pasts. But
funerary inscriptions illuminate how freedwomen frequently used their
legal status to define their personal identity and social relationships,
even in cases where it did not seem necessary. Freedwomen were individuals who benefited from positive relationships with a range of people: fellow slaves, former owners, and kin who continued to be slaves.
Freedwomen remained intimately connected to their former household by these personal relationships even after manumission permitted
them to form households of their own. As these relationships conveyed
a degree of respectability, inscription writers used status indicators to
express what kind of woman a freedwoman had been.

Nowhere was the idea that freedwomen's relationships with their
former households influenced their standing more evident than in the
inclusion of the patron-freedwoman relationship on both freedwomen's
and patrons' funerary monuments. These monuments were principally
about family, and therefore reassertion of the patron-freedwoman bond,
even in death, was an extraordinary testament to its importance in both
parties' lives. Moreover, these inscriptions suggest that Romans used
reference to the patron-freedwoman relationship as a powerful tool
to express the depth of their connection to each other. Including the
patron-freedwoman relationship in an epitaph was such a powerful statement that it explained, legitimized, and possibly subsumed other types
of social relationships, most notably marriage. This suggests that some
freedwomen understood their enslavement as a critical means to express
their status as citizens. For many freedwomen, it was not about hiding
their slavish origins, but rather using their servile experiences to justify
and validate their belonging to the citizen community.

5   The Slavish Free Woman and
the Citizen Community

More than any other figure, the freedwoman demonstrated the extraordinariness of Roman manumission as a pervasive social ritual; her transition demanded not only the expansion, but in many ways a reversal, of fundamental behaviors and values associated with her legal status. As slaves, freedwomen's lives had been defined by an expectation of sexual availability; as a category of people they possessed a sexuality incompatible with the social norms governing respectable Roman women. Embedded in the manumission process was a complicated concern about the creation of personal integrity and respectability that the endowment of citizenship entailed. Moving beyond the simple question of whether or not only worthy slaves were being manumitted, elite Romans considered the extent to which any female slave could escape the stigma of her servile experiences. How was it possible for a sexualized woman to recover her chastity, sexual virtue, and respectability? Fundamentally, the standards for female slaves and female citizens were so different that this transition necessarily required an examination of citizenship, its definition, and its significance. Freedwomen's standing in Roman society was a critical lens through which elites explored inequalities built into citizenship and the extent to which slaves could be elevated to this status.

This chapter expands upon the preceding evaluation of the representation of freedwomen in the epigraphic record by analyzing how Roman elites interpreted and shaped the meaning of ex-slaves' presence in the citizen community. In a variety of texts, ranging from erotic poetry to historical narratives to juridical opinions, authors participated in a communal discourse scrutinizing the lives of these women. They consistently imagined freedwomen as a discrete group, set apart from other female citizens on account of their indissoluble connection to their previous servitude. Different types of thinkers nonetheless reached diverse conclusions about the significance of freedwomen's distinction and how it should influence their standing as citizens. Within this multiplicity of views, it is possible to see two broad patterns emerge. The first, found primarily in legal sources, represents freedwomen as a socially inferior class of individuals, but also as citizens capable of attaining a moral equality with freeborn women. In contrast, literary authors overwhelmingly depict freedwomen as persons living lives at odds with the values and practices characteristic of the Roman *matrona*, the archetype of the female citizen.

In both law and literature, Roman elites debated the relationship between the persistence of servile ignominy and the idea of legal equality against the backdrop of new dialogues about family and morality, concerns about women's personal authority and their control of financial assets, and the inclusion of a broader spectrum of individuals in Roman citizenship. They struggled to reconcile competing interests: It was important to guarantee the standing of freedwomen as citizens, but it was also vital to distinguish this population from their social superiors. While immediate debates took the form of a discussion about whether Roman freedwomen were perpetually tarnished by their servitude and the limitations of manumission as a citizen-making process, they also alluded to a much more complicated question: What *should* freedwomen be doing as members of the community? Linked to both slavery and citizenship, degrading service and respectability, freedwomen lived under conflicting societal expectations. Given their past experiences and their license to engage in less than reputable activities, was it possible for ex-slaves to achieve and maintain the moral standards characteristic of female citizenship? Essentially, Roman elites were exploring a tension between legal equity and social equality by examining the rights, obligations, and status citizenship entailed.

THE LEGAL STANDING OF FREEDWOMEN: AN EQUALITY OF RESPECTABILITY

Roman law articulated an idealized vision of freedwomen integrated into the citizen community with the same honor and civic standing as their freeborn counterparts. This view was premised on the belief that former slaves could possess the respectability and social prestige intrinsic to all female citizens. At the same time, policymakers also established freedpersons as a separate – and lesser – legal category than freeborn citizens. The establishment of "freedperson" as a distinct legal status for ex-slaves reinforced the alterity of the ex-slave. However, the realities of this distinction – the specific legal and financial deficiencies assigned to freedpersons – did not entirely differentiate them from the great bulk of the citizen population.[1]

The most significant evidence of this equality of respectability is jurists' explicit inclusion of freedwomen within the rank of *matres familias*, which, by the time of Augustus, had become a sociolegal category characterized by moral probity and sexual honor. Roman authors generally used the title *mater familias* in reference to a married woman, often in the context of highlighting her dignity and social decorum. They frequently juxtaposed *matres familias* with less reputable women such as prostitutes, concubines, and female slaves, furthering the association of the title with the possession of feminine honor, especially a sexual integrity worthy of protection from violation.[2]

Around 18 BCE, the *lex Iulia de adulteriis coercendis* seemingly codified the category of *matres familias* when it criminalized adultery and other forms of socially unacceptable extramarital sexual relations (*stuprum*). In their attempts to clarify the latter, juridical commentators created a category of Roman women exempt from the law, with whom extramarital sexual affairs were permitted: female slaves, prostitutes, procuresses, and actresses.[3] Lawmakers seem to have classified the group of women liable under the *lex Iulia*, a category that included freedwomen, according to the title *mater familias*, further reinforcing the title's association with respectability and sexual honor.[4]

Defining the legal meaning of the term, Ulpian explained:

'Matrem familias' accipere debemus eam, quae non inhoneste vixit: matrem enim familias a ceteris feminis mores discernunt atque separant. Proinde nihil intererit, nupta sit an vidua, ingenua sit an libertina: nam neque nuptiae neque natales faciunt matrem familias, sed boni mores.

We ought to regard as "*mater familias*" a woman who has not lived dishonorably; for her moral conduct distinguishes and separates a *mater familias* from other women. Accordingly, it will make no difference whether she is married or a widow, freeborn or freed. For neither marital status nor status at birth make a *mater famil-ias*, but good moral conduct (*Dig.* 50.16.46.1).

According to the jurist, the determining factors of the title *mater famil-ias* were an "honorable way of life" (*non inhoneste vivere*) and "good moral conduct" (*boni mores*), rather than marital status, social standing, or even free birth.[5] The central role of sexual integrity in determining female honor in general, and the link between the title *matres familias* and the *lex Iulia*, would suggest that proper sexual behavior was an essential aspect of the required "good moral conduct." By including female ex-slaves among the rank of *matres familias*, Roman jurists were effectively classi-fying freedwomen within the highest, honor-based sociolegal status for women. In doing so, they linked freedwomen to their freeborn counter-parts within a moral equality defined by their shared citizenship.

The Augustan interpretation of a freedwoman's capacity for honor appears to have roots in republican beliefs. An anecdote preserved in Macrobius's *Saturnalia* describes an episode occurring during the Second Punic War (218–201 BCE) when state officials ordered a day of public prayer and feasting after a series of portentous occurrences. This festi-val was to be funded by offerings collected from the entire community (*ex conlata stirpe*), to which freedwomen who wore the *vestis longa* were allowed to contribute (1.6.13). *Vestis longa* was a phrase used to describe the apparel of a respectable matron, the prominent item being the *stola*. More than simply a garment, the *vestis longa* was a visual indication of a woman's *pudicitia* and her moral standing in the community.[6] While the later date of Macrobius makes it difficult to accept this evidence as conclusive proof, the narrative does suggest that freedwomen had access to this garment in the republican era and thus had the right to claim the sexual honor and moral rectitude that defined a *mater familias*.[7] Given the long-standing association of citizenship with manumission, it seems probable that from the time of the Republic, Romans believed that freedwomen could achieve respectability – and thus official stand-ing in the citizen community – on par with that of a freeborn woman.[8]

However, the examples from Ulpian and Macrobius also introduce possible confusion and debate regarding the status of freedwomen. Macrobius's example begs the question of why freedwomen were not automatically considered part of the civic community supporting the

festival. The very fact that Ulpian believed it necessary to clarify explicitly the definition of *mater familias* suggests that the association of
freedwomen with this moral status may have been a contested point.
The two inclusions under the *lex Iulia* that the jurist felt compelled
to elucidate were unmarried women and former slaves. Given that the
term *mater familias* had been historically tied to the idea of marriage, it
is logical to assume that some jurists may have contested the association of this title with an unmarried woman. This could suggest that
the idea of including ex-slaves within the rank of *matres familias* may
have been just as "illogical" and may have controverted common –
but less formal – notions of status categories. While Ulpian's opinion
(and its acceptance into Justinian's canon of law) indicates a prevailing
belief among legal authorities that freedwomen should be included in
the category of respectable Roman women, it also suggests that this
moral equality was not necessarily self-evident. Thus, the leaders of the
Roman community needed to determine the extent to which the possession of a citizen-level respectability translated into civic equity and
social equality.

An anecdote related by Livy about the Second Punic War illustrates
the perceived separation between freedwomen and freeborn citizens in
the Republic. In his account of 217 BCE, the author describes a series
of terrible disasters that had plagued Roman territory. The state magistrates interpreted these catastrophes as ominous portents and ordered
all of the matrons in the city to make an offering to Juno Regina and
all of the freedwomen to the old Etruscan deity Feronia (22.1.18).[9] The
straightforward separation of matrons and freedwomen in Livy's account
suggests a strict division in civic/religious practice based on legal status. Both sacrifices were essential to the well-being of the community,
but the separation of the participants into two groups and the obvious
hierarchy of the two goddesses only reinforced the idea of a social hierarchy among the women themselves.

The perceived difference in standing between freeborn women and
freedwomen during the republican era is most evident in the official
sanction against marriages between female ex-slaves and freeborn men.
The primary evidence for this discriminatory regulation is Livy's account
of Hispala Faecenia, the freedwoman *meretrix* who aided the city in suppressing the Bacchanalian rites in the second century BCE. The author

reports that, as a reward for her meritorious service to the state, Hispala received a special package of rights, which included the ability to marry a freeborn citizen without causing her husband to suffer disgrace from the union (39.19).[10] From this account, modern historians have supposed the existence of a prohibition – or at least a dissuasion – against marriages between freedwomen and freeborn males. Such a marriage would not have been declared void under republican law, but it would have conferred an official mark of disgrace (*nota*).[11] Roman elites must have implemented this measure to discourage unions between freeborn citizens and individuals perceived as their social inferiors. This chauvinism is confirmed by Hispala's reward; her meritorious actions elevated her status to the point that a marriage with a freeborn male was no longer considered disreputable.[12]

Since freedmen suffered restrictions on their civic participation in the republican era, limiting the marriage opportunities of freedwomen constrained these women to a social and political status distinct from freeborn citizens.[13] Freedmen – and hence their wives and children – were generally assigned to one of the four urban tribes, although this was a contentious issue for Roman politicians at various times throughout the history of the Republic. Furthermore, Roman law prohibited freedmen from entering the Senate or holding civic magistracies.[14] These practices limited the political power of freedpersons and their ability to attain elite status in the citizen community. Yet one could also argue that these practices were part of an effort of rural-based elite to hold on to power in general.

In one of the most important pieces of legislation involving freedwomen, the *lex Iulia de maritandis ordinibus* prohibited a male member of the senatorial order from marrying a freedwoman, an actress, or the daughter of an actor/actress.[15] This law had a clear purpose: to protect the exclusive status of the senatorial order. In the process of doing so, it continued to assure that no individual freedwoman could achieve a degree of social prestige that would allow her the most elite standing in the Roman community. Furthermore, the *lex Iulia* (or the subsequent *lex Papia Poppaea*) prohibited pimps and male prostitutes from marrying any female citizens other than freedwomen.[16] While the provisions delineating the marriages to senators or pimps clearly did consider ex-slaves as a subordinate rank, the practical applications of these restrictions were rather limited; the number of senators and pimps desiring to marry ex-slaves cannot have been significant compared to the total number of marriages involving freedwomen. The implications of this legislation lay less in the pragmatic and tangible effects of its application, and more in how it reinforced freedwomen as having a distinct and degraded rank within the body of female citizens.[17]

Yet this discriminatory legislation excluding freedwomen from the senatorial order might also reflect a growing sense of civic equity between nonelite freeborn citizens and ex-slaves. The *lex Iulia de maritandis ordinibus* appears to have removed any official stigma and prohibitions from marriages between freeborn men and freedwomen.[18] As the Roman elite distanced itself from the more common citizens through the development of *honestiores* and *humiliores*, and as the Roman Empire expanded, citizenship and the basic package of rights and institutions traditionally affiliated with it began to lose prestige. This evolving notion of the meaning and stakes of citizenship, coupled with the increasing power and resources of freedpersons, contributed to narrowing the perceived social gap between ex-slave and freeborn.[19] Accordingly, the very category where the difference between freedwomen and freeborn women remained the most pronounced – the rarified stratum of the senatorial elite – bespoke less Romans' belief that freedwomen lacked the honor necessary for respectable citizenship and more their enfolding ex-slaves into the category of average citizens. Rome was never an egalitarian society, even among its citizens; status and social standing were influenced by myriad factors, including birth, wealth, and occupation. If freedwomen were inferior to senators and their wives, then they shared this inferiority with the overwhelming bulk of Roman citizens; in terms of practical application, the law did not entail freedwomen being treated all that differently than the majority of free female citizens.

The belief that freedwomen and freeborn women shared a moral equality under the law did not preclude mounting differences in their legal and economic rights; throughout Roman history, lawmakers imposed significant obligations on freedwomen that had tangible financial repercussions. In the Republic, these differences were less substantial than they would later be. Since early law classified former owners as agnatic relatives, treating the legal relationship between a freedwoman and her patron nearly identically to that of a daughter and her parent, there were few differences in the legal rights of freedwomen and freeborn women with one surviving agnate.[20] In this situation, a male agnate/patron would function as a *tutor legitimus*, whom lawmakers vested with significant authority because of his personal stake in the woman's estate – he was the primary heir to the woman's property and possessed the authority to approve or reject the creation of a will.[21] The most significant difference between these two relationships was a patron's privilege of exacting *operae*, which presented freedwomen with a unique financial liability, although not necessarily a strenuous one.[22]

The inequalities between these classes became more pronounced during the early Principate as lawmakers and jurists struggled to protect the economic rights of patrons. In altering the regulations governing *tutela mulierum* and the testamentary powers of women, the Augustan legislation created two important distinctions between the financial rights of freedwomen and those of freeborn women: the number of children required to earn exemption from *tutela* and the requirement that a share of the estate of a deceased freedwoman go to her patron. As was discussed in Chapter 3, the *lex Papia Poppaea*, ostensibly to increase the birth rate among Roman citizens, created the first process by which women could earn a full exemption from *tutela* by producing a requisite number of children (*ius liberorum*). Whereas ex-slaves in the *tutela legitima* of their male patrons needed four children to attain the exemption, freeborn women needed three children.[23]

Given the rigors of childbirth in the ancient world and the advanced starting age for freedwomen, the need to produce an extra child most likely represented a significant obstacle.[24] Moreover, whereas a freeborn woman with the *ius liberorum* would have possessed full capacity to administer and distribute her estate by means of a will, the *lex Papia* ruled that all freedwomen owed their patrons an obligatory share of their estate, proportional to the number of children surviving them.[25] Finally, after the *lex Claudia* abolished agnatic guardianship through *tutela legitima*, freedwomen with male patrons possessed significantly less control over their money than other women.[26] As imperial legislators continued to alter the framework of *tutela* and women's rights to fiscal management, they effectively relegated freedwomen to a secondary status below freeborn women, who received increased capacities and protections.

While lawmakers and jurists generally held freedwomen to more constrictive standards than those governing freeborn women, they did not design these obligations to punish former slaves or mark them as second-class citizens; the diminished legal capacity of freedwomen remained a by-product of the judicial and fiscal protection granted to patrons. Even though the end result was the same – that freedwomen suffered greater legal disabilities than their freeborn counterparts – it is significant that these restrictions were related more to aiding patrons than discriminating against freedwomen.[27] The distinction between the civic abilities of freeborn women and those of ex-slaves increased over time as lawmakers continued to protect the financial interests of patrons in the face of increased economic rights for women, yet this separation never challenged a freedwoman's claim to respectability and standing in the citizen community. More often than not, Roman lawmakers conceived of the legal condition of freedwomen and freeborn women as being nearly identical, rooted in the same framework of rights and obligations.

Nonetheless, there was still an enduring perception during the Principate that freedwomen possessed a social status inferior to that of freeborn women. This is perhaps best illustrated by the *senatus consultum Claudianum* of 52 CE, which addressed the sexual relationships between male slaves and free women and the legal status of any children produced by this union.[28] The edict decreed that if the male slave's owner did not approve of the relationship, he was to issue warnings to the woman; if the woman disregarded these warnings, then she became the owner's slave herself. In cases where the owner approved of the relationship, the woman's legal status was reduced to that of a freedwoman (if she was not a freedwoman already).[29] Not only did the authors of the edict identify "freedwoman" as a lesser social status than "freeborn," they also reinforced the degraded nature of this status when they assigned it as a penalty for a free woman engaging in a sexual relationship with a male slave.

Although the sources considering the legal standing of freedwomen reveal the prevalent bias against ex-slaves as being socially inferior to freeborn women, they consistently indicate that Roman elites believed freedwomen capable of achieving the respectability and honor intrinsic to female citizens. Lawmakers and jurists were compelled to consider ex-slaves as a discrete rank by virtue of their unique juridical status. The references to both *ingenuae* and *libertinae*, necessary for the sake of both clarity and completeness, would also unavoidably reinforce the perception that freedwomen were inherently different from their freeborn counterparts. Thus, the same juridical opinion that declared freedwomen to be included in the category of *matres familias* also reinforced the idea that they were entities distinct from their freeborn counterparts. It was impossible to introduce freedwomen into legal discourse without creating a means for discrimination against them; difference inevitably became inferiority. By explicitly denying freedwomen access to the full range of citizen abilities and institutions – even in cases with little practical application or consequence – Roman lawmakers and jurists effectively marginalized ex-slaves as a discrete rank within this body of citizens. Accordingly, the legal categorization of freedwomen as a group with diminished rights and the degraded status of this group were interconnected.

Yet lawmakers and jurists steadfastly maintained that this inferiority, both actual and perceived, did not preclude freedwomen's ability and right to obtain the personal honor that defined the female citizen. Legal analysts displayed and reinforced many of the same biases found in literary texts but explicitly rejected the separation of freedwoman from *matrona*. Ultimately, legal sources suggest an idealized, elite vision of Roman society. While it is impossible to determine whether an individual freedwoman could truly attain the status and honor imbued by citizenship, the law insists that this is what *should* happen.[30]

THE PROBLEM WITH EX-SLAVES: THE SLAVISH FREEDWOMAN IN ROMAN LITERATURE

If one were unaware that ex-slaves could become ordinary, respectable citizens, a survey of Roman literature would suggest that all freedwomen were low-status, libidinous individuals located on the margins of the community. Authors perpetuated images of freedwomen that stressed their distinction from other female citizens, most notably in terms of their moral and sexual behavior. They associated the status of freedwoman with extramarital sexual conduct that occurred outside the boundaries of the household.[31] This sexualization contributed to a categorization of freedwomen as a social rank distinct from respectable freeborn women, especially the idealized figure of the Roman matron.

This trend was apparent in Horace's appraisal of the liabilities of various types of extramarital sexual affairs in *Satire* 1.2. The premise of this poem is that foolish men trying to avoid vices often fall into converse behaviors that are just as problematic.[32] Horace first recounted the potential dangers of sexual relations with *matronae* and then turned to adultery's contrary vice – affairs with women of "the second class" (*classis secunda*, 47), which he clarified to mean freedwomen (*libertinae*, 48).[33] The following lines of the poem indicate that the term *libertinae* served as a metonym for low-status, sexually promiscuous women such as actresses (*mimae*) and prostitutes (*meretrices*, 55–63). The poet made this association even clearer in his critique of this countervice: These types of relationships can seriously drain a man's financial resources. Horace did not simply include freedwomen in the category of disreputable women, but rather used the status to define and title the larger group of women for hire. In doing so, he completely dissociated ex-slaves from the idea of marriage; sex with "freedwomen" did not fall under the crime of adultery (the first vice) because "freedwomen" were not wives. Rather, these individuals were prostitutes and professional companions, whose company required gifts and payment. By using the label "freedwomen" to describe this category of antimatronal figures, Horace was not literally proclaiming *all* freedwomen to be prostitutes but rather was drawing upon what must have been a prominent associative stereotype in elite Roman life and thought.[34]

For philanderers in search of adventure, the accessible sexual nature of freedwomen made them more common and thus less desirable romantic partners. In Plautus's *Miles Gloriosus*, the slave Palaestrio approaches his master with a ring, telling him that it is a pledge of affection from a beautiful young woman. Pyrgopolinices receives the token and asks whether the woman is freeborn or a freed slave. Palaestrio replies, with a touch of indignation, that he certainly would not be the envoy of a freedwoman when his master lacks the time to respond to all the free-born ladies who seek his attention (962).[35] Martial echoed these sentiments in an epigram reproducing a perceived hierarchy of sexual value that ranked freedwomen as less desirable partners than freeborn women for extramarital sexual liaisons (3.33).[36] The best explanation for the evaluative sentiments of Pyrgopolinices and Martial's poetic persona – men characterized as sexual adventurers – was the availability and challenge of the affair; freedwomen were less desirable partners because, like female slaves, they were more common and easier to obtain. By portraying freedwomen as sexually accessible and mundane, authors essentially classified them as being sexually available in a way that freeborn Roman women were not.

This generalizing categorization of freedwomen was reinforced by the fact that the vast majority of freedwomen characters existing in Roman literature adhered to these categorical boundaries, exhibiting conduct oppositional to the idealized lifestyle of the Roman *matrona*. Nearly all of these freedwomen, whether historical or fictional, appeared as prostitutes, courtesans, or extramarital mistresses.[37] As in the example from Horace's *Satire* quoted, authors often employed the label "freedwoman" to suggest public promiscuity and/or prostitution. Valerius Maximus considered the case of Q. Antistius Vetus, who divorced his wife after he spied her speaking secretly in public with a certain common freedwoman (*quaedam libertina vulgari*, 6.3.11). The insinuation is that this specific freedwoman was somehow engaged in illicit or disreputable sexual activities, as is emphasized by the sexual connotations of the term *vulgaris*.[38] Similarly, Horace wrote of his love for the freedwomen Myrtale (*Carm.* 1.33.13–15) and Phryne (*Epod.* 14.15), both of whom he described as low and promiscuous; he remarked that he chose the former over a mistress of a better sort (*melior ... Venus*) and noted that the latter was not content being with just one man.[39] The majority of literary freedwomen displayed a sexuality that reinforced the perception of ex-slaves as marginal citizens, who were closely linked to prostitution and other types of extramarital affairs.

Further indicating the presence of a pervasive stereotype of freedwomen, authors employed sexually charged terms even when describing individuals not immediately connected with sexual activities. Cicero attacked the politically ambitious senator L. Gellius Poplicola for marrying a freedwoman, not to satisfy lust (*libido*), but rather solely to increase his standing with the plebs (*Sest.* 110). The orator's condemnation of Poplicola's political motives suggests that his audience would have viewed lust as the most likely explanation for a relationship with a freedwoman.[40] In another example, the freedwoman Epicharis attempts to gain the support of the *navarchus* Volusius Proculus for a revolt against Nero. Tacitus did not label Epicharis a freedwoman until her death in a later scene but initially described her as a woman never before concerned about "honorable matters" (*res honestae*, *Ann.* 15.51). Commenting on her exchange with Proculus, the historian expressed uncertainty about whether they had known each other previously or whether this was a new relationship (*is mulieri olim cognitus, seu recens orta amicitia*, *Ann.* 15.51). Tacitus never described the exact nature of the relationship between these two individuals, but both *cognitus* and *amicitia* have strong sexual connotations.[41]

Elite writers also implied a freedwoman's slavish lifestyle and questionable sexual *mores* through her close relationship with another morally problematic woman. Suetonius wrote that Augustus expressed his shame over his daughter Julia's promiscuous behavior by remarking that he would have preferred to have been the father of one of her attendants (*conscii*), a freedwoman named Phoebe who had recently hanged herself (*Aug.* 65.2). The emotive power of such a comparison relied on the reader's acceptance of Phoebe as a shameful figure. The term *conscius* also connotes illicitness, suggesting an individual privy to secret or criminal knowledge, and even the presence of guilt.[42] The fact that the freedwoman chose to commit suicide suggests some sort of perceived complicity or association with the scandalous sexual conduct of Julia.

In a similar example, Pliny considered the case of Licinianus, whom Domitian arrested for harboring a fugitive freedwoman. This fugitive was a freedwoman of the chief Vestal, who had been accused of breaking her vow of chastity with Licinianus (*Ep.* 4.11.11). The supposed flight of the freedwoman and her choice of hideout suggest her connection to the illicit sexual conduct of her patron. In both of these examples, the conduct of the freedwomen must have invoked images of the *ancillae* who facilitated the moral downfall of their mistresses.[43] Suetonius and Pliny did not represent these freedwomen as overtly sexual individuals themselves. Instead, they insinuated the women's slavish, disreputable, and immoral sexuality by their implicit complicity in the scandalous behavior of their sexually problematic female patrons.

The degraded and promiscuous sexuality of literary freedwomen distinguished them from Roman matrons, and authors criticized men who transgressed the bounds of propriety by treating their mistress in the manner of a wife. Cicero insulted Antonius by noting how the man treated the freedwoman Volumnia Cytheris, an infamous actress and courtesan, as a "second wife" (*altera uxor, Att.* 10.10.5) and by ridiculing her queenly reception by the Italian municipalities (*Phil.* 2.58).[44] Similarly, Suetonius commented that Nero all but made the freedwoman Acte his lawful wife, after bribing certain ex-consuls to commit perjury by swearing that she was of royal birth (*Ner.* 28.1). The author included this pretense in a list of the emperor's sexual crimes, indicating his abhorrence of the act.[45] By criticizing men who treated freedwomen mistresses in the manner of wives, Cicero and Suetonius strengthened the perception of "freedwoman" and "wife" as opposing categories.

Ovid vividly dissociated the freedwoman from the respectable Roman matron by portraying a freedwoman's marriage as an insignificant and unworthy obstacle to an amorous liaison.

> Qua vafer eludi possit ratione maritus,
> quaque vigil custos, praeteriturus eram.
> Nupta virum timeat: rata sit custodia nuptae;
> hoc decet, hoc leges iusque pudorque iubent.
> Te quoque servari, modo quam vindicta redemit,
> quis ferat? Ut fallas, ad mea sacra veni!

> I was going to omit the method by which a clever husband or a watchful guardian can be deceived. Let a bride fear her husband, let the guarding of a bride be secure. This is appropriate, this the laws, righteousness, and modesty command. But who can bear that you be guarded, you who were just freed by the rod? Adopt my practices so that you may deceive (*Ars am.* 3.611–616)!

Here the poet prioritized the low social standing of the freedwoman – and thus her suitability as a potential sexual partner – over her marital status. Fundamentally, Ovid invalidated any notion of a married freedwoman by deeming the marital vows of an ex-slave as unworthy of either protection or regard.

The paucity of ordinary, respectably married freedwomen appearing in literary texts reinforced the dissociation of ex-slaves from the role of matron. Literary freedwomen rarely appeared as wives and mothers, and when they did, they were often presented as flawed because of their illicit or disreputable sexual conduct.[46] In his attack on Poplicola, Cicero discredited the man's freedwoman wife by explaining marriages between freedwomen and freeborn men in terms of lust (*libido, Sest.* 110).[47] A household report delivered to Trimalchio mentions a watchman who divorced his freedwoman wife because of her adulterous affair with a bath attendant (Petron. *Sat.* 53.10). Finally, Tacitus described the mother of Nymphidius Sabinus as a freedwoman who had prostituted herself (*vulgaverat*) among the slaves and freedmen of the imperial court (*Ann.* 15.72). As in the case of Ovid's appeal to freedwomen, these images of flawed and adulterous marriages devalued the idea of freedwoman marriages in general.

Authors did not label the extramarital sexual conduct of freedwomen, and its accompanying influence on male affairs, as being inherently problematic; there were relatively few negative value judgments placed on such behavior, as the servile past of these individuals created a sense of appropriateness. Although writers stereotyped freedwomen as sexualized individuals inferior to the idealized Roman matron, they did not necessarily represent these individuals as wholly depraved or objectionable. The prevalent opinion in Roman society was that prostitution and other licit forms of extramarital sexual conduct served necessary social purposes.[48] As former slaves and lower-status citizens, freedwomen were viewed by elites as suitable candidates to fill these roles. The lack of condemnation in literary sources effectively validated the appropriateness of such conduct and reinforced the distancing of the category of freedwomen from the moral status of other female citizens.

Even the limited virtue of a literary freedwoman remained contingent upon her lack of sexual integrity. Livy's treatment of the heroic freedwoman prostitute Hispala Faecenia, who helped reveal the practice of the Bacchic rites at Rome, reflects the potential tension in valorizing a low-status ex-slave.[49] Described as a "well-known prostitute" (*scortum nobile*, 39.9.5; *non ignotam viciniae*, 39.12.1), Hispala had developed an intimate relationship (*consuetudo*) with the young *eques* Publius Aebutius. The mother and stepfather of Aebutius, who had mismanaged the young man's patrimony, planned to exert increased influence over the youth by introducing him into the Bacchic rites. When Aebutius mentioned his scheduled initiation to Hispala, who had attended the rites as a slave, she grew alarmed and encouraged him to avoid the rituals at all costs. Eventually, the consul called upon Hispala to disclose the details of the Bacchic rituals and granted her singular civic honors for her cooperation.

Hispala's status as a freedwoman prostitute is simultaneously critical to her role in the suppression of the rites and a low social position to be transcended. It is precisely because of her marginal status that Hispala was able to protect Aebutius and Rome from the salacious Bacchic cult. Having attended the rituals as a slave attendant, Hispala was able to gain the insider knowledge necessary to save Aebutius and at the same time protect her own reputation as an unwilling participant. Most importantly, her position as a prostitute provided her close access to the young aristocrat and thus put her in a position to save him from the nefarious plans of his parents. Yet there is also a sense that this woman rose above her status in helping the Roman magistrates. Livy qualified her role as a prostitute in several ways to ensure the acceptance of Hispala as a positive figure. He initially described her as unworthy of the profession that she had grown accustomed to as a young slave and explicitly noted that Aebutius's relationship with Hispala did not injure the young man's reputation or his pocketbook (39.9.5).[50] Not only was she a prostitute who did not charge her client, she even supported him when his funds ran low and eventually made him the sole heir to her estate (39.9.6–7). Hispala's position as a prostitute was necessary to the narrative of Aebutius and the Bacchic rites, but nonetheless Livy attempted to dissociate her conduct and reputation from the realities of her professional status.

In contrast to these texts, Roman comedy used the idea of the freedwoman as a figure of respectability despite her distinction from freeborn women. The standing of "freedwoman" is a desired goal for female slaves, which represented significant social advancement compared to the woman's previous status as a *meretrix*. The term "freedwoman" is associated with monogamous, seemingly stable relationships, often characterized by expressions of mutual love – albeit as a concubine/mistress rather than as a legitimate wife.[51] While these women possess a lower standing, it is not a denigrated status; "freedwoman" is the highest level of achievement for the lowest women in Roman comedy.

Later authors expressed similar views when considering imperial concubines. The freedwoman Caenis, the concubine of Vespasian, appeared as a respectable figure who possesses a significant measure of prestige and authority. Suetonius approvingly remarked that Vespasian treated her almost as his lawful wife, even after he became emperor (*habuitque etiam imperator paene iustae uxoris loco*, *Vesp.* 3.1). Cassius Dio, however, called attention to a freedwoman concubine's unique abilities by portraying Caenis more as a business partner than a traditional Roman matron; she engages in less-reputable backroom negotiations on behalf of the emperor (66.14.3).[52] Authors recognized that freedwomen could obtain a respectable standing in Roman society without becoming wives but still emphasized crucial differences between these two social roles.

To a certain extent, it was the demands of genre that explain the dominant portrayal of freedwomen as highly sexualized characters. As each genre of texts has its own purpose, voice, and structure, the type of text impacted the representation of characters.[53] It is unsurprising that freedwomen appeared as low, sexualized individuals in a genre such as elegiac poetry, which often addressed situations involving low sexual behavior. However, these examples take on new meaning given the number of sexualized freedwoman who appeared across other genres and the near-total absence of any alternate depiction of female ex-slaves in the surviving corpus of Roman literature.

Roman literature's overwhelming number of sexualized and scandalous freedwomen indicates that Roman elites – the authors and readers of these texts – widely believed that freedwomen's servile pasts distinguished them from other female citizens. Eventually the terms "freedwomen" and "extramarital sexual partners" became synonymous, the idea being so well entrenched in Roman literature that it rarely needed to be articulated explicitly. This stereotype's perpetuation involved a substitution wherein the idea that most freedwomen were prostitutes and mistresses was substituted for the actuality that many prostitutes and mistresses were freedwomen.[54] Being a prostitute or mistress could be socially acceptable for freedwomen because they were both ex-slaves and low in status; as such they were prominent and appreciated elements of elite society. Fundamentally, what remains most intriguing about the characterization of freedwomen as prostitutes is not its existence, but its dominance over competing images of them as ordinary low-status women. Alternative and/or countercultural beliefs might have emerged to challenge this stereotype, but it would have proven difficult for other citizens to avoid it completely. The political and social influence of elite men meant that their culture became the dominant or mainstream culture.[55]

Accordingly, Roman literature does not prove that all freedwomen were low, sexually promiscuous individuals as much as it indicates that authors and their readers found it useful to represent freedwomen in this manner.[56] For these educated and well-to-do Romans, freedwomen who worked as prostitutes and mistresses were appropriate subjects for male desire, with which they were already familiar. These male citizens had less exposure to – or even interest in – counterexamples of freedwomen who were not extramarital companions; they did not seek ex-slaves as wives, and the ordinary freedwomen within the lower-class population were not individuals with whom elite citizens would have had much personal contact.[57] Therefore, on one level it should be unsurprising that Roman literature, which focused on the affairs, desires, and thoughts of elite men, only addressed this specific segment of the freedwomen rank; the social reality of elite Roman men allowed them to conflate "freedwomen" and "sexually available women" as a common category. This is not to say that the actualities of elite social networks fully explain the sexualized representation of freedwomen in literary sources. One must assume that, at the very least, Horace, the son of a freedman, had personal contact with a variety of freedwomen. Yet even with this wider social awareness, he still reduced the rank of former slaves to a group of prostitutes, courtesans, and mistresses. He did so largely because freedwomen were easily identifiable to his audience as characters who could become appropriate objects for their sexual desires.

For Roman audiences, the existence of sexualized female characters not only presented an opportunity for the exploration of male lust, but also identified unstable and troubling situations that created dramatic tension. Authors commonly portrayed women from all ranks as sexual beings, heavily influenced and motivated by their passions rather than by rationality. Where good women were able to master these passions and adhere to chaste, respectable norms, bad women acted on their sexual desires. Since positive female sexuality was absent from the public gaze, depictions of the sexual behavior of women in literature were intrinsically negative and thus associated with wicked or low-status individuals.[58] Overtly sexualizing a woman, transforming the meaning of her sexual conduct from private-oriented reproduction to public-oriented pleasure, provided a means to discredit an individual, to mark her as a degraded or morally problematic character.

What made freedwomen distinct from matrons was that they were permitted to be sexual outside marriage and to enjoy their sexual affairs in a way that matrons were not; such behavior by matrons would have resulted in disgrace and a significant loss of standing. Therefore, while the sexual conduct of literary freedwomen identified these individuals as low-status and occasionally disreputable figures, it did not necessarily imply a deeper depravity or wickedness, qualities often associated with other literary women who transgressed the boundaries of societal expectations. In this way, freedwomen resembled female slaves.

Most of the sexual scenarios in literary sources relied on a simple distinction between two groups: women with whom affairs were not permitted and those with whom they were. The *matrona* and the *virgo* dominated the first group, whereas the second group consisted of the overlapping assortment of girlfriends, courtesans, and prostitutes.[59] Authors were not concerned with legal or even social precision when describing categories of women; the use of generalizations could be an expedient literary device.[60] When they appeared in these texts, freedwomen were mapped onto the second group, which simultaneously affiliated them with lower-class women and distinguished them from respectable matrons.[61]

The most obvious example of this mapping occured in Horace's *Satire* 1.2 (quoted and discussed previously), where the author introduced the entire category of low-status, sexually available women – later described as girlfriends, actresses, courtesans, and prostitutes – as "freedwomen." This satire also provides an explanation for the prevalence of this literary stereotype: "Freedwomen" was the only categorizing term that could have possibly encompassed all types of public, extramarital affairs. "Freedwomen" could and did mean anything; their legal and social status allowed these women access to the full spectrum of professions and behaviors. All ex-slaves were available to Roman men as safe and appropriate sexual partners – with one notable exception: The stereotype necessarily required the elision of the married freedwoman.[62]

The significance of Roman literature's representation of freedwomen as universally sexualized characters lies in the capacity of these depictions to reinforce and reproduce a stereotype of actual freedwomen within the ranks of Roman society. Freedwomen derived their symbolic meaning – and their dramatic value – from ex-slaves' precarious position at the nexus between promiscuity and chastity, obscurity and distinction. They represented an ambiguity in the moral ideology espoused by the Roman elite, and, especially as this ideology acquired increased emphasis and greater meaning during the reign of Augustus, posed an intriguing and critical topic for authors, jurists, and social commentators to consider. Freedwomen provided a compelling lens through which to explore female sexuality and its relationship to social standing. Literary depictions both suggested that the lack of sexual honor that freedwomen experienced during their tenure as slaves somehow carried into their free lives and assured that it would continue. These women may have obtained their freedom, but they were unable or unwilling to progress beyond the sexual norms established during servitude.[63] Nor was there any indication that they *should*; the unbounded, public sexuality and diminished sexual honor found in literary depictions of freedwomen effectively established these women as a discrete rank contrasting with respectable Roman matrons.

MARRIAGE AND THE TRANSCENDENCE OF THE SLAVISH FREEDWOMAN

Legal and literary sources from classical Rome offer two complementary, but also contradictory, views on the social inferiority of freedwomen; both views were part of a larger cultural discourse about a woman's ability to transform from slave to citizen. Thus, it is noteworthy that jurists and literary authors both indicate that marriage was essential to understanding and resolving this complicated transition. Nowhere was the significance of marriage more apparent than in legal opinions that upheld the exploitative control that patrons possessed over their freedwomen; in this blatantly coercive structure of obligations and restrictions jurists consistently protected a freedwoman's ability to marry, even offering incentives for these unions.[64] Recall that one of few absolute precepts guiding legal opinions on manumission was that if a female slave was going to be freed, she *must* possess the ability to marry. Jurists understood marriage to have been a fundamental right crucial to the creation of female citizens.

Jurists so valued marriage as a critical institution for freedwomen that they created a quasi-marital category for those freedwomen who sought to enter into a conjugal union with a man whose social status precluded matrimony: respectable concubinage.[65] Marriage and concubinage were similar not only in structure, but also in terms of the woman's status under the law; the honorable concubine was also a *mater familias*.[66] By elevating the concubine to the same moral – if not social – status as the wife, jurists essentially created a connubial status for women who, according to social norms, should not marry (as it was more respectable for them to become the concubine of their patron). Indeed, Ulpian noted that the only difference between a wife and a concubine was the *dignitas* of the woman (*Dig.* 32.49.4). The fact that jurists envisioned respectable concubinage as being so similar to marriage, especially in the context of the *lex Iulia et Papia*, emphasizes the significance of marriage to freedwomen's status as Roman citizens.

Literary sources also suggest that marriage contributed to the establishment of a freedwoman's respectability. Trimalchio remarks that he bought his wife, Fortunata, who was a courtesan and singing girl (*ambubaia*), and, in his own words, made her as good as the next person (*hominem inter homines*, Petron. *Sat.* 74.13).[67] Given the satiric nature of the character and text, this statement about the status of Fortunata, like many of Trimalchio's assertions, should be read with reservation. Yet Trimalchio's gaffes are usually not due to factual inaccuracy, but instead to his gross lack of sophistication and nuance. Thus, to an upper-class reader, the boastful freedman may have been laughably naive in assuming that he could elevate his ex-singing-girl wife to the level of the social elite that they wished to emulate. However, this does not mean that the idea of marriage as a redemptive institution should be discounted. Valerius Maximus similarly suggests marriage's significance to the manumission process in his aforementioned account of the slave mistress of Scipio Africanus (6.7.1).[68] The author reports not only that the widow of Scipio decided to free the slave after her husband's death, but also that she provided a husband for the freedwoman; marriage completes the woman's transition from slave to free. The sexualized stereotypes of freedwomen in literary texts further speak to this connection between marriage and respectability: The vast majority of freedwomen characters appear outside any marital context and, in some cases, are explicitly contrasted with matrons. All of these examples imply that a woman's marriage was the logical end to the manumission process and her transition from slavery.

The roots of the belief that marriage could perfect ex-slaves' transformation into citizens were grounded in the relationship between sexuality and female citizenship. The idea that female honor and sexual integrity were linked to the welfare of the state was a prevalent theme in Roman literature. For example, Livy used the sexual assaults against Lucretia and Verginia as focal points for his accounts of political upheaval and revolution.[69] Authors commonly employed the trope of uncontrolled female sexuality to indicate the general breakdown of Roman social order.[70] Augustus validated the association between female sexuality and the welfare of the state when he deemed adultery and other forms of illicit sexual conduct to be public, criminal offenses.[71] Roman lawmakers expected, and even compelled, men to avoid unchaste women as potential wives and to divorce adulterous spouses.[72] The Augustan legislation lessened the gap between moral rhetoric and social reality as it legally delineated the separation between honorable and shameful conduct and provided a mechanism to enforce an individual's official civic reclassification.[73] As a result, engaging in dishonorable sexual behavior could affect the package of rights and legal abilities available to free women.[74] The significance of marriage in defining proper female behavior is evident in the Augustan legislation, which described all respectable women under the term *mater familias*, a term traditionally associated with the *matrona*. Appropriate and respectable sexual conduct was part of a woman's civic responsibilities, and marriage institutionalized her compliance with this standard.

Sexual disgrace was not linked solely to a woman's current conduct; illicit actions and disreputable behavior had the potential to create indelible disgrace that could result in a loss of status. Under the Augustan laws, the practice of illicit or debased sexual acts tainted the practitioner in such a way that stopping the activity did not necessarily remove the dishonor. Considering the case of prostitution under the *leges Iulia et Papia*, Ulpian wrote:

(4) Non solum autem ea quae facit, verum ea quoque fecit, etsi facere desiit, lege notatur: neque enim aboletur turpitudo, quae postea intermissa est. (5) Non est ignoscendum ei, quae obtentu paupertatis turpissimam vitam egit.

(4) Moreover, the law registers as disgraced not only a woman who practices prostitution, but also a woman who has done so in the past, even if she has ceased to practice prostitution; for disgrace is not erased by later discontinuing the behavior. (5) She is not to be forgiven, who has led a very shameful life with the excuse of poverty (*Dig.* 23.2.43.4–5).

Similarly, Roman law denied women convicted of adultery the rights to inherit or to remarry.[75] These examples indicate a prevalent belief among lawmakers and jurists that once lost, a woman's sexual honor was impossible to regain.[76] Yet even here, some authors so validated marriage's potential to redefine and legitimize previous sexual conduct that they viewed it as a possible means of redemption. There was a prevalent belief that a woman's sexual honor could be repaired by a wedding; marriage effectively enfolded previous behavior into the appropriate sexual relationship between husband and wife.[77]

The relationship between a woman's sexual conduct and her standing as a Roman citizen posed a particular problem for freedwomen, who had been sexualized and sexually exploited as slaves. Whereas freeborn women had lived their entire lives within a social system that prized chastity and sexual integrity, freedwomen had lived under a different set of sexual norms. Female slaves had little control over the conditions of their lifestyles, yet the context of their servitude would affect their status as Roman citizens if they were fortunate enough to obtain manumission. Accordingly, a primary question in the discourse about freedwomen's standing in the citizen community was the extent to which it was possible for these women to transcend the sexual exploitation of slavery and to gain a respectability that was potentially at odds with their previous conduct. The stereotype that sustained the image of the literary freedwoman was derived in part from the anxiety and bias of Roman elites concerning the introduction of sexualized individuals into the chaste and virtuous citizen community.

Some legal analysts suggested that the compulsory nature of slavery could be a mitigating factor that reduced the stigma of sexual duties. Most notably, jurists did not include prostitutes among the list of *dediticii*, freedpersons denied citizenship on the basis of their dishonorable conduct as slaves.[78] Similarly, Seneca describes a *controversia* that considered the extent to which forced enslavement in a brothel may have

affected the honor and purity of a female slave (1.2). The orators arguing against the young woman's position all agreed that her experiences
as a brothel slave left her unchaste and impure to the point that she
was ineligible for a priesthood. However, one of these speakers conceded that she was chaste enough for marriage; she was only considered
"impure" under the stringent conventions regulating religious offices
(1.2.8). By the third century CE, the emperor Septimius Severus issued
a rescript declaring that a woman's reputation (*fama*) was not harmed by
the profession she had followed as a slave (*Dig.* 3.2.24, Ulpian).[79] Given
that Roman authors and lawmakers viewed prostitution as the most
disgraceful of slave sexual duties, it is reasonable to assume that they
did believe that a female slave's sexual conduct within the household
would not necessarily restrict her from attaining the idealized respectability of a female citizen.

The idea of marriage was a crucial element in rationalizing the standing of ex-slaves in the citizen community because it allowed Roman
elites to reconcile a freedwoman's newfound respectability with the sexual exploitation of her past. There is a sense that Romans believed that
marriage could redeem freedwomen by legitimizing certain types of
slavish sexual conduct. Elements of this belief can be found in various types of sources that valorized and prioritized unions between male
patrons and their former slaves; a freedwoman's sexual conduct as a slave
meant something different if the relationship persisted beyond manumission.[80] Furthermore, the act of marriage retroactively validated a
freedwoman by marking her as someone worthy of matrimony and thus
respectable. Hence, Trimalchio speaks of redeeming the debased and
disreputable Fortunata, who is now his wife.[81]

Most importantly, both marriage and honorable concubinage effectively placed an ex-slave into a social category with clearly defined
expectations about sexual conduct. Unmarried freedwomen possessed
a nebulous status in the Roman world. As former slaves and low-status
individuals, but also citizens, freedwomen were subject to conflicting
expectations. According to elite ideology, ex-slaves were supposed to
join the citizen community, and thereby adopt standards of respectability, and at the same time staff the disreputable, yet crucial, social roles
such as actress, courtesan, and prostitute. Their inferior social status
and exposure to similar duties during slavery made them acceptable

and desirable candidates for these roles. Furthermore, at the moment of manumission, freedwomen had no legally recognized family, a condition that reduced the wider social stakes of a woman's illicit sexuality. Accordingly, there was no institution in place to regulate freedwomen's behavior, nor any clear answer to the question of how freedwomen *should* behave.

Marriage not only functioned as an expression of respectability – demonstrating that an ex-slave chose to embrace the moral rigors of female citizenship – but also created a firm set of boundaries and expectations for a freedwoman's conduct and her relationships with other Romans. While it was perfectly acceptable for a freedwoman to continue acting in a slavish manner, such behavior was clearly inappropriate for a *mater familias*.[82] The institution of marriage was fundamental to solving the dilemma of the slavish freedwoman; it was a symbol of an ex-slave's virtue, marking her as one worthy of being married and at the same time a social mechanism that conferred respectability upon freedwomen.[83]

CONCLUSION

Freedwomen occupied a precarious position within the Roman community. Officially, these women possessed full Roman citizenship, with legal and economic rights nearly equal to those of freeborn women. Jurists consistently declared that these individuals could rise above ignominious conduct endured during servitude and earn sufficient honor and social prestige to lay claim to the respectability intrinsic to Roman matrons. Conversely, Roman elites contributed to a literary discourse that portrayed freedwomen as a degraded rank, permanently tainted by their servile experiences. Authors reproduced and reinforced this valuation by consistently representing freedwomen as low, sexualized individuals, whose lifestyles were fundamentally at odds with the reserved chastity characteristic of the respectable *matrona*. As much as the literary sources would suggest the maligned and marginalized standing of freedwomen, legal sources often echoed this sentiment in the process of protecting patrons' rights and the perceived integrity of the elite social orders. The dominance of these images suggests a burden on freedwomen to escape these stereotypes and the desire of others to perpetuate them.

The literary image of freedwomen was part of a wider discourse about legal equity and social distinction that fundamentally spoke to Romans' concerns about whether or not manumission could create citizens from slaves. From the strict legal perspective, the answer was affirmative: Formal manumission by a Roman citizen resulted in Roman citizenship.[84] However, Roman elites drew a sharp distinction between women who merely possessed this legal status and authentic female citizens – women whose *pudicitia* functioned as a pillar of the state. Hence they structured the law to compel women to proper action; those women who failed to adhere to the desired standards of modesty and conduct were incrementally marginalized within the citizen community. Freedwomen posed a particular problem since law and popular opinion encouraged them toward both respectability and licentiousness. At the heart of the literary stereotype distinguishing freedwomen from freeborn matrons was the belief that the absence of the moral framework that had structured the lives of freeborn citizens from birth could lead ex-slaves to remain mired in the sexualized, unmatronlike status of their former servile lifestyles.

It was the idea of marriage that allowed freedwomen to bridge the gap between slavishness and citizenship in the elite mind. Both literary and legal sources reinforced the belief that freedwomen belonged to a discrete rank, socially inferior to that of their freeborn counterparts. Literary authors structured this social distinction in terms of freedwoman and matron, completely excluding ex-slaves from the order of authentic female citizens. In contrast, lawmakers and jurists differentiated between freed and freeborn, a necessary legal distinction that at times validated the literary stereotype. But even though a freedwoman did not possess full legal equity with her freeborn counterparts, she had the right and the capacity to join the citizen community in full standing as a *mater familias*. The institution of marriage allowed Romans to resolve the nebulous social status faced by ex-slaves by inserting freedwomen into the moral framework of the Roman matron. As marriage imbued a freedwoman with a new civic status, possessing the ability to marry designated a recently manumitted ex-slave as a woman capable of becoming a *mater familias* and thus worthy of Roman citizenship.

Conclusion

Throughout this study, I have argued that Romans' conceptualization of manumission was more complicated than suggested by its legal simplicity. What was in practice a relatively straightforward transaction that freed an individual from bondage required a dramatic and incredibly meaningful transition between two incompatible categories. Roman manumission was not just about freeing a slave; it was also about incorporating a former slave into the citizen community. Above all, I have attempted to identify the inherent complexity of Roman manumission and to explain how different types of people understood and rationalized this institution. I have also stressed the importance of gender in such an analysis. Gendered assumptions about sexuality, labor, and citizenship structured not only the experiences of female slaves and freedwomen, but also the transition between the two categories. Female slaves had an identity thrust upon them, an identity that continued to shape their existence after manumission.

From the perspective of literary authors and legal analysts evaluating the manumission process, this transition from female slave to female citizen raised several critical concerns, not only about the worthiness of the individual slaves being freed, but also about the efficacy of the institution itself. Perhaps the most significant issue concerning the manumission of women was the incompatible sexual norms assigned to female slaves and to female citizens; the accessible sexuality of the female slave was wholly at odds with the chastity and sexual integrity expected of a respectable female citizen. When they chose to incorporate ex-slaves into the citizen community, Romans encountered the problem of how to reconcile these two dialectical statuses.

The conceptual complexity of Roman manumission and the social anxiety associated with this process was most clearly expressed by the existence of contradictory interpretations of the freedwoman and her standing in Roman society. "Freedwoman" was a status that conveyed a sense of social elevation and personal success, indicating the worthiness of a woman who was somehow able to gain her freedom from slavery. At the same time, the title instantly degraded the woman, marking her as socially inferior to her freeborn counterparts. In various texts, the freedwoman appears as both a slavish and a citizen-worthy figure, just as the patron-freedwoman relationship appears as both an indicator of exploitation and an expression of intimacy and legitimacy. I believe that these disparate representations of freedwomen and their social relationships were part of an ongoing discussion about freedwomen's proper place in the citizen community and their ability to fully escape their servile past.

The discourse that problematized and reconciled manumission was more a discussion about slavery, citizenship, and Roman identity than about the specific experiences of the individuals involved. Early in its history, the Roman state made a decision to admit former slaves into the citizen community, a practice that continued for centuries with the sanction of the Roman people. I believe that the discourse on manumission informs our understanding not only of the expectations of Roman citizenship, but also of how Romans managed their own understanding of slavery in order to consider these individuals as potential citizens.

The accessible sexuality imposed on female slaves characterized these women as low-status, degraded individuals, whose sexual activity was closely associated with the dishonorable and shameful behavior of disreputable free women. However, the exclusion of female slaves from the honor-shame model that governed the lives of freeborn women changed the meaning of their sexual conduct. Romans effectively created a unique framework of sexual expectations for female slaves by denying these women self-interest and assigning them *en masse* to a sexualized category of people. While this set of sexual standards separated female slaves from the category of Roman women, it nonetheless adopted a prime assumption of the female honor-shame model: a woman's distance from illicit or public sexual conduct increased her perceived worth and standing. This assumption had two significant ramifications for female slaves. First, despite the unambiguous expectation that female slaves in general should be sexually accessible, there was a prominent belief that sexual conduct could still damage a slave and diminish her value. Second, lawmakers and jurists frequently drew upon the concepts and language of honor and shame to describe potentially damaging sexual conduct.

The assumption that all slave sexual activity did not mean the same thing created an opportunity to recast certain conduct as more or less respectable. Here, prevalent biases in Roman law and social values against prostitutes and, perhaps more importantly, pimps contributed to the development of a hierarchy of slave sexual standards centered on the household. Slave owners fearing the degradation and dishonor of being classified a pimp would have needed to be cautious about the context of their slaves' sexual conduct, lest these women be branded as prostitutes. As prostitution was the consummate low status sexual activity for women in the Roman world, female slaves who performed sexual duties that could not be construed as prostitution were inevitably elevated through the comparison. This book has explored how jurists attributed a greater economic value and moral worth to slaves who were not made to perform more public sexual duties.[1] I have also argued that female slaves who maintained monogamous relationships, and thus effectively adhered to the sexual standards of female citizens, possessed even greater standing and esteem. Whereas all female slaves were necessarily sexualized by virtue of their legal status, owners, authors and jurists assigned different values to different types of sexual activity, allowing certain conduct to be understood as more or less respectable, and thus more or less citizen-worthy.

Gendered assumptions about labor contributed to conceptualizations of slave respectability by typically associating female slaves with social and economic roles similar to those of freeborn women, most notably that of wife and mother. While female slaves possessed only limited access to the more prestigious or lucrative occupational positions, they benefited from their close adherence to traditional female roles. Furthermore, Roman lawmakers valorized the performance of these roles as being particularly citizen-worthy, allowing these slaves special access to manumission and its benefits. By creating a framework of sexual standards for female slaves that categorized conduct as more or less respectable, and by assigning value to female slaves fulfilling traditional female social roles, Roman law and social convention helped to reconcile the dramatic transition between slavery and citizenship.

The patron-freedwoman relationship also contributed to the social integration of female slaves and their legitimization as members of the citizen community. As freedwomen needed the opportunity to achieve the respectability and personal honor defining the female citizen, lawmakers and jurists carefully structured the exploitative relationship between patrons and their ex-slaves in order to allow freedwomen to avoid potentially shameful situations that could damage or impede their newly-won status. But it was not simply about restraining patrons, as this relationship had clear beneficial implications. Both patrons and freedwomen used their relationship to designate the woman's place in the community, marking her as an individual deserving of citizenship. It was an identity that indicated past servitude, but also spoke powerfully of intimate relationships, good character, and worthy service. The inscriptions celebrating individuals as *liberta et coniunx* or *patronus et coniunx* reveal both the private and public significance of this relationship. Individuals used the patron-freedwoman relationship to communicate the citizen-worthiness of the woman; freedwomen referred to their servile origins not only to explain their place in the citizen community, but also to legitimate it. The patron-freedwoman relationship permitted ex-slaves to become respectable matrons and also served as evidence for their social worth.

Even though Roman law and social convention encouraged an understanding of slavery and manumission that allowed female slaves to become female citizens, there was still significant cultural dialogue about the efficacy and even the validity of this process. Freedwomen were potentially problematic figures because their ideal place in Roman society was ambiguous. While accorded the rights and respectability of the female citizen, they were also expected to staff low status female social roles, such as prostitute or actress. The fact that freedwomen were not wholly constrained by the traditional moral boundaries of the female citizen contributed to their ambiguous status, a status potentially at odds with the ideals of female citizenship.

   Throughout the course of this study, I have argued that marriage
was a critical element in Romans' understanding of the manumission
process. Perhaps most importantly, Roman law ensured that if an owner
was going to free a female slave, she must possess the ability to marry.
Sources also speak to the redemptive power of marriage, which not only
assigned boundaries to freedwomen, but also had the potential to recast
the meaning of their previous sexual conduct by enveloping it within
a conjugal context. Whereas freedwomen often used their legal status
to explain and legitimize a marital relationship, the elision of the married freedwoman from literary texts suggests that, for Roman authors
evaluating the system of manumission and the standing of ex-slaves,
being a *matrona* subsumed a woman's legal status. Marriage helped to
reconcile the problematic status of the ex-slave by creating a definite set
of expectations and boundaries, and thus removing any ambiguity from
the freedwoman's standing in the citizen community. While manumission released a freedwoman from bondage, transforming a woman from
property to person, it was marriage that ultimately completed her transition from slave to citizen.

Appendix A: Approximate Dates for Jurists Mentioned in the Text

SCAEVOLA (Q. Mucius Scaevola)	late second/early first century BCE
TREBATIUS (G. Trebatius Testa)	mid-first century BCE
NERATIUS (L. Neratius Priscus)	late first/early second century CE
CELSUS (P. Iuventius Celsus)	early second century CE
GAIUS	mid-second century CE
JULIAN (P. Salvius Iulianus)	mid-second century CE
MARCELLUS (Ulpius Marcellus)	mid-second century CE
POMPONIUS (Sextus Pomponius)	mid-second century CE
TERENTIUS CLEMENS	mid-second century CE
VALENS (L. Aburnius Valens)	mid-second century CE
CALLISTRATUS	late second/early third century CE
PAPINIAN (Aemilius Papinianus)	late second/early third century CE
PAUL (Iulius Paulus)	late second/early third century CE
TRYPHONINUS (Claudius Tryphoninus)	late second/early third century CE
ULPIAN (Domitius Ulpianus)	late second/early third century CE
LICINNIUS RUFINUS	early third century BCE
MARCIAN (Aelius Marcianus)	early third century BCE
MODESTINUS (Herennius Modestinus)	early/mid-third century CE
HERMOGENIAN (Aurelius? Hermogenianus)	late third/early fourth century CE

Appendix B: Inscriptions from *CIL* 6 Commemorating "Patrons" and "Husbands"

Inscription Number	Freedwoman	Patron	Husband	Patron Precedes Husband	Husband Precedes Patron
6194	Afinia Tyche	L. Afinius Felix	T. Flavius Nicomedes	X	
6612	Valeria Prima	C. Valerius Cosanus	P. Camelius Salvillus	X	
8829	Claudia Ge	(Claudius) Nymphius	Donatus (Imperial Freedman)	X	
9133	Porcia Chreste	M. Porcius Artemidorus	M. Porcius Sodalis	X	
15540	Claudia Chrysanthis	Claudia Philumene	A. Oppius Tertius	X	
16744	Iulia Nice	C. Iulius Rufus	Q. Dasianius Superus		X
16956	Domitia Eutychia	Cn. Domitius Paederos	Cn. Domitius Diogenes	X	
17562	Fabia Severa	Q. Fabius Secundus	Sergius Sulpicius Celer	X	
18042	Flavia Helpis	Flavius Dius	Lucanus (Imperial Slave)	X	
19234	[...]ria Anatole	[...]ria Helpis	M. Antonius Atimetus	X	

Inscription Number	Freedwoman	Patron	Husband	Patron Precedes Husband	Husband Precedes Patron
19239	[Cloeli]a Helpis	M. Cloelius Felix	[...I]ulius Faustus		X
20819	Iunia Venusta	M. Iunius Persus	M. Iunius Satyrus	X	
23665	Paccia Tyche	L. Paccius Rhodo	P. Aelius Hellen	X	
26286	Septueia Dionysias	Q. Septueius Salvius	L. Licinius Epaphroditus		X
28373	Vateria Agathemeris	Vateria Pamphila	M'. Clodius Pol	X	
29607	Ustia Helena	P. Ustius Erotis	P. Aninius Icarus	X	
34401	Annia Euhodia	P. Annius Communis	Ti. Claudius Patroclus	X	
37826	[Camer]ia Iarine	[L. Cam]erius Thraso	[L. C]amerius Onesimus	X	

Appendix C: Inscriptions from *CIL* 6 Commemorating an Individual as "Patron and Husband" or "Freedwoman and Wife"

Inscriptions with "Patron and Husband" ("Husband" precedes "Patron")

01833a	9251	13491	24177
2470	11207	20682	28432
5254	13157	23223	

Inscriptions with "Patron and Husband" ("Patron" precedes "Husband")

2584	11440	16824	22749
2884	11840	17951	23048
2962	11978	17994	23897
5360	13819	18212	24445
6788	14592	18470	24711
7368	14970	19539	25585
7788	15129	19818	27900
8449	15215	20037	28040
8604	15600	20270	28221
9590	15624	20331	28375
9609	15687	21508	28670
9683	16305	21539	28964
9975	16306	21996	29272
10214	16618	22137	29527
11368	16796	22299	32678

34768	34853	35702	38610
34774	34890	37373	38674
34775	34966	38264	

Inscriptions with "Freedwoman and Wife" ("Wife" precedes "Freedwoman")

7515	13491	16413	29386
7673	14930	18208	35444
11770	15965	23295	
12162	16342	23848	

Inscriptions with "Freedwoman and Wife" ("Freedwoman" precedes "Wife")

1886	12003	17621	25319
1949	12286	18017	25485
3118	12537	18215	25832
3178	12589	18461	26281
3490	12660	18861	26843
7790	13670	19131	26920
8159	13844	19827	27196
8801	14215	20402	28285
9263	14494	20675	28809
9567	14529	20867	28881
9569	14712	21325	28953
10108	15383	21370	29256
10173	15389	22765	29345
10219	15603	22767	29378
10522	16233	23251	33880
10584	16753	23255	35503
10586	16899	24049	36558
10693	17082	25108	37566
11176	17588	25146	38565

Inscriptions with Split Status (One Individual Commemorated as "Patron/Freedwoman," the Other as "Husband/Wife")

| 1886 | 3118 | 3490 | 8159 |
| 1949 | 3178 | 7790 | 8801 |

9263	14215	19827	26920
9567	14494	20402	27196
9569	14529	20675	28285
10108	14712	20867	28809
10173	15383	21325	28881
10219	15389	21370	28953
10522	15603	22765	29256
10584	16233	22767	29345
10586	16753	23251	29378
10693	16899	23255	33880
11176	17082	24049	35503
12003	17588	25108	36558
12286	17621	25146	37566
12537	18017	25319	38565
12589	18215	25485	
12660	18461	25832	
13670	18861	26281	
13844	19131	26843	

Notes

INTRODUCTION

1   In his recent book on the Roman freedman, Mouritsen provides an excellent analysis of the perceived "stain" of slavery (2011: 10–35).

2   For a similar discussion on the significance of discourse and its relationship to lived reality, see Milnor (2005): 37–38.

3   As a partial resolution, he suggests that the exchange of citizenship between the ancient Latin communities may explain the enfranchisement of freedmen in early Rome, and that the "influence of time and precedent" may then explain the extension of this practice to freedmen of non-Latin origin (1973: 322–331, esp. 323–324).

4   Official policy began to shift in the first century CE as the imperial government began to extend citizenship rights to larger segments of the subject population. As Roman citizenship became more commonplace throughout the empire, and thus less prestigious, status distinctions among citizens began to take on greater legal significance (most notably the distinction between *honestiores* and *humiliores*). See Garnsey (1970), esp. 267–271; Sherwin-White (1973), esp. 225–251.

5   See Treggiari (1969): 11–20; Hopkins (1978): 99–132; Fabre (1981): 330–352; Bradley (1987): 83.

6   Wallace-Hadrill (1989): 71–78, esp. 76.

7   Gardner (1993): 19; cf. Mouritsen (2011): 31–35.

8   Mouritsen (2011), esp. 206–247; cf. D'Arms (1981).

9   Modern scholars have evaluated and illustrated freedpersons' ability to gain their freedom, attain some measure of respectability, and integrate themselves successfully into Roman society. Works central to understanding manumission in the Roman world include Duff (1958);

Treggiari (1969); Weaver (1972); Alföldy (1972); Hopkins (1978):
1–171; Fabre (1981); Bradley (1984, 1994); Andreau (1993); Gardner
(1993): 7–51; Herrmann-Otto (1994); Finley (1998); Kleijwegt
(2006); Mouritsen (2011). For the somewhat unique circumstances
of imperial freedmen, the standard works remain Chantraine (1967);
Boulvert (1970, 1974); Weaver (1972).

10 Seminal studies of women in the classical world that address the
situation of female slaves and freedwomen include Balsdon (1962);
Pomeroy (1975); Gardner (1986). Susan Treggiari has also written a
series of articles dealing with the experiences of female slaves and freedwomen in general (1979b, 1982) and the work commonly performed
by these individuals (1975a, 1975b, 1976, 1979a). More recently, the
work and status of female slaves and freedwomen have been explicitly
addressed in articles by Saller (2003, 2007); Roth (2002, 2004, 2005,
2007); and Kleijwegt (2012).

1 GENDER, SEXUALITY, AND THE STATUS OF FEMALE SLAVES

1 In this book, I use the term "sexuality" in its broadest sense: sexual
desire and behavior, and popular interpretation of such desire and
behavior. In this sense, "sexuality" implies a sexual identity – both
self-fashioned and imposed by the community – but not necessarily a
"sexual orientation" in the more modern sense.

2 For example, see Osiek (2003); Saller (1998); Fantham (1991). One
notable exception is McGinn (1998).

3 Most notably for this project, see Cohen (1991a): 109–126; Cohen
(1991b): esp. 54–69; Saller (1991): 144–165; Saller (1994): 71–153;
McGinn (1998): esp. 10–14. Some of the major works discussing the
honor-shame model in general include Peristiany (1966); Pitt-Rivers
(1977); Gilmore (1987a); Stewart (1994). For a synopsis of key arguments, criticisms, and debates in honor-shame theory, and their relevance (or lack thereof) for understanding the Greco-Roman world, see
Z. Crook (2009); Osiek (2008); Horden and Purcell (2000: 485–523);
Golden (1992).

4 The definition of honor devised by Pitt-Rivers provides the starting
point for nearly all scholarly discussions of the honor-shame model:
"Honour is the value of a person in his own eyes, but also in the eyes
of his society. It is the estimation of his own worth, his *claim* to pride,

but it is also the acknowledgement of that claim, his excellence recognized by society, his *right* to pride" (1966: 21). It is important to note that the comparative study of honor and shame relies on two imprecise "translations" enacted by the scholarly observer: the translation of local dialects into a common language and the translation of local concepts and practices into an anthropological model. Just provides an excellent illustration of these "translations" (2001).

5   In this respect, both men and women experienced both honor and shame (see later discussion).

6   See Cohen (1991a): 115–117. Cf. Pitt-Rivers's account of male honor and the protection of the sexual integrity of female family members in Andalusia (1977: 23). For the view that female sexuality was a fundamental aspect of male honor and shame in Mediterranean societies, including ancient Rome, see Horden and Purcell (2000): 507.

7   The most prominent criticism has come from Michael Herzfeld (1980, 1984, 1987). See also the synopses in n.3.

8   See McGinn (1998): 12–13. Cf. n.11.

9   See Gilmore (1987b): 4–5. See also the synopses in n.3. This categorization stems from observed social ideals that require men actively to pursue honor in the public sphere and women to protect their (sexual) virtue by remaining modestly aloof or secluded. Thus, the flawed paradigm of masculine honor and feminine shame is in fact a product of the gendered implementation of the basic honor-shame model – essentially how men and women conceptualized and experienced honor and shame in different ways (or, perhaps more accurately in many historical cases, how men believed that men and women conceptualized and experienced honor and shame in different ways).

10 The strongest objection against using even this basic framework in the study of ancient Rome is from Treggiari, who accepts the existence of the interrelated concepts of honor and shame, but rejects the idea of the interconnectedness of honor between family members. As evidence, she points to the specific vocabulary used to describe the family members of shamed women, the lack of a classical Latin word for "cuckold," the lack of emphasis on revenge as a requirement for redress, the absence of duels, and the absence of admiration for successful adulterers. She argues that male relatives may have experienced grief, resentment, and anger on account of the shameful conduct of their female relatives, but that there is no evidence of direct injury to their honor (1991: 311–313). However, as McGinn notes, these criticisms do not preclude the existence of a Roman version of the honor-shame

model, but instead caution against the "crude application" of that model to Roman evidence (1998: 12–13); cf. Bradley (1993): 243. A useful compromise can be found in Kaster's broader study of *pudor* in Roman society. Kaster agrees that individuals felt shame "by association" on account of the actions and experiences of other people connected to them, but he argues that the *pudor* experienced by an individual due to the conduct of his or her associates was "differently nuanced and felt," depending on how the individual identified with his or her associates (2005: 38–41). Thus one may say that a Roman man perceived or experienced the "shame" caused by his own mistakes differently than the "shame" caused by the actions of his wife – but in both cases the internal emotions and social repercussions suffered by the man were similar enough to warrant classification as "shame."

11 When considering elite attitudes toward female sexual misconduct and male honor, Evans Grubbs distinguishes between the beliefs of the urban aristocracy in Rome and those of upper-class individuals with small town and provincial backgrounds. She argues that most of the evidence for an honor-shame culture in the late Republic and early Principate is from the latter group: men such as Cicero, Juvenal, Seneca the Elder, Seneca the Younger, Pliny, and Augustus (described as "a product of 'small-town' Italy"). She argues that these voices were at odds with the beliefs and practices of urban aristocrats, who were "inclined to turn a blind eye to the sexual adventures of their womenfolk, or to go no further than divorcing a wife of dubious reputation" – behavior that represents a "decline of the ancient 'code based on honour'" (1995: 212). McGinn, however, rejects this distinction, finding no reliable evidence of actual differences in urban and rural/provincial beliefs about moral standards (1998: 12–13). I would attribute the apparent decline of the "code based on honour" to the oft-observed incongruity between ideal and practice (see later discussion), rather than an alternative moral system advanced by the urban elite.

12 There was an obvious double standard for Roman men, for whom extramarital affairs were socially permitted so long as they were conducted in an appropriate manner. This double standard carried direct consequences for female slaves, whom Romans generally considered to be acceptable partners for male infidelity (see later discussion). For more on this double standard in general, see Treggiari (1991): 299–309.

13 Saller (1999): 196. He contrasts these insults to women with the standard insults to men, which focused on physical blows and forcible entry into another's *domus*. Cf. Gardner (1995).

14 For example, Dixon admits that Romans idealized female honor, but argues that adherence to these cultural norms was tempered in the classical era by Romans' unwillingness to apply serious sanctions such as divorce and prosecution for adultery (2001b: 36). See also Evans Grubbs (1995): 212–213; Treggiari (1991): 297–298; Fantham (1991): 272–273. The extent to which the rest of the Roman population would have agreed with these beliefs is, of course, difficult to determine given the paucity of evidence. However, the prevalence of the language of chastity and sexual virtue in epitaphs would suggest that the ideals permeated multiple levels of society.

15 For an extensive survey of the various uses and meanings of the term *pudicitia*, see Langlands (2006). Langlands notes that, unlike other Latin terms connected with sexual virtue, *pudicitia* always referred to sexual behavior (2006: 2). She compares *pudicitia* to related terms such as *castitas*, *sanctitas*, *abstinentia*, *continentia*, *verecundia*, and *modestia*, which Latin authors used in both sexual and nonsexual contexts. Langlands also notes that *pudicitia* became a key legal term (2006: 21).

16 Langlands (2006), esp. 37–38.

17 For proper dress as a sign of *pudicitia*, see V. Max. 6.3.10; Plut. *Mor.* 267C. The relationship between a woman's garments and her legal/moral status will be discussed further in Chapter 5. Juridical opinions often made reference to women traveling with slave attendants (e.g. *Dig.* 47.10.15.15–16, Ulpian). For a recommendation in favor of an unattractive escort so as not to attract more attention from male bystanders, see Plaut. *Merc.* 415. In comparison, comedic sources suggest that a woman traveling alone may have been mistaken for a prostitute (McGinn 1998: 334).

18 For *pudor* as a Roman concept, see Kaster (2005): 28–65.

19 For the relationship between *pudicitia* and *stuprum*, see Williams (2010): 103–136; Langlands (2006); Fantham (1991); Gardner (1986): 121–125.

20 *Adulterium* (adultery) was a form of *stuprum* that involved the sexual penetration of a married female citizen. After the passage of the *lex Iulia de adulteriis coercendis*, which ostensibly focused on this particular form of *stuprum*, jurists often juxtaposed the terms *adulterium* and *stuprum*, with the latter denoting sex with an unmarried female citizen. For example, see *Dig.* 48.5.6.pr, Papinian (quoted and discussed in the following section); 48.5.13(12), Ulpian. Noting that the law used the two terms indiscriminately and at times improperly, Papinian

clarified that a man committed adultery by having sex with a married woman (*nupta*) and *stuprum* by having sex with an unmarried woman (*virgo*) or a widow (*vidua*). For the general use of the term *stuprum* to describe any irregular or promiscuous sexual acts, see Treggiari (1991): 264; Fantham (1991): 269. There is also evidence that prior to the late Republic writers used the term *stuprum* to indicate a general sense of shame or disgrace in nonsexual contexts (Williams 2010: 105).

21 The *lex Scantinia* definitely addressed *stuprum* committed against citizen males and almost certainly all other forms of *stuprum* as well. See Fantham (1991); Ryan (1994); Williams (2010): 130–136.

22 While the *lex Iulia de adulteriis coercendis* classified adultery and other forms of sexual misconduct as criminal offenses, it is uncertain whether the *lex Scantinia* fell under criminal or civil procedure (McGinn 1991; Ryan 1994). Moreover, the extent to which the *lex Iulia* complemented and/or superseded the *lex Scantinia* is also unclear. For illicit sex as a public concern in general, see Milnor (2007): 10–14; Milnor (2005): 140–154; Edwards (1993): 42–47; Cantarella (1991): 229–230; Galinsky (1981): 128. The reform program of Augustus will be discussed in Chapter 2.

23 Gaius 3.220; *Dig.* 47.10.1.2, Ulpian; 47.10.15.15, Ulpian.

24 Livy 1.58; V. Max. 6.1.1; Ov. *Fast.* 2.741–834; cf. Cic. *Fin.* 5.64. For female morality as part of the ideological agenda of Augustus, see Milnor (2005). The reforms of Augustus will be discussed in greater detail in Chapter 2.

25 For her decision to kill herself, Valerius Maximus named Lucretia as the leader of Roman (sexual) virtue (*dux Romanae pudicitiae*, 6.1.1). Cicero also praised Lucretia for "atoning" (*luere*) for her rape (*Fin.* 5.64).

26 Kaster (2005): 37.

27 For example, *Dig.* 48.5.30(29).9, Ulpian; 48.6.3.4, Marcian. Papinian stated that a woman who had been raped did not commit an offense against the Augustan adultery law (*Dig.* 48.5.40(39).pr). The legal phrase corresponding to forcible sexual assault was *stuprum/stuprare per vim*.

28 For other examples of the shame experienced by a raped woman, see Kaster (2005): 35–37.

29 All translations are my own unless otherwise noted.

30 *Non persuadeo tamen mihi ut crediderit. Neque enim irritare tam delicatas eius cupiditates potuisset ancilla, nec fecit quod adversus hanc condicionem fieri fortasse potuisset: rapuit tamquam ingenuam* (*Dec. Min.* 301.7).

31 *Quis Veneris famulae conubia liber inire / tergaque conplecti verbere secta velit?* (*Am.* 2.7.21–22). *Quid, quod in ancilla siquis delinquere possit, / illum ego contendi mente carere bona?* (*Am.* 2.8.9–10). For *delinquere* referring to sexual affairs, see McKeown (1998): 161. McKeown suggests that the harsh assonance of 2.7.21–22 was meant to convey an impression of whipping and perhaps a sense of disgust about the notion of a sexual affair with a female slave (1998: 154).

32 Cf. Jerome *Ep.* 77.3. The only other attested use of the title *ancillariolus* is in an epigram of Martial: "Your wife calls you a lover of female slaves (*ancillariolus*), and she herself is a lover of litter-bearers. You are a pair, Alauda" (12.58). Both of these examples make sense only if the term *ancillariolus* carries a negative connotation.

33 Cf. *AP* 5.18.7–8 (Rufinus); Curt. 8.4.26.

34 The narrator uses the arguments of the slave in opposition to language such as *casta* and *pudicitia* (111–112). See also Ovid *Ars am.* 1.351–398.

35 Catullus indicated that free women often spoke of their affairs to their *ancillae* (47.41–42). Similarly, one of the most famous "slave facilitators" is Nape, who carries messages from Ovid to Corinna (*Am.* 1.11). See also *Am.* 2.19.41; Petron. *Sat.* 16, 126. Even if female slaves were not directly involved in the affair, their close connection to their mistress could suggest an awareness of illicit actions to outside observers (see Sen. *Contr.* 6.6).

36 For representations of male slaves as objects of desire, see Kamen (2011): 192–196; Williams (2010): 19–38; Richlin (1992): 34–44.

37 For ancient theories of natural slavery and the perceived humanity of slaves, see Mouritsen (2011): 13–26; Klees (2002); Papadis (2001); Finley (1998): 140–145; Garnsey (1996), esp. 11–14, 23–52, 107–127; Brunt (1993): 343–388; Patterson (1982): 21–27. The idea of slaves being the intellectual and moral equals of free citizens became an increasingly prevalent topic of discussion in Stoic and Christian texts. See Bradley (1994): 132–153 for the "change and continuity" wrought by these beliefs.

38 In contrast, if an individual purchased a mature woman thinking that she was a virgin, the sale was not void unless the seller had let the buyer knowingly persist in the error (*Dig.* 18.1.11.1, Ulpian; 19.1.11.5, Ulpian).

39 A point raised by Saller in his analysis of female labor in the household (2003: 190) and Thalmann in his discussion of female slaves in

the *Odyssey* (1998: 27). The issue of gender and the labor of female slaves will be discussed in detail in Chapter 2.

40   The jurist Gaius noted that the primary distinction (*summa divisio*) in the law of persons was between free individuals and slaves (1.9; cf. *Dig.* 1.5.3). Of course, such a distinction arose from the complicated property issues affecting the lives of slaves.

41   It goes without saying that male slaves were just as vulnerable as female slaves to the demands and whims of their owners. For the "dehumanization" of slaves in general, see Finley (1998): 161–164; Bradley (2000).

42   Patterson popularized the idea of slavery as a social death, where enslaved individuals had no social existence or place in the community apart from their relationship with their masters (1982: 35–76, esp. 38). This idea also appears in Roman legal texts. Ulpian wrote that "slavery was similar to death" (*servitus morti adsimulatur, Dig.* 35.1.59.1) and "we compare slavery closely with death" (*servitutem mortalitati fere comparamus, Dig.* 50.17.207). Cf. *Dig.* 50.17.32, in which Ulpian declared that under civil law (*ius civile*), "slaves were held to have no standing (*pro nullis*)."

43   Spelman contends that in the social order outlined by Aristotle in the *Politics*, the legal status of female slaves effectively rendered them genderless. This analysis is part of a larger argument on the inextricable intersection of gender and race/class (1988: 37–56, esp. 52–55); cf. Thalmann (1998); Osiek (2003): 255–256. Nonetheless, I would argue that gender never fully disappeared and, as I hope to demonstrate in this book, always had the potential to loom large.

44   Saller (1998): 87–88. See Scullard for the details of the Compitalia ritual (1981: 58–60).

45   In a later Christian critique, Jerome wrote: "Among the Romans the restraints of chastity are relaxed for men, and with only *stuprum* and adultery (*adulterium*) condemned, sexual activity (*libido*) is permitted far and wide in the brothels and with female slaves, as if status (*dignitas*) created the offense, not sexual desire" (*voluptas, Ep.* 77.3). Barton advocates for a slave sensitivity to notions of honor and status (2001: 11–13). However, it is impossible to understand fully how the redefinition of shameful conduct as expected duties may have affected slaves' perceptions of specific acts. This question is taken up again in the discussion of "freedwoman and wife" commemorations in Chapter 4.

46   Williams (2010): 104–108; Mueller (1998): 226; Fantham (1991): 270. Noting this phenomenon, Langlands suggests that the Romans understood the issue of slave *pudicitia* as being "open to debate"

(2006: 22). The use of the language of *pudicitia* and *stuprum* in reference to female slaves will be discussed in depth in the section that follows.

47   For *pudicitia* as the province of the free, see Williams's comments on Valerius Maximus 6.1.pr. (2010: 106). For slaves' inability to suffer *stuprum*, see *Dig.* 48.5.6.pr, Papinian (quoted and discussed in the following section).

48   Kaster (2005): 23, 157n.35, 160n.3. He found only one example of *verecundia* (*Dig.* 1.12.1.8, Ulpian) and one example of *pudor* (Curt. 10.2.20) being ascribed to slaves. He notes that the latter example may suggest a belief that slaves were expected to feel *verecundia* or *pudor* toward one another.

49   Descriptions of these events are found in Plut. *Rom.* 29, *Cam.* 33; Macrob. *Sat.* 1.11.36–40. Ovid also mentioned the incursion (although he claimed that it was the Gauls, not the Latins, who were invading) and the resulting festival (*Ars am.* 2.257–258).

50   The sources do not reveal precisely what happened to the female slaves during their day with the Latin soldiers. After describing the decision to send the women to the enemy camp, the authors skip ahead to the events of the evening, when Philotis and her compatriots collect the weapons from the sleeping army.

51   Saller (1998): 88–89; (1999): 195n.35.

52   ... *in memoriam benignae virtutis quae in ancillarum animis pro conservatione publicae dignitatis apparuit* (Macrob. *Sat.* 1.11.36).

53   For legal status as a key variable in cases of injury and assault, see *Dig.* 47.10.15.44, Ulpian. Ulpian went so far as to argue that not only was legal status significant, but also the slave's character or type (*qualitas*).

54   *Ancillarum sane stuprum, nisi deteriores fiant, aut per eas dominam adfectet, citra noxam habetur* (PS 2.26.16). The charge of making a slave worse and the ways that offenses toward female slaves affected their owners will be discussed in detail later.

55   This opinion is quoted and discussed in more detail later.

56   On the exclusion of slaves, see also McGinn (1998): 196.

57   See *Dig.* 47.1.2.5, Ulpian; *PS* 1.13a.6. For the *lex Aquilia* in general, see Buckland (1963): 585–589; Watson (1965): 234–247; J. Crook (1984); Crawford (1996): 723–728. Most likely established in the third century BCE, it seems to have initially considered only slaves and herd animals, but was later extended to cover physical damage to inanimate objects. Gaius noted that the law treated slaves and herd animals equally (*Dig.* 9.2.2.2).

58 For physical damage or loss as a necessary requirement of the *lex Aquilia*, see Buckland (1963): 589.

59 An opinion by Ulpian suggests that the idea of physical damage may have been a debatable concept (*Dig.* 47.10.25). He declared that illicit sex (*stuprum*) with a female slave was a case of *iniuria*, but added that some jurists also believed that if the slave was a young maiden (*virgo immatura*), action under the *lex Aquilia* was also applicable. In the case of a young *virgo*, the physical damage seems apparent – the loss of her virginity. The specification of a *virgo* as victim and the reference to "some jurists" suggests that the applicability of the *lex Aquilia* to cases involving *stuprum* and adult female slaves may have been contested on the grounds of a lack of physical damage.

60 *Dig.* 11.3.1.pr, Ulpian. For the range of conduct covered under *servi corruptio*, see *Dig.* 11.3 and in general, Buckland (1908): 33–36; Watson (1965): 264–265; Bonfiglio (1998).

61 The jurist Paul noted that corrupting behavior could hurt the essential quality (*substantia*) of the slave (*Dig.* 1.18.21). When considering the rescission of purchased slaves, Ulpian declared that the purchaser (who was returning the slave to the original owner) would have to make additional financial restitution if he or she had made the slave worse, either mentally or physically (*si deterius mancipium sive animo sive corpore ab emptore factum est*). One example of this deterioration was debauching (*stupratum*) a slave (*Dig.* 21.1.23.pr).

62 Sexual corruption could be argued for both male and female slaves, but one passage suggests that jurists associated it predominantly with female slaves. In a lengthy excerpt on multiple delicts, Ulpian provided six examples of incidents where offenders could be prosecuted for the theft, insult, or direct harm of a slave (*Dig.* 47.1.2). In each case, the jurist referred to the masculine *servus*, except in the one example involving theft and sexual corruption, where he employed an *ancilla* as the example's subject (*Dig.* 47.1.2.5). This single exception among a body of similar examples implies its deliberateness, suggesting a perceived relevance of sexual corruption to female slaves.

63 *Dig.* 11.3.2, Paul; 21.1.23.pr, Ulpian.

64 *Dig.* 47.1.2.5, Ulpian; 11.3.1.5, Ulpian. The exact legal meaning of *amator* is unclear, as this is its only appearance in surviving juridical sources. This example is particularly notable because it treated the slave as an active agent and suggests that the corruptor need not have been personally involved in the actual sexual affair. Cf. *Dig.* 48.5.13(12), Ulpian on encouraging *stuprum*.

65 Juridical opinions also mention persuading slaves to injure, steal, mis-
manage financial accounts, run away, or become lazy, defiant, or sedi-
tious as examples of corruption (*Dig.* 11.3.1.5, Ulpian; 11.3.2, Paul).

66 Similar actions did not always yield the same outcomes; nor were
all injurious actions of equal consequence, for the level of insult was
derived from the context of the conduct and the status of the recipient.
As in the case of free individuals, the status of the victim determined
the degree to which conduct was insulting. For Ulpian, factors such
as the slave's character, occupation, and past behavior all contributed
to this reckoning (*Dig.* 47.10.15.15, 44).

67 Jurists recognized that such behavior may or may not have been a
deliberate attempt to insult the slave's owner. They described actions
in response to the former as *actio iniuriarum suo nomine* and those in
response to the latter as *actio iniuriarum servi nomine*. The action *servi
nomine* was a juristic creation designed to justify the charge of insult
without intention. Despite the title, there was neither consideration
of damage done to the slave nor any recognition of the slave's possessing a sense of honor able to be injured. See Buckland (1908): 79–82;
cf. *Dig.* 47.10.15.35, 44, Ulpian.

68 *Dig.* 47.10.15.15, 20, Ulpian; cf. *Dig.* 47.10.15–23, Ulpian.

69 Saller (1994): 93–94.

70 Both Treggiari (1991: 300) and Fantham (1991: 274–275) infer this
from the *pro Caelio* passage. Cf. Hor. *Epist.* 1.18.72–75; Ps.-Quint.
Dec. Min. 301.17. Seneca criticized a man who showed no consideration for his own *pudicitia* but did not want others to make an attempt
on the chastity of his female slaves (*Ira* 2.28.7). Patterson also examines how sexual offenses against female slaves injured the honor of
their owners in slaveholding societies (1982): 81–85, esp. 82, 85.

71 Buckland (1908): 76; McGinn (1998): 314. Kolendo emphasizes that
these regulations, while enforced in the interests of the owner, still
carried tangible benefits for slaves by protecting them from rape and
assault (1981: 293).

72 Roman law did place some restrictions on owners' ability to prostitute
their slaves. See the following section for the restrictions and the differences between sexual conduct and prostitution.

73 *Dig.* 48.5.6.pr-1; cf. *Dig.* 48.5.35(34), Modestinus; 50.16.101.pr,
Modestinus.

74 *Dig.* 11.3.2, Paul; 47.10.25, Ulpian; *PS* 2.26.16; cf. *Dig.* 1.18.21,
Paul (*servo stuprato*). In comparison, see *CJ* 9.9.24(25), Diocletian and
Maximian (291 CE), where the author used the verb *stuprare* in the

case of a free woman and *comprehendere* in the case of a female slave, emphasizing the difference between the two offenses.

75 *Dig.* 47.10.10, amending *Dig.* 47.10.9.4, Ulpian. Ulpian's opinion used similar, but slightly different phrases to describe injurious acts against free individuals and those against slaves. Paul then redefined the phrase describing the offense involving slaves by using the same language that Ulpian used to describe the offense involving free women. This seems to suggest that Paul was attempting to link the acts. Furthermore, the placement of Paul's opinion directly after that of Ulpian suggests that the compilers of the *Digest* also read Paul's explanation as a clarification or correction of Ulpian's definition.

76 *Servi ob violatum contubernium adulterii accusare non possunt*, *CJ* 9.9.23, Diocletian and Maximian (290 CE); cf. *HA Aurel.* 49.4. The category of extramarital sex did not technically exist for female slaves, who were legally incapable of marriage. Hence, a slave could not bring a legal charge of adultery against his partner (*contubernalis*).

77 Paul defined the phrase *pudicitia adtemptata* as *ut ex pudico inpudicus fiat* (*Dig.* 47.10.10). Cf. *Dig.* 47.10.15.15, 20. It is unclear exactly what Ulpian meant by *impudicitia* in the second opinion. The opinion concerns the cruel treatment of slaves, so this may have been left to the interpretation of the magistrate, or it may have been a reference to compulsory prostitution (see later discussion). While there is no evidence from legal sources that Romans denied the existence of slave *pudicitia*, popular use of the term indicates a clear association with free women (see earlier discussion).

78 Later jurists commonly treated the *lex Iulia de maritandis ordinibus* (18 BCE) and the *lex Papia Poppaea* (9 CE), which refined the earlier legislation, as a single law: the *lex Iulia et Papia*.

79 McGinn reconstructs this phrase by comparing relevant juridical opinions. He notes that lawmakers used a similar phrase in earlier legislation, and that Roman authors had long associated the words *quaestum facere* with prostitution (1998: 99–100). As a useful point of comparison, McGinn provides a general definition of prostitution that encompasses three elements: "promiscuity, payment, and emotional indifference between the partners" (1998: 17–18).

80 As a useful point of comparison, Karras and Boyd argue that medieval European writers and lawmakers understood a prostitute as "a certain type of person rather than as a person who did certain things" and therefore understood prostitution as "a sexual orientation, an important component of personal identity" (1996: 104).

81 Cf. *Dig.* 23.2.41.pr. Marcellus read *palam* to mean "openly" in the sense of "in public," but argued that this quality was not necessary for defining a prostitute.

82 Roman law considered prostitutes among the category of those branded by *infamia* or *ignominia*. Not all prostitutes would have been Roman citizens; a prostitute must have achieved Roman citizenship by birth or enfranchisement. For the civil and legal disabilities suffered by prostitutes, see McGinn (1998): 21–69.

83 This appears to have been a matter of custom rather than law until the Augustan legislation, which may have made the toga a formal requirement. See McGinn (1998): 156–171.

84 *Dig.* 11.3.14.4, Paul; 9.2.18, Paul. A partial explanation was that prostitution lowered the market value of a female slave. Consider the poem of Martial, in which he described an auctioneer having trouble trying to sell a slave girl of "none too good reputation, such as those who sit in the middle of the Subura" (*famae non nimium bonae puellam, / quales in media sedent Subura*), because people feared she was not clean (*pura*, 6.66). For the Subura as a noted locale for prostitutes, see Welch (1999), esp. 382; McGinn (2004a): 21, 80–81.

85 *Si quis virgines appellasset, si tamen ancillari veste vestitas, minus peccare videtur: multo minus, si meretricia veste feminae, non matrum familiarum vestitae fuissent* (*Dig.* 47.10.15.15, Ulpian).

86 See McGinn (1998): 326–337. It is likely that such limited liability for transgressive conduct against slave prostitutes existed in part to discourage owners from acting as pimps. McGinn argues that "unlike other slave owners, the pimp has betrayed the honor of his female slaves; indeed, he profits from their sexual disgrace" (1998: 327–328).

87 Calp. *Decl.* 5.

88 Horace blended together the idea of the female slave and the prostitute in *Satire* 1.2. Cf. Jerome *Ep.* 77.3.

89 There is evidence of prostitutes of all social statuses in ancient Rome: slave, freed, and freeborn (including women from elite families). While it is impossible to determine the ratio of slave to free prostitutes accurately, it is clear that Roman authors and lawmakers closely associated slavery and prostitution. McGinn notes that when an ancient source mentioned the status of a female prostitute, more often than not she was a slave (2004a: 59). However, he concedes that evidence may be skewed because Roman authors were more interested in female slaves than in the free poor (citing Scheidel 1995; 1996).

90 Flemming (1999): 40–43, 57–58.

91 McGinn remarks that the focus on slaves in this juridical opinion means one of two things: Either the ownership of slave prostitutes was more significant as a socioeconomic phenomenon in the Roman world, or there was a special legal reason requiring this particular emphasis. He believes the former to be the likely explanation (1998: 54–55). Cf. *Dig.* 23.2.43.9, where Ulpian described prostitutes being kept under the pretext of being *instrumenti*, a word often used to denote slaves as owned property.

92 Nowhere in the juridical opinions concerned with this covenant is the term "prostitution" defined. Rather, jurists treated the term as a known, clearly delineated action, most likely drawing upon established legal definitions and social norms. The *ne serva prostituatur* restriction was one of four restrictive covenants recognized by Roman law. The others were *ut manumittatur*, *ne manumittatur*, and *ut exportetur*. For a summary of these restrictive covenants, see Buckland (1908): 68–72. For more details on the structure and enforcement of the *ne serva prostituatur* covenant in particular, see McGinn (1990); (1998): 288–319.

93 According to Modestinus, Vespasian made a decision in a case involving a slave protected by a *ne serva prostituatur* clause (*Dig.* 37.14.7.pr). Papinian also cited an opinion of Masurius Sabinus, whose life has been dated to the first century CE, on the topic (*Dig.* 18.7.6.pr).

94 *Dig.* 37.14.7.pr, Modestinus. According to this opinion, Vespasian decreed that the new buyer would be liable for violating the covenant, even if he was ignorant of its existence. See also *Dig.* 18.1.56, Paul. Unsurprisingly, female slaves themselves possessed little agency in this process, as enforcement of the covenant would have relied almost entirely on the action of the original vendor.

95 *CJ.* 4.56.1, Alexander Severus (223 CE). See also *Dig.* 2.4.10.1, Ulpian; 21.2.34.pr, Pomponius; 40.8.7, Paul. Alexander Severus referred to a decree enacted by Hadrian as the foundation for his ruling. The exact policy prior to Hadrian is unclear. For McGinn, this represented a critical shift in that the law now recognized the interests of a slave independent of those of her master (but not necessarily independent of the interests of slave owners as a group; see n.97).

96 For the link between *contumelia* and *iniuria*, see McGinn (1998: 315n.147). Building on analysis by Treggiari, McGinn persuasively argues that *affectio* did not predicate the existence of a sexual relationship between the vendor and his slave (1998: 314n.145, 315).

97 See Watson (1987); McGinn (1998): 307. McGinn theorizes that in the case of *ne serva prostituatur*, the interests of the female slave were

in line with those of the owners as a group, since it was validating the practice of offering slaves a tangible reward as an incentive for good-quality service (1998: 310).

98 McGinn (1998): 314–315. On the basis of this language, McGinn argues that the *ne serva prostituatur* covenant is a rare example of juristic acknowledgment of personal honor in slaves.

99 The veracity of this statement is impossible to ascertain. The *Historia Augusta* is a notoriously dubious historical source and no surviving legal text makes reference to such a law. McGinn, who is inclined to accept the existence of such a law, argues that *Dig.* 18.1.42, Marcian and *Dig.* 48.8.11.1–2, Modestinus, which discuss limitations placed on the sale of slaves to fight wild beasts, may support the presence of similar legislation concerning the sale of female slaves to pimps/brothels (1998: 305n.81). It is also unclear what circumstances would have constituted "just cause." According to Modestinus, a *lex Petronia* (most likely dating from the early Principate) and related *senatus consulta* forbade the sale of slaves to fight beasts unless they had appeared before a judge (*Dig.* 48.8.11.1–2).

100 McGinn (1998): 309–310. Therefore, McGinn assumes that the opinion refers only to the enforcement of the *ne serva prostituatur* covenants. Flemming supports this interpretation, suggesting that the final words of the paragraph (*ne prostituatur*) reference the phrase *ne serva prostituatur* (1999: 53n.77). Alternatively, Robinson adopts a more literal interpretation, asserting that Severus's decree forbade compulsory slave prostitution – thus implying that voluntary slave prostitution continued (1981: 242). This interpretation raises the larger question of any slave's ability to exercise truly "voluntary" actions. Cf. *Dig.* 1.6.2, where Ulpian included the compulsion of unchaste acts and base sexual violation (*ad impudicitia turpemque violationem compellat*) among the behaviors prohibited to slave owners.

101 A common motif in both comedy and romantic poetry was the lover who is attracted to the female slave of his girlfriend. In these examples, affairs with slaves must occur in secret, lest the men anger their girlfriends. See Yardley (1974): 432–434. Examples include Plaut. *Truc.* 94; Aristaenetus 2.7; Prop. 3.15 (if one accepts Lycinna as the slave of Cynthia); Ovid *Ars am.* 1.383–386, 3.665–666; *Am.* 2.7–8. Even the more innocuous affairs between a man and a female slave who did not belong to his household retain elements of surreptitiousness. For example, the relationship between Lucius and Photis in Apuleius's *Metamorphoses* endured for a significant amount of time in a rather

small household. Yet the author's narrative still suggests a degree of
furtiveness in the actions of the two lovers. Beginning the description
of their first embrace, Apuleius explicitly notes that both Milo and
Pamphile (Lucius's host and hostess, and the only other members of
the household) were absent – a situation that seems to spur Lucius into
action (2.7). Furthermore, Photis always joins Lucius in his bedroom
later in the evening, after putting her mistress to bed (2.16, 3.13).
However, there was clearly a belief that an affair with a female slave
was a less transgressive and safer alternative to adultery or *stuprum* with
a free woman belonging to the household (Apul. *Met.* 2.6).

102 For men purchasing slaves out of love or desire, see Plaut. *Epidi.* 463–
466; *Poen.* 102–103; Mart. 2.63, 6.71; cf. Watson (1967): 6–7. An
underlying sentiment is the man's desire to be the only individual to
have access to the female slave.

103 The scholiast Pseudo-Acro understood "small gift" to mean a sexual act (*obscenitas*, *coitus*), rather than the slave herself (Hor. *Epist.*
1.18.75).

104 *Ac si forte cepisset oculos tuos, quid opus erat vi? Non munusculo sollicitasses?*
Non, si contumacior esset, pro tua illa comitate a domino petisses? (*Dec. Min.*
301.17)

105 In the *Satyrica*, Encolpius meets a female slave who only has sex with
equites, and whose female owner only has sex with male slaves (126).
One can infer that the female slave is having sex with men outside the
household with her owner's consent. However, it seems unlikely that
this should be read as a socially condoned practice, especially when
coupled with the scandalous sexual conduct of her owner.

106 For the civic disabilities of pimps, see McGinn (1998): 21–69.

107 Veyne attributes the prevalence of sexual relations to the combination
of subordination and intimacy in the master-slave interactions within
households (1961: 219). A related, but rarely mentioned, aspect of
these relationships was reproduction, and specifically the creation of
new household slaves. See Chapter 2.

108 Musonius Rufus noted that many people saw no fault with a man's
sleeping with his female slaves, since owners had the authority to use
their own slaves as they wished (*fr.* 12). In these cases, "owner" can also
be applied to free members of the household who did not have legal
possession of the slave. For example, Valerius Maximus recorded that
Scipio Africanus began an affair with one of his wife's female slaves
(6.7.1). Kolendo attributes the lack of positive evidence about casual
affairs with slaves to the popularity of the practice and naturalness of

such sexual exploitation in the Roman world (1981: 288). In contrast, Treggiari argues that the moral sanctions against sexual affairs with slaves suggest a sense of feminine disapproval that would have limited the sexual exploitation of slaves (1979b: 192; cf. Saller 1987: 78–79 for a response to Treggiari's argument).

109 See Chapter 2.

110 See Muson. *fr.* 12; V. Max. 6.7.1; Gell. *NA* 2.23.10. Cf. Sen. *Ep.* 94.26, 95.37, 123.10. In these examples, Seneca did not write specifically about female slaves, but about having a mistress (*paelex, amica*) in general – a category that often included unfree women. Seneca used the term *iniuria* to describe the affront to one's wife caused by such an extramarital affair (95.37).

111 Critics of these affairs focused not so much on the women involved as on owners who became subservient to their female slaves. For example, see Prop. 1.9.4. Kamen notes how Martial used the trope of slave agency and control over the master as a means of critiquing and insulting particular slave owners (2011).

112 Treggiari (1981a): 72; Rawson (1974): 289. Cf. Plaut. *Epidi.* 463–466; Watson (1967): 7. There is a significant amount of evidence for both concubinage and marriage between male owners and their female former slaves. The concern over slave concubines was closely tied to the reputation of the owner; elevating the legal status of his partner through manumission was a means to protect his own social standing.

113 *Lucillae concu/binae piissimae / quae vixit / annis XV / diebus XXX / fecit P. Coe/lius Abasca/ntianus do/minus ben(e)/merenti et / castae (CIL* 6.21607).

114 *Tit. Ulp.* 5.5; *PS* 2.19.6. Inscriptional evidence indicates that there were female slaves who had a freedman as their *contubernalis*, but most of the examples appear to represent relationships begun when both partners were slaves, and then continued after the man's manumission (Treggiari 1981b: 53–54). It is important to note that, despite the absence of *conubium*, many slaves (and ex-slaves looking backward) described their partners/spouses in funerary epitaphs using the terminology of legitimate marriage. I will return to this point in Chapters 2 and 4.

115 The connection between *contubernium* and legal marriage is evident, as many *contubernales* entered formal matrimony after manumission (see Treggiari 1981b). Despite the growing recognition of *contubernium* as a union worthy of preserving, dissolution of the relationship was always a very real danger given slaves' status as property. See Rawson

(1966): 78–79. The stability of slave families will be discussed in
more depth in Chapter 2.

116 Treggiari found only six inscriptions involving slave *contubernales* in
which it was possible to discern the ownership of both partners. There
were three couples of *conservi* and three who possessed different owners. Of these last three, Treggiari theorizes that one pair were from
different households within the extended imperial *familia*, and that
the final two pairs both involved owners who were married to each
other (1981b: 46). See also Edmondson (2011): 349. While there is
evidence of married freedpersons who appear to have been slaves in
different households, it is often impossible to discern whether these
relationships began before or after manumission.

117 The *Historia Augusta* recorded that the emperor Aurelian punished
one of his female slaves who had committed adultery (*adulterium*) with
another slave (*Aurel.* 49.4). Cf. *Dig.* 48.5.6.pr, Papinian; *CJ* 9.9.23,
Diocletian and Maximian (290 CE), which restrict the charge of *adulterium* to married partners, thus excluding *contubernales*. McGinn suggests
that the passage from the *Historia Augusta* may indicate a temporary
change to this law (1998: 196n.446). However, the fact that Aurelian
chose to punish the female slave personally while turning over other
slaves to the courts for trial (49.5) may indicate that his penalty was not
technically supported under contemporary Roman law.

118 Roman law recognized the existence of *contubernium* between slaves
and suggests that partners received certain considerations and benefits. Most notably, Ulpian asserted that *contubernales* counted as family
members, in that they could not be separated without great inconve-
nience (*magno incommodo*, *Dig.* 21.1.35); cf. *Dig.* 33.7.12.6–7, Ulpian.

2 GENDER, LABOR, AND THE MANUMISSION OF FEMALE SLAVES

1 For the gendered division of labor in Roman society, see Brunt (1971):
143–144; Scheidel (1995): 205–06; Saller (2003, 2007, 2012: 79–80).
For the best example of this ideal division of labor on a Roman agricultural estate, see Col. 12.pref.1–6.

2 For example, the jurist Hermogenian noted that a woman's sex prevented her from performing physical civic duties (*corporalia munera*,
Dig. 50.4.3.3); cf. Ps.-Arist. *Oik.* 1.1344a3–6; *CJ* 5.35.1, Alexander

Severus (224 CE). These edified stereotypes still possessed power in light of contrasting evidence (e.g., Gaius 1.144, 190 on *tutela*). Dixon argues that the "womanly weakness" commented on in Roman legal sources did not have roots in the Republic, but rather was created later to rationalize the existence of *tutela mulierum*. She concludes, then, the idea of female financial helplessness did not represent a true belief in the intellectual deficiency of women, but rather an attempt to exclude women from traditional masculine spheres (2001b: 73–88, esp. 76). Dixon's argument illustrates how the idea of female intellectual and physical deficiency could reinforce the prestigious/exclusive nature of masculine work (see later discussion).

3   There is substantial evidence from other cultures for female slaves being employed in "masculine" agricultural labor (Scheidel 1995: 208–210; Saller 2007: 103–104). Given this evidence from other slave societies, Scheidel remarks that there is no reason to assume that Roman slave owners did not treat their female agricultural slaves in such a manner (213; cf. Erdkamp 1999: 571). Scheidel's point has merit, especially considering the economic needs of less prosperous slave owners. Nonetheless, it is still significant that Roman authors promoted a vision of female slave labor in accord with standard gender norms. This was not true in the case of male slaves, whom owners frequently used for "female" duties as a display of status. The underlying message of such staffing decisions was that owners were wealthy enough to use more expensive commodities (male slaves) than the work required. In contrast, classical authors often associated female rural labor with barbarians and other marginalized peoples (Scheidel 1996: 5–8; Saller 2003: 198; 2007: 102–103).

4   Male slaves may have actually outnumbered females in the early Republic when the primary source of slaves was military conquest (although Scheidel offers a persuasive argument why this may not have been the case, 2005: 72; see also Roth 2002, 2007, 2008). However, during the Principate, natural reproduction, which demands a more equal sex ratio, was the primary source of new slaves (Scheidel 1997). Harris agrees that natural reproduction was the most important source of new slaves during this period (albeit not as important as in Scheidel's model) but contends that factors such as the irregular sexual habits and extended nursing duties of female slaves severely limited the effectiveness of this model. He suggests that the necessary import of male slaves and the exposure of newborn female slaves could support the sex ratio appearing in textual and epigraphic evidence,

where male slaves greatly outnumbered females (Harris 1999, esp. 65, 69–70). It seems to me that the large number of slaves in the Roman world would have rendered the factors inhibiting natural reproduction less significant, and thus I am inclined to accept the more equal sex ratio proposed by Scheidel. In addition, Bagnall and Frier's demographic analysis of Roman Egypt seems to support arguments in favor of a balanced ratio (1994: 158).

5   Treggiari (1975a): 395, on the basis of her study of the households of Livia, the Volusii, and the Statilii. The tomb of each household reflects an approximate 2:1 male:female ratio; see also Hasegawa (2005): 65. Weaver found a similar ratio in three separate groups tied to the *familia Caesaris* (1972: 172).

6   For the imbalanced sex ratio in agricultural sources, see later discussion. Hopkins admits that the evidence for female agricultural slaves is ambiguous as ancient authors seem to assume that most slaves were male and celibate (e.g., only the *vilici* had female partners) but at the same time also encourage the production of slave offspring. He leaves the matter unresolved but does note that comparative evidence indicates the possibility of running an economy with a predominantly male labor force (1978: 106n.16). Scheidel concludes that the numerous references to slave children on rural estates imply the existence of a considerable number of unfree women (1996: 3). Similarly, Roth points to the substantial calorie content of the proposed slave rations and the existence of female-oriented equipment such as (hand) grain mills and looms in Cato's treatise as an implicit acknowledgment of the female slaves working on an agricultural estate (2002).

7   In this respect, the treatment of female agricultural slaves by ancient authors does not differ from that of rural women in general. For the work performed by women in rural/agricultural settings, see Scheidel (1995, 1996); Erdkamp (1999); Roth (2004); Saller (2007): 102–104.

8   A *vilica* need not necessarily have been a slave, but slaves frequently fulfilled this role (see later discussion on the *vilica* as a reward).

9   Cato *Agr.* 143; Col. 12.1–3; *Dig.* 40.5.41.15, Scaevola; Carlsen (1993); Roth (2004). Columella remarked that in previous times, the wife of the head of the household had performed these supervisory duties whereas the *vilica* had little to do. However, as contemporary women chose to live lives of idleness and luxury, these duties fell to the *vilica* (12.pref.8–10). Roth cautions against viewing the *vilica* simply as the wife of the *vilicus* (or even assuming the *vilicus* was always married to the *vilica*). She stresses that the sources treat the *vilica* as a professional

manager in her own right (2004). As a point of comparison, Garrido-Hory notes that Martial broadly used the term *vilica* to describe a female slave performing unspecialized labor (1999: 303).

10 The *vilica* is the only female slave included on Cato's inventory of ideal farm staffs (*Agr.* 10–11; see later discussion). Varro noted that some larger farms may have required two *vilicae* (*Rust.* 1.18).

11 This definition is a simplification of a complicated and somewhat nebulous legal distinction. See *Dig.* 33.7 and Saller (2003): 192–193 for more details.

12 *Dig.* 33.7.12.7, 33, Ulpian; *PS* 3.6.38. *Contubernales*, the children of male slaves, and the categories of *fundus* with *instrumentum* and *fundus instructus* are discussed in more depth later.

13 Col. 12.3.6–8, 12.4.3; *Dig.* 33.7.12.6, Ulpian. For a detailed study of the role and significance of female slaves in agricultural slavery, see Roth (2007).

14 In particular, Columella briefly alluded to female slaves working as chicken tenders (8.2.7). de Ste. Croix believes that the specific references to women's work in Columella (compared to its near-absence in Cato and Varro) reflects an increased interest in the labor of female slaves on a societal level (1981: 234–237, 587–588n.14); cf. Smadja (1999): 356–357. Harris rightly questions whether such meager references can support such a bold claim (1999: 70n.60); cf. Roth (2007).

15 Scheidel (1996): 4–5; Saller (2003): 200. Roth agrees with this assessment of assigned duties, yet cautions against discounting the economic potential of female labor on agricultural states, especially the industrial production of textiles (2007, esp. 53–118). Individual female slaves serving poorer families may have been forced to participate in agricultural labor out of necessity, but larger households would have been less likely to require additional labor support. The willingness of farmers to ignore gendered labor norms in situations of need is a primary argument of Scheidel (1995, 1996).

16 See Treggiari (1975b, 1976, 1979b); Kampen (1981); Günther (1987): 40–137, esp. 135–137; Joshel (1992), esp. 69–71; Clarke (2003): 105–125; Hasegawa (2005): 69–71; Saller (2007): 104–107.

17 Treggiari (1976). There are examples of women fulfilling a few "male" positions such as doorkeeper and waiter, but such assignments do not appear to have been common.

18 For slaves working in these professions, see the references to female labor in general in n.16. See also Garrido-Hory (1999); McGinn (2004a): 57–60 for female slaves as prostitutes and entertainers, and

Dixon (2000–2001, 2004: 65–68) for slaves in the textile industry. Interestingly, artisanal training for the textile industry may have been an area where the labor experiences of female slaves diverged from the gendered expectations of free women. In his survey of thirty apprenticeship contracts from Roman Egypt, Bradley found evidence of free and slave boys, but only slave girls (1991: 107–08; see also Saller 2012: 79–80). Career options and opportunities may have been even more limited for female members of the *familia Caesaris*. See Herrmann-Otto (1994): 117–118, 346–347.

19   A complicating factor in assessing the work performed by female slaves – and the representation of this work in the historical record – is the treatment of freedwomen, whose presence in commercial and manufacturing ventures is much more visible (see Pomeroy 1975: 198–202; Joshel 1992: 128–145; Dixon 2001a). It is logical to assume that many, if not most, of these women were continuing in occupational paths that they had begun as slaves – but of course it is impossible to say for certain. In my opinion, the increasing commercial visibility of freedwomen (which is still limited compared to that of freedmen) makes the occupational/economic marginalization of female slaves (if only representational) all the more interesting.

20   See Treggiari (1976): 82–83, who mitigates the supervisory role of *lanipendae* by casting them as deputies of the *mater familias*.

21   Aubert found only a few examples of women in general who served as business or estate managers (1994: 193, 224, 268, 292, 372, 419); cf. Setälä (1998).

22   The *peculium* was a fund granted by a *pater familias* to an individual in his *potestas* (usually a child, grandchild, or slave) in order to mitigate the latter's inability to own property formally. This individual possessed full control over the use of the fund – either for his or her own maintenance or to act as a financial agent of the *pater familias* – but the *pater familias* retained ownership and could revoke the fund at any time. For more on the *peculium*, see Buckland (1908): 187–206; Crook (1967): 110–111, 188–191; Fabre (1981): 271–278; Żeber (1981); Thomas (1982); Kirschenbaum (1987): 31–88; Roth (2005, 2010); Mouritsen (2011): 159–180.

23   Two other opinions mentioned female slaves as part of the complete list of individuals who could possess a *peculium* (*Dig* 13.6.3.4, Ulpian; 21.1.23.4, Ulpian). Another discussed a female slave transferring a "dowry" from her *peculium* to that of her *contubernalis* but provided

no other context (*Dig.* 23.3.39.pr, Ulpian). Cf. *CJ* 7.66.5, Gordianus (238 CE).

24 Roman literary authors and jurists generally considered slaves trained in a skill (*artificium*) to be more valuable than those occupying a general position. To illustrate, the jurist Marcian mentioned a cook as an example of a skilled slave, and a litter bearer as one without a skill (*Dig.* 32.65.1). Given the gendered attitudes toward labor, it seems likely that slave owners would have allocated very little of the limited resources dedicated to educating and training slaves for women. See Saller (2003): 197.

25 Treggiari notes that no female staff appear in Cicero's writings, and only very few in the correspondence of Pliny, Sidonius Apollinaris, Fronto, and Symmachus (1976: 100n.5).

26 Joshel (1992): 49–50; Harris (1999): 67 (citing Tac. *Ger.* 25). Cato's elision of female slaves from his estate rubrics supports this assertion. Furthermore, occupational titles were an essential aspect of slave and freedperson self-identification (Treggiari 1975b: 57; Flory 1978: 80; Joshel 1992; George 2006; Verboven 2012: 92–93).

27 Smadja (1999): 362; Harris (1999): 69. Cf. Saller, who suggests that many female slaves may have been "underemployed" (2003: 197).

28 cf. Gell. *NA* 4.1.17.

29 Female weavers may not have been included in this category (*Dig.* 33.9.3.6, Ulpian).

30 Saller argues that as rural labor (*opus rusticum*) was the defining example of slave labor, the household *ancilla* was the quintessential example of a slave "who does not work" (2003: 191); cf. Ter. *Haut.* 142–143.

31 While there is significant dispute over the exact percentage of new slaves created through internal reproduction, all scholars recognize the importance of procreation in the Roman slave supply, especially during the late Republic and early Principate. See Bradley (1987); Scheidel (1997); and Harris (1999) for three different perspectives on this issue. Cf. Biezunska-Malowist and Malowist (1966); Herrmann-Otto (1994), esp. 1–3, 287; Roth (2007), esp. 1–24.

32 Although the evidence for slave prices in the Roman world is limited, there are a few sources that suggest the value placed on reproductive ability. For example, according to Diocletian's Price Edict, unskilled female slaves reach their highest value in the sixteen to forty age range. Perhaps even more illuminating is that the only age cohort where unskilled female slaves have the same maximum price as unskilled male

slaves is eight to sixteen, where female slaves are just entering their childbearing years and male slaves still have not reached their peak productivity as laborers (Saller 2003: 202–204). Bradley notes that the maximum age recorded for the sale of a female slave in Egyptian papyri was thirty-five. This suggests the importance of reproductive ability to their value (1978, 1984: 55); cf. Dalby (1979).

33 For example, *Dig.* 33.8.3, Paul; 33.8.8, Ulpian; 40.5.26.2, Ulpian.

34 *Dig.* 21.1, esp. 21.1.14.1, Ulpian. This opinion contrasted with the view of Vitruvius, who maintained that a pregnant slave was not judged sound (*integra*) for the purposes of sale because the fetus sapped the health of the mother (2.9.1). Bradley suggests that Ulpian's stance may have superseded that of Vitruvius (1984: 62n.54).

35 Herrmann-Otto thoroughly explores the usage (or lack thereof) of the term *verna* among Roman authors, jurists, and inscription writers (1994). She notes how the term was used primarily by private owners to designate affection or the means by which the slave was acquired, whereas it functioned more as an indicator of elite status within the *familia Caesaris*. Cf. Chantraine (1967): 171; Weaver (1972): 51–53.

36 Nep. *Att.* 13.4; Stat. *Silv.* 5.5.66–70; Plin. *Ep.* 5.86. As a result, being a *verna* must have helped to build a bond with one's owner and increase one's chances of manumission. For the status of *vernae* (and other "home-born" slaves), see Herrmann-Otto (1994); B. Rawson (1986, 2010); Laes (2003, 2010).

37 *Ancillarum etiam partus et partuum partus quamquam fructus esse non exis- timantur, quia non temere ancillae eius rei causa comparantur ut pariant, augent tamen hereditatem*: (*Dig.* 5.3.27.pr, Ulpian). *Fructus* (fruits/pro- duce/profits) was a legal category, although there was some debate by jurists over its exact contents. See *Dig.* 7.1.68, where Ulpian echoed the sentiment of Gaius (*Dig.* 22.1.28.1) that humans cannot be fruits. Cf. Basanoff (1929): 29–33, 61–90; Treggiari (1979b): 188; Bradley (1984): 63n.54 and n.55; Herrmann-Otto (1994): 268–272; Rodger (2007): 446–448; Roth (2008).

38 Treggiari paraphrases *temere* as "without due consideration," argu- ing that breeding was not the *main* function of female slaves (1979b: 187–188, her italics). Kinsey (in Watson, ed., *The Digest of Justinian*) has a similar interpretation, translating *temere* as "solely." Harris con- tends that this translation is erroneous, instead favoring "commonly" (1999: 66n.31). He uses this translation in support of his assertion that the acquisition of female slaves with the intention of profiting from their fertility seems to have been rare (1999: 66). Furthermore,

he maintains that his argument is not contradicted by *Dig.* 19.1.21.pr, Paul and 21.1.14.1, Ulpian, which indicate that owners were sometimes interested in the fertility of their slaves (66n.31). Herrmann-Otto adopts the translation of *leicht*, which she believes reflects the absence of a systematic slave-breeding plan executed at any type of state or societal level (1994: 411). She attributes this to a general lack of awareness of the economic potential of exploiting slave fertility (1994: 269–287). Bradley, on the other hand, adopts a paraphrase along the lines of "not rashly," arguing that the passage merely suggests that individuals who purchased slaves with breeding in mind would have done so with due caution (1984: 63n.54).

39 Rodger (2007).

40 For example, Ov. *Am.* 1.11; Mart. 11.23, 11.27; Petron. *Sat.* 111–112; *Dig.* 24.1.31.1, Pomponius. Alternatively, a male character in Terence's *Heauton Timorumenos* refers to the *ancillae* responsible for dressing him (130). Treggiari's survey of female slave labor found seventy female slaves working for women and only twelve working for men (1976: 92).

41 Consider a quote by the philosopher Favorinus, who remarked rather derisively that some families simply handed over their children to whichever slave was currently lactating (as quoted by Aulus Gellius, *NA* 12.1.17). For ancient authors' sentiments about nursing in general, and examples of meritorious and poor conduct by nurses, see Bradley (1986); Joshel (1986).

42 It is, of course, impossible to ascertain the validity of any of these emotional claims. Moreover, given the immense power disparity resulting from the slave's status as owned property, a woman would have possessed no ability to resist, and a vested interest in acquiescing to, the desires of her owner. See Bradley (1986): 220–222; Joshel (1986): 20–22. It is significant, however, that both elite authors and ex-slaves themselves frequently represented relationships in such a manner. This issue will be discussed again in Chapters 3 and 4.

43 Kolendo (1981): 290. Such relationships were not exclusive to female slaves. Although Roman social mores discouraged sexual affairs between female owners and their male slaves (Quint. *Inst.* 5.11.34–35; Evans Grubbs 1993), male slaves could gain favor with their male owners through amorous relationships (e.g. Petron. *Sat.* 75–76).

44 Taking full advantage of this economic opportunity would have required some degree of emotional detachment from one's own children.

45 Treggiari (1979b): 192. It is interesting to note that all of the surviving accounts exemplifying the dangers of a master's sexual affair with

his slave involve male slaves. Martial also highlights the potential tension resulting from master-slave relationships in his exaggerated picture of the ideal wife – a woman who will send her *ancilla* to her husband's bed without care (11.23).

46 Consider Diocletian's Price Edict, where the maximum price for an unskilled, ordinary female slave was, at its lowest point, still two-thirds the price of a male slave of equivalent age and training. Furthermore, female slaves continued to have value after their child-bearing years (see Saller 2003: 202).

47 Ulpian founded an opinion on legacies of *fundus* with *instrumentum* with the assumption that a testator would not want a slave family to be separated unless explicitly indicated (*Dig.* 33.7.12.7); cf. Buckland (1908): 77; Treggiari (1979b): 198.

48 Cato *Agr.* 143; Col. 1.8.5. Cf. *Dig.* 40.4.59.pr, where Scaevola referenced a female slave attendant (*pedisequa*) given to an agent as a *contubernalis*. Plutarch related a similar story about Cato the Elder, who sold the sexual services of his female slaves as a reward for male slaves (*Cat. Mai.* 21.1).

49 The term *praefecti* generally referred to the slaves who held supervisory/managerial positions on an estate, which included the *vilicus*. See Carlsen (1995): 121.

50 Although Roman law did not recognize slave marriages, authors and jurists clearly viewed many slave relationships as conjugal unions. For example, the prologue proclaims the existence of slave marriages in various locations in defense of the plot of Plautus's *Casina* (67–78). While it is unclear how seriously the author intended this statement to be received, the support for slave unions appears genuine. Bradley reads Martial 4.13 as a marriage blessing for two slaves (1984: 47), but the exact status of the couple is unclear. In later sources, Tertullian mentioned slaves marrying (*nubere, Ad ux.* 2.8.1) and Ammianus referred to a female slave as the "wife" (*coniunx*) of a male slave (28.1.49). For the recognition granted to slave families in juridical sources, see Treggiari (1979b): 197–198; Morabito (1981): 194–196. Eventually, Constantine banned the partition and sale of slave families (Bradley 1984: 48).

51 *Contubernales* and the children of slaves were clearly part of *fundus instructus* (*Dig.* 33.7.12.33, Ulpian). It is important to note that these debates were over categories – the wife and/or children of a male slave were not automatically included in the bequest of a male slave (*Dig.* 33.7.20.4, Scaevola).

52 Although the text does not explicitly identify the husband of the *vilica*, it seems safe to assume that the author was referring to the *vilicus*. The other women included by Trebatius in the *instrumentum* all had specific household duties: "the women who cook bread and maintain the villa" (*mulieres quae panem coquant quaeque villam servent*), "the kitchen-maid" (*focaria*), the "textile workers" (*lanificae*), and "the women who cook relishes" (*quae pulmentaria ... coquant*). Roth notes how the conditional inclusion of the *vilica* through her husband discounts the professional nature of the position and thus is at odds with depictions of the *vilica* from other sources. As the grammatical verb structure that follows the phrase containing *focaria* and *vilica* is in the singular, she reads the phrase "*et vilica*" as a later interpolation (2004: 116–118). If this is true, it remains that jurists classified the vast majority of female agricultural slaves solely as "wives" and "mothers."

53 Treggiari draws a similar conclusion from *Dig.* 40.4.59.pr, Scaevola (1976: 93–94). It is important to note that emphasizing the occupational roles of "wife" and "mother" did not preclude owners from using (and profiting from) female slaves as supplemental/ancillary laborers.

54 There has been significant scholarly debate about the rate of manumission in the Roman world. Drawing primarily upon epigraphic evidence supported by literary and legal sources, Alföldy concludes that most urban slaves would have been manumitted near the age of 30 (1972, esp. 128–129; cf. Weaver 1972: 97–104 on the *familia Caesaris*). Using the data gathered by Szilagyi, Harper notes that the average age of death for freedpersons – 25.2 years – was higher than that of both slaves and freeborn. Recognizing the flaws in using epigraphic evidence to determine actual life expectancy, he nonetheless theorizes that the comparison of the ages of death for slaves, freedpersons, and freeborn individuals indicates a substantial rate of manumission (1972: 341–342). Using the research of Alföldy, Hopkins theorizes that a significant number of slaves were freed before the age of 30, including a large number of women (1978: 127n.63). Critiquing these optimistic conclusions, Wiedemann argues for a lower – yet still significant – rate of manumission, stressing the need to distinguish between idealization and practice (1985). Mouritsen supports this critique on the basis that the epigraphic evidence does not represent an accurate demographic sample (2011: 133–139; cf. Scheidel 2011: 307–308; 2012: 94). Scheidel asserts that there was a much lower rate of manumission

than the epigraphic and legal evidence might suggest. He contends that, in order for the Roman slave population to replenish itself through natural reproduction – the primary source of slaves during the Principate – female slaves cannot have regularly been manumitted while still of childbearing age (a fact that seems to be substantiated by Egyptian census data, 1997: 160–161). Scheidel's demographic estimates suggest a low rate of manumission in the early Roman Empire at 1 percent of the total slave population per year, something like sixty thousand manumissions per year (1997: 167n.43). Given Scheidel's calculations, I feel that it is safe to assert that, no matter what the rate of manumission actually was in terms of a percentage of slaves, the total number of female slaves manumitted – both before and after the age of 30 – was nevertheless substantial. Thus, it should not be surprising that literary authors, lawmakers, and jurists all viewed manumission as a significant social institution that profoundly affected both the Roman slave system and the citizen community.

55 See Kleijwegt (2012): 113–114 for the possibility of slave owners' reneging on promises to manumit.

56 However, as Mouritsen rightly warns, manumission was not always governed by any "strict economic logic" (2011: 196).

57 The "loyal slave" was a popular trope in Roman *exemplum* literature, serving to bolster owners' comfort and confidence in the institution of slavery and to provide a model of obedience for other slaves (Parker 1998: 163).

58 Hopkins (1978): 99–132, esp. 131–132.

59 Deemphasizing the significance of self-purchase, Mouritsen stresses the importance of personal relationships – primarily with the master, but also with outsiders willing to provide funds – for manumission in general (2011: 159–180).

60 It bears mentioning that close proximity did not necessarily produce intimacy and could even lead to animosity and/or abuse. See *CIL* 6.14930 (quoted and discussed later).

61 Treggiari notes that there is little evidence for the manumission of rural slaves (1969: 107). However, this is in part due to the lack of evidence concerning rural slavery in general.

62 Treggiari (1979b): 191–192. Treggiari theorizes that these factors may explain why women may have had a higher manumission rate than men, whose work in the household would have been less likely to gain their master's attention.

63 Perhaps speaking to the dangers of such affairs mentioned in Chapter 1, the freedwoman betrayed Fulvius because she was jealous of the woman whom he had married after their relationship ended.

64 In his survey of the 700 inscriptions from *CIL* 6 that mentioned marriages involving at least one partner of slave or freed status, Weaver found 143 examples of a patron who married his freedwoman (1972: 181). Such marriages may have occurred when the woman was still a child: Two freedwomen were married to their patrons at the ages of thirteen and ten (183). In some cases, the patron may have been a *collibertus* who purchased his partner and then freed her, legally becoming her patron. These specific circumstances will be discussed later.

65 See also Kleiner (1987): 132–134 for an in-depth analysis of this altar.

66 Evans Grubbs (2002): 230–236. It is unclear from what evidence she deduces Acte's evident youth. Most likely it is Euphrosynus's self-identification as a *senex*, which may indeed imply a difference in the ages of husband and wife. If Acte was indeed young, manumission *causa matrimonii* would have been necessary in light of the age requirements established by the *lex Aelia Sentia* (see later discussion).

67 There is only one other explicit reference to manumission *gratis* in *CIL* 6 (2211).

68 Roman law echoed this sentiment, forbidding a female slave manumitted for the sake of marriage to wed a man other than her patron, unless her patron renounced his right to marry her (*Dig.* 23.2.51.pr, Licinnius Rufinus).

69 Alföldy (1972); Hopkins (1978): 115–132; Fabre (1981): 272–278; Roth (2010). All of these scholars stress the importance of payment (usually via the *peculium*) in the manumission process. However, Mouritsen argues that the evidence for self-payment is extremely limited, and that this mode of manumission was probably "the exception and not the rule and probably concentrated in certain professions" (2011: 180). The existence of a 5 percent manumission tax (*vicesima libertatis*) would have added to the financial stakes of this transaction. For details on the tax, see Nicolet (1980): 170; Bradley (1987): 104–106, 149–150.

70 Cf. Hasegawa (2005): 70.

71 A wealthy prostitute able to purchase her freedom was almost certainly the exception to the norm. For the humble earnings and lifestyle of most slave prostitutes, see McGinn (2004a): 40–55. For the status of slave prostitutes in general, see Chapter 1.

72   According to Cicero, the celebrated mime actress Dionysia earned two hundred thousand *sesterces* annually (*Rosc. Com.* 23). Also, a funerary inscription speaks of the attention and praise earned by the stage performances of a young freedwoman (who died at the age of fourteen) (*CIL* 6.10096 = *CIL* 1².1214 = *ILLRP* 803 = *ILS* 5213= *CLE* 55).

73   In addition to the degraded status associated with these professions, McGinn suggests that ex-prostitutes may have become Junian Latins after manumission (1998: 331). See later discussion.

74   It should be noted that in this example the female slave is in the midst of childbirth, necessitating the intervention of another payer. Tryphoninus was primarily concerned with the timing of the manumission rather than the contingent circumstances.

75   In this opinion, Gaius considered the case of a female slave who provided a guarantor to cover the cost of her manumission and then undertook the debt afterward. The jurist ruled that this case did not violate the *senatus consultum Velleianum* of 46 CE, which forbade women to undertake the financial liabilities of another individual, because the liability actually belonged to the ex-slave. It is important to note that Roman law did allow slaves to form contracts toward obtaining their manumission (*Dig.* 4.3.7.8, Ulpian). Cf. *FIRA* 3.11. This document recorded the manumission of the slave Helen, whose freedom was purchased as a "gift" by Aurelius Ales.

76   However, this may also be due to the limited evidence that exists for self-payment manumission in general (Mouritsen 2011: 162–172). Epigraphic evidence indicates that female slaves who obtained their freedom sometimes were able to purchase and manumit their partners (e.g. *CIL* 6.37826). However, it is unclear exactly how these freedwomen achieved their manumission.

77   Hopkins raises the question of how female slaves raised enough money to pay for their manumission and suggests men's financial assistance as a possible solution (1978: 168–169); cf. Brunt (1971): 144.

78   Smadja suggests that Columella's theoretical practice may have been influenced by Augustus's legislation granting benefits to freeborn women who gave birth to three children (1999: 358).

79   *Dig.* 1.5.15, Tryphoninus; 40.7.3.16, Ulpian. The phrase *si tres pepererit* used in the legal sources indicates that it was not necessary for slaves to give birth to three sons, but simply three children. In these cases, the act of manumission occurred instantly. Tryphoninus ruled that if a woman possessing such an agreement gave birth to triplets, after already having produced one child, the last triplet was born free

since he/she was born of a free mother (*Dig.* 1.5.15). A precedent for stipulations offering manumission in exchange for producing children is found in the practice of conditional manumission (*paramonē*) that was commonly used in the Greek world. *Paramonē* was a contractual obligation for freed slaves to remain in the service of their ex-owners for a specified period, generally until the manumitter died. There are several examples of contracts where women in *paramonē* could hand over a child in exchange for their own full freedom. See Hopkins (1978); Tucker (1982): 233–235. For *paramonē* in general, see Weiler (2003): 184–189; Zelnick-Abramovitz (2005): 222–248; cf. Mouritsen (2011): 167–169.

80 Cf. *Dig.* 40.7.3.16, where Ulpian's phrase *si tres servos pepererit* highlighted childbirth as the production of a new labor supply.

81 Smadja argues that the large number of freedwoman–male slave "marriages" collected by Rawson in her study of *contubernales* and other de facto marriages (1974, esp. 294, 302) indicates that in cases of slave "marriages," the woman was usually manumitted first (1999: 365). However, such a conclusion is problematic because it does not take into account the larger set of freedman-freedwoman marriages. This data could indicate that freedmen were manumitted first and were better at securing the freedom of their *contubernales* (although any such conclusion would be speculation). Smadja, on the basis of private correspondence with Kolendo, surmises that a male slave may have worked to secure his wife's manumission first, in order to use her as an occupational intermediary (1999: 365). While I find the conclusion unpersuasive, the initial supposition is intriguing. By securing the freedom of his *contubernalis* first, a male slave might allow for his children to be born free (albeit illegitimate under the law). Cf. Herrmann-Otto (1994): 253–255. For details on the status of such children, see Buckland (1908): 412–413; Weaver (1986); Rawson (1989).

82 *Omnibus autem libertis meis et quos vivus et quos his codicillis manumissi vel postea manumisero, contubernales suas, item filios filias lego* (*Dig.* 32.41.2); cf. *Dig.* 34.1.20.pr, Scaevola for a similar bequest.

83 Weaver notes that female slaves of the *familia Caesaris* had a higher rate of early manumission (before the age of twenty-six) than male slaves. Similarly, Hopkins found that the inscriptional evidence collected by Alföldy (1972) indicates that three-fifths of all slaves freed before the age of thirty were female (1978: 127). However, it is unclear to what extent these percentages reflect the total percentages of all slaves freed, given the possible skewing of early manumission

due to the *lex Aelia Sentia* and *causa matrimonii* (the *lex Aelia*, which is discussed in greater detail later, prohibited the manumission of slaves below the age of thirty except in a few special cases, most notably manumitting a slave for the purpose of marrying him or her; since Roman mores discouraged marriages between a female patron and her male freedman, one would expect the majority of slaves freed before the age of thirty to have been female). Smadja argues that the fact that freedwomen made up a larger percentage of the total women attested in the household data collected by Treggiari than the percentage of freedmen to total men suggests a higher rate of manumission for women (1999: 361). Furthermore, she argues that the data collected by Rawson on *contubernales* in *CIL* 6 (1974: 294) support this supposition, as there are a greater number of freedwomen–male slave relationships attested than freedmen–female slave relationships (if one includes the categories of both certain and probable freedpersons and slaves) (364–365). However, this final supposition is problematic. Cf. Gardner (1986): 225–226; Weiler (2001); Wacke (2001). As comparative figures, Hopkins and Roscoe found that 61 percent of the manumitted slaves recorded in the inscriptions at Delphi were female (Hopkins 1978: 139–140; cf. Tucker 1982: 225). Mouritsen, however, concludes that there is little actual evidence to suggest that female slaves were freed earlier or more frequently than male slaves, and that the Delphic inscriptions are not representative of Roman practices (2011: 190–192). In his analysis of Egyptian census data, Bagnall found more evidence of female slaves older than thirty than male slaves, which may suggest that the manumission of males was more common (1997: 127; cf. Harris 1999: 71). Furthermore, Scheidel argues that the existence of natural reproduction as the primary source of new slaves in the Principate meant that few female slaves could have been freed while still being of childbearing age and finds that the Egyptian census data support this supposition (1997: 160–161). Nonetheless, he acknowledges the considerable presence of young, fecund freedwomen in the epigraphic record of the western regions of the empire (2011: 307–308).

84 Both Plautus and Ovid mentioned a female slave freed by manumission *vindicta* (they used the phrase "by the rod") (*Mil.* 962; *Ars am.* 3.615). Additionally, all the material concerning the Augustan manumission legislation (see later discussion) is contained within the *Digest* chapter on manumission *vindicta* (40.1).

85 A will could contain conditions for manumission; once the conditions were fulfilled, manumission occurred immediately (*Dig.* 1.5.15, Tryphoninus).

86 For the citizen rights of freedwomen and the legal disabilities imposed on ex-slaves, see Chapters 3 and 5. The third option was manumission *censu* (by census), which involved slaves being enrolled directly onto the census roll of Roman citizens, thus officially transforming their legal status from property to citizen. As the extent to which women in general were listed in the census is unclear, Gardner believes manumission *censu* did not apply to female slaves (1986: 222). The census was conducted sporadically during the late Republic and eventually fell out of practice in the early Principate, thus limiting the use of this form of manumission. For a full discussion of the evolution of the manumission process in Roman history and the procedural details in general, see Buckland (1908): 437–512; Daube (1946); Watson (1967): 185–200; cf. Duff (1958): 12–35; Treggiari (1969): 20–31; Mouritsen (2011): 120–205.

87 Gaius 1.44. There is some debate whether the phrase *inter amicos* means "among friends" (i.e., in the presence of witnesses) or "as between friends" (referring to the informal nature of this agreement between freedperson and ex-owner). See Treggiari (1969): 29; cf. Buckland (1963): 77.

88 Gaius 3.56.

89 The liberty of informally freed slaves does not appear to have been recognized formally under Roman law, but only by the praetor, who might intervene to protect their freed status.

90 As evidence, Treggiari cautiously (and with appropriate reservations) cites an example from Plautus's *Menaechmi*, where the informally manumitted Messenio volunteers to work for and live with his ex-owner (1034; 1969: 30). The implication is that an informally manumitted slave must volunteer to enter into such an arrangement and could not be compelled. Sirks (citing Wlassak 1905: 376) suggests that the praetor may have prevented patrons from demanding personal services from informally freed slaves, judging these duties to be representative of the master-slave relationship (1981: 249). However, this supposition does not seem to be substantiated given the personal obligations that all freedpersons owed their patrons.

91 The specific reforms of the *lex Iunia* and the legal status of Junian Latins are discussed in detail later.

92 Modern scholars highlight the financial interests of owners as a primary motive for informal manumission (Weaver 1990, 1997; Roth 2010). Others note the limited accessibility to magistrates and the infrequency of the Roman census as possible complications (Sirks 1981: 248; Bradley 1984: 100–103).

93 For the remainder of this chapter, the term "manumission" will refer to the formal modes of manumission.

94 See Buckland (1963: 72) on *Dig.* 38.2.1.pr, Ulpian and *Tit. Ulp* 1.6. Cf. Treggiari (1969): 19–20. Cicero made the connection between liberty and citizenship several times (*Caecin.* 96; *Balb.* 24; *Top.* 2.10). Since ex-slaves took the citizenship of their former owners, these views only apply to slaves manumitted by Roman citizens.

95 The role of the state in manumission *censu* and manumission *vindicta* is obvious. In the early Republic, wills had to be ratified by the Comitia Calata – which could function as a means of public oversight on manumission *testamento*. Eventually, the Comitia Calata ceased to operate and this potential form of state regulation disappeared (Treggiari 1969: 28).

96 *Servos denique, quorum ius, fortuna, condicio infima est, bene de re publica meritos, persaepe libertate, id est civitate, publice donari videmus (Balb.* 24); cf. Watson (1975): 88–89. The origins of citizen manumission seem to lie in the practice of *postliminium* – allowing war captives to transfer their citizenship to join their new community – among the early Latin states (see Sherwin-White 1973: 323–334).

97 Conversely, slaves (as a stereotyped group) displayed qualities incompatible with citizenship (see Mouritsen 2011: 19).

98 Cf. Ps.-Quint. *Dec. Min.* 311.9. In this declamation, the orator defends a debtor's decision to manumit certain slaves by stating: "It is clear why he freed these slaves: he was pleased with their dutiful service and wished to repay their respectful compliance." (*Servos cur manumiserit manifestum est: delectatus est officiis, referre voluit gratiam obsequio.*)

99 Dittenberger, *SIG³* 543, lines 30–35; Dionysius of Halicarnassus *Ant. Rom.* 4.22; cf. Weiler (2003): 173–180. Of course, it is difficult to determine exactly how well these outside commentators understood Roman attitudes and practices.

100 *quod vero scribis oblata occasione proconsulis plurimos manumissos, unice laetor. Cupio enim patriam nostram omnibus quidem rebus augeri, maxime tamen civium numero: id enim oppidis firmissimum ornamentum (Ep.* 7.32).

101 *Sumne probus, sum lepidus civis, qui Atticam hodie civitatem / maximam maiorem feci atque auxi civi femina?* (*Per.* 474–475). Even though the play is set in Athens, Plautus must have surely been referring to Roman manumission, as the Greek city-states did not grant their ex-slaves citizenship. Furthermore, Dordalus mentions making a trip to see "the praetor" regarding the status of the manumission (487).

102 See Treggiari (1969): 37–68; Sherwin-White (1973): 322–324. The most notable attack on the institution of citizen manumission occurred in 169 BCE, when the censors attempted to deprive freedmen of the vote (Livy 45.14.1–7). According to Livy, this legislation was unsuccessful precisely because it amounted to a loss of citizenship (3–4). Cf. Tac. *Ann.* 13.27 (quoted later) on the senatorial debate to grant patrons the right of reenslaving ungrateful and insolent freedpersons. Opponents of the measure, who ultimately prevailed, argued that freedom, once granted, should be irrevocable.

103 For the significance of individual virtue and social responsibility in the Augustan program, see Milnor (2005), esp. 12–16; Galinsky (1996): 80–140, esp. 138. For the evolution of Roman ethical discourse and its connection to the rise of the Principate, see Roller (2001): 17–126.

104 For the significance of gender, feminine virtue, and domesticity to the whole Augustan program, see Milnor (2005); Severy (2003), esp. 44–56, 153–157; Edwards (1993): 34–62.

105 The law set the limit for the number of slaves manumitted as a fraction of the total number of slaves owned, with a maximum of one hundred individuals (Gaius 1.40–46; *Tit. Ulp.* 1.24).

106 For the *lex Aelia Sentia*, see Gaius 1.18–19, 36–41.

107 Gaius 1.19, 39; *Dig.* 40.2.11–13, Ulpian. Paul also mentioned a slave's heroic service on behalf of his or her owner as *iusta causa* (*Dig.* 40.2.15). Some jurists believed that a woman could manumit a male slave in order to marry him, but only if the male slave had been legated to her for that purpose (implying that he used to be her *conservus*, *Dig.* 40.2.14.1, Marcian). Given the frequency of marriages between freedwomen and their ex-masters, it seems likely that women possessed a decisive advantage over men in earning early manumission (see Weaver 1972:70; Wacke 2001). However, it is difficult to ascertain to what extent such relationships would have given female slaves an advantage in gaining manumission over men in general.

108 *Dig.* 40.2.13, Ulpian.

109 Buckland (1963): 79n.2. Outside the city of Rome, the committee consisted of twenty citizen assessors.

110 Gaius 1.26–27. *Dediticii* included slaves who had suffered serious punishments (chains, branding, torture) for their criminal actions, and those who had fought in gladiatorial arenas (Gaius 1.13).

111 Commenting on the *lex Aelia Sentia*, Ulpian noted that just cause for manumission resulted from affection (*affectus*) not from luxury (*luxuria*); accordingly, the law granted freedom not for self-indulgence (*deliciae*) but rather for just affection (*iustae affectiones*, *Dig.* 40.2.16).

112 Some scholars have argued that these measures did not reduce the total number of slaves manumitted, but only the number of slaves manumitted formally (see López Baria de Quiroga 2008). A comment by Suetonius suggests that the ethnicity of the slave may have contributed to this perception of deservedness. He writes that Augustus attempted to restrict manumission in order to protect against the taint of servile/foreign blood and to maintain the elite prestige of Roman citizenship (*Aug.* 40.3–4; cf. Dio Cass. 55.13.7). While such sentiments (which are not corroborated by any legal evidence) do not support the existence of an extreme xenophobic backlash against ex-slaves depicted by some modern scholars, they do suggest the significance that some Romans may have placed on slave ethnicity.

113 Although the date of the *lex Iunia* is uncertain (17 BCE, 15 CE, or 19 CE), Weaver makes a persuasive case for a date prior to the *lex Aelia Sentia* (1997: 58–60); cf. Duff (1958): 210–214; Sherwin-White (1973): 332–334; Sirks (1981): 251n.9. The processes for Junian Latins becoming full Roman citizens were most likely established by later legislation, including the *lex Aelia Sentia*. For the various reasons behind the creation of the *lex Iunia* and the implications of its passage, see Sirks (1981); Weaver (1997); B. Rawson (2010); Roth (2010); Mouritsen (2011): 88–92. Weaver argues that the number of Junian Latins must have been significant (and greater than previous scholars have estimated) (1990, 1991, 1997, 2001); cf. n.114. However, given the limitations of the surviving epigraphic evidence, it is impossible to determine exactly what percentage of manumissions were informal and what percentage were formal.

114 Gaius 1.23, 55–56; *Tit. Ulp.* 11.16. Roth suggests that, for this reason, informal manumission may have been significantly more popular than modern scholars have previously suspected (2010: 118).

115 One legal source refers to Junian Latins as "citizens of no certain state" (*cives nullius certae civitatis*, *Tit. Ulp.* 20.14); cf. Tac. *Ann.* 13.27; Salvian *Ad ecc.* 3.7.31.

116 Gaius 1.29; *Tit. Ulp.* 3.3. Gaius attributed this procedure to the *lex Aelia Sentia* whereas the *Tituli ex corpore Ulpiani* attributed it to the *lex Iunia*. The *anniculi probatio* would have made the entire nuclear family – husband, wife, and any freeborn children – Roman citizens. However, there is strong evidence to suggest that, whereas a male Junian Latin could marry either a Latin or a Roman citizen, a female Latin could only marry another Latin (Gaius 1.67–71, 79–80; cf. Gardner 1986: 223–224). Gardner concludes that this restriction would have made it more difficult for Latin women to satisfy the *anniculi probatio* procedure than men. Weaver, in turn, emphasizes the general difficulty in fulfilling any of these requirements and believes that a large number of Junian Latins were never able to attain full Roman citizenship (1997).

117 Gaius 1.28–34; *Tit. Ulp.* 3.1–6. Claudius specifically addressed freed-women as possible candidates for the shipbuilding option (Suet. *Cl.* 18.2–19; cf. Sirks 1980; Kleijwegt 2012: 117–118). Other options for Junian Latins to gain citizenship included *interatio* (being formally manumitted at a later date) and appealing directly to the emperor. For example, Pliny petitioned Trajan to grant full citizenship (*ius Quiritium*) to two freedwomen at the request of their female patron (*Ep.* 10.5.2).

118 The epitome appears to be listing various options by the date of their enactment. If so, this method of gaining citizenship would have taken effect during the reign of Trajan or later. Gaius did not mention this option, although there are three illegible lines in the manuscript where it would be expected to appear (1.34).

119 Cf. n.9.

3 THE PATRON-FREEDWOMAN RELATIONSHIP IN ROMAN LAW

1 For an outline of the fundamental elements of patronage, see Saller (1982): 1.

2 Gardner (1993): 28–29; Waldstein (1986): 19–42; Fabre (1981): 217–265; Watson (1975): 104–110; Treggiari (1969): 68–81, esp. 80–81; Duff (1958): 37. Several factors contributed to the formaliza-tion of the patron-freedperson relationship, the most important being the growth and development of Roman law. Another possible stim-ulus for change was the increase in wealth, status, and influence of

freedpersons in the late Republic, which made ex-slaves less dependent on the financial support of their patrons (see Gardner 1993: 28;
Duff 1958: 37).

3 For example, MacMullen (1974): 104.

4 Wallace-Hadrill (1989): 76. Gardner rightly comments that ideas
such as conditional membership and sponsorship effectively illustrate
the element of social control in the patron-freedperson relationship
but can be potentially misleading if taken too literally (1993: 20). Cf.
Łoś (1995) for the positive correlation between the social status of a
patron and the status of his freedman.

5 Gardner (1993): 19–20; cf. Corbier (2008); Mouritsen (2011): 51–65.

6 Roman jurists associated the rights accorded to patrons with an individual's decision to release a slave as opposed to the actual fulfillment of the
legal act of manumission. Those who were in some way compelled to
manumit a slave received only limited benefits. For example, manumitters who acted out of obligation by fulfilling a *fideicommissum* could not
demand services but could still claim the property of a deceased freedperson (*Dig.* 38.1.7.4, Ulpian; 38.1.13.pr-1, Ulpian; 38.2.29.pr, Marcian).
Similarly, Roman law allowed only the person who had decided to manumit the slave to prosecute for ingratitude (*Dig.* 40.9.30, Ulpian).

7 For the *matrona* as the iconic Roman woman, see Treggiari (1991):
58; McGinn (2004a): 68. For sexual honor as an essential element of
female respectability and social standing, see Chapter 1.

8 The absence of surviving, contemporary legal sources obscures any
specific obligations that freedpersons owed to their ex-owners.

9 Gardner (1993: 28), drawing from the theories of Duff (1958: 37) and
Kirschenbaum (1987: 133–134). Cf. Watson (1987): 43. While these
are logical assumptions, the lack of any surviving evidence makes
proof difficult. Going one step further, Fabre reasons that Roman law
bound freedpersons to continue residing with their patrons until the
end of the second century BCE (1981: 131–132). Waldstein, however,
questions the limited evidence supporting this assertion (1986: 85).
Moreover, E. Rawson finds positive evidence for freedpersons living
apart from their patrons (1993: 222–223). Alternatively, Pomeroy
suggests that many freedwomen may have continued to live and work
with their ex-masters even into the imperial era because female slaves
were rarely taught marketable labor skills (1975: 202). For the training and duties of female slaves, see Chapter 2.

10 Cicero famously described the experience of early freedpersons as continued slavery (*Accensus sit eo numero quo eum mariores nostri esse voluerunt,*

qui hoc non in benefici loco sed in laboris ac muneris non temere nisi libertis suis deferebant, quibus illi quidem non multo secus ac servis imperabant, Cic. *Q. fr.* 1.1.13). Treggiari rightly cautions against taking this phrase out of context and using it as evidence of state-sanctioned subjugation of freedpersons (1969: 68–69). Whereas all modern scholars recognize the constraints imposed on ex-slaves during the republican era, Fabre goes so far as to characterize freedpersons' status as little better than slaves' and their relationship with their patrons as a form of continued servitude (1981). However, this argument perhaps overestimates the nature and burden of freedpersons' obligations to their patrons and certainly underestimates both the range of freedperson experiences and the very real (and very tangible) benefits of freedom and citizenship. Indeed, Waldstein argues that there is no evidence to suggest that Roman law required freedpersons to remain in a state of dependence vis-à-vis their patrons (1986).

11 Watson (1975): 108; Treggiari (1969): 80–81; cf. Fabre (1981): 226–232; E. Rawson (1993): 223. However, both Watson and Treggiari note that individual patrons could impose standards of *obsequium* on their freedpersons by *stipulatio* at the time of manumission.

12 There has been serious debate over what exactly the edict of Rutilius (or, more specifically, Ulpian's analysis of the edict) proves about the situation of freedpersons in the early Republic. Modern scholars generally agree that that the purpose of the edict was to detail (and, to a certain extent, restrict) the obligations of ex-slaves but differ in their assessments of the underlying motives of this measure and its impact on the lives of freedpersons. For details on this scholarly debate, see Treggiari (1969): 69–71; Fabre (1981): 309–315; Waldstein (1986): 131–153; Gardner (1993): 25–30. Rutilius is normally identified as P. Rutilius Rufus, who was praetor in 118 BCE, thus establishing the date for the edict. For the dating of Rutilius's praetorship, see Broughton (1951): 527; Brennan (2000): 742.

13 *Dig.* 38.1.36.pr, Ulpian. The lack of detailed evidence has made the *societas* a difficult topic for modern scholars to evaluate. See Fabre (1981): 296–299; Waldstein (1986): 131–153, esp. 138–149; Masi Doria (1989); Gardner (1993): 26–28. Concurrently, jurists increased patrons' right to share in the estates of deceased freedpersons (mentioned in *Dig.* 38.2.1.2). This will be discussed in detail later.

14 Some scholars also associate the concept/term *officium* with the general reverence owed by freedpersons to their ex-masters (although it varies

slightly in definition from author to author). See Duff (1958): 40; Crook (1967): 51–52; Treggiari (1969): 80; Fabre (1981): 229.

15 The word *obsequium* appears in the title of *Digest* 37.15, but the jurists never explicitly define the term. Modern scholars tend to use the term "respect" (or an equivalent translation) when translating *obsequium*. In comparison, Treggiari notes that in republican sources, *obsequium* generally meant "compliance" or "allegiance" and was used most frequently to denote political loyalty. It is never used in any of the surviving texts to describe the behavior of a freedperson toward a patron (1969: 73); cf. Waldstein (1986): 51–80, esp. 79.

16 Historians have debated about the origins of these obligations and how this concept of reverence may have evolved over time. See Treggiari (1969): 68–71; Gardner (1993): 23–28 for summaries of this discussion.

17 *Dig.* 37.15.2, Julian. See also Duff (1958): 38–40; Buckland (1963): 88; Watson (1987): 39; Gardner (1993): 24.

18 *Dig.* 22.5.4.pr, Paul.

19 *Dig.* 25.3.5.18–26, Ulpian; 25.3.9.pr, Paul; 37.14.19, pr, Paul. Since Roman law required guardians to be male, freedwomen would not have been required to fulfill this service.

20 This does not appear to have been a female-specific issue, but rather a response to an actual inquiry from a freedwoman or her female patron. See Watson (1987): 40; Gardner (1993): 45. It may be significant that the one example that explicitly addresses female *obsequium* involved a freedwoman's relationship with a *female* patron.

21 *Dig.* 25.3.6.1, Modestinus; cf. Tac. *Ann.* 13.26.

22 Buckland (1908): 422–424; Watson (1987): 17. Reenslavement became a possible penalty for certain offenses during the reign of Claudius (*Dig.* 37.14.5, Marcellus) and appears to become part of the standard punishment during the reign of Commodus (*Dig.* 25.3.6.1, Modestinus). For the sources on reenslavement, see Buckland (1908): 423–424; Watson (1987): 17–18. There is no evidence that ungrateful freedpersons could be reenslaved during the republican era (Watson 1987: 17; 1967: 229).

23 *Dig.* 38.2.33.pr, Modestinus. A later imperial rescript ruled that patrons lost all of their patronal rights (*ius patroni*) in such cases (*Dig.* 37.14.5.1, Marcellus). See Waldstein (1986): 284.

24 *CJ* 6.6.6, Gordianus (242 CE).

25 There were also penalties for individuals who attempted to reenslave their freedpersons unlawfully (see *Dig.* 38.2.9.pr, Paul).

26 Buckland (1963): 589–590; Watson (1965): 250–251.

27 Gaius 3.221; *Dig.* 47.10.1.3, Ulpian. While it is clear that individuals could suffer *iniuria* from transgressions against their spouses and kin, modern scholars are divided about exactly how this injury affected the personal honor of the affiliated parties. See discussion in Chapter 1.

28 The difference between *atrox* and ordinary *iniuria* was a formal, but subjective, legal distinction. An offense might be *atrox* if the insult was extreme, in a very public setting, or aimed at an individual who warranted special respect (Buckland 1963: 592).

29 *Dig.* 2.4.4.1, Ulpian; *CJ* 6.6.1, Alexander Severus (223 CE).

30 In situations not involving a patron and a freedwoman, there was nothing to stop a husband from initiating *actiones* in his wife's name as well as in his own.

31 Gardner believes that Ulpian constructed this example of "slightly injurious behavior" by a patron as an extreme case to provide an obvious counter to the views of Marcellus (1993: 47).

32 *OLD* 1, 2. Cf. *Dig.* 47.10.7.2, Ulpian.

33 *Dig.* 47.10.15.12. Insults (*maledictum*) that were neither loud nor public were not *convicium*, but rather "defaming abuse" (*infamandi causa dictum*).

34 *Plane si forte filius liberti vel uxor velint iniuriarum experiri: quia patri maritove non datur, denegandum non erit, quia suo nomine experiuntur* (*Dig.* 47.10.11.8, Ulpian).

35 Note how the jurist began the following statement with the word *plane*, which suggests a logical deduction from the previous section.

36 *Dig.* 38.1.1.pr, Paul. Gardner believes that the imposition of *operae* was primarily economic in nature because Roman law allowed owners to exact monetary payments instead of general services, or in lieu of promised labor that remained unperformed (1993: 20). Mouritsen, while recognizing that many freedpersons would have continued working with (or for) their patrons, questions the prominence of *operae* (as formalized days of service) in everyday life. He argues that such a system was too rigid and inflexible to be successful in business affairs (2011: 225–226).

37 Treggiari (1969): 75. *Operae* were voluntary insomuch as freedpersons agreed to accept these services in exchange for their freedom. However, if the only alternative was to remain in slavery, individuals did not have much choice. Since oaths sworn by slaves were not legally valid, masters usually extracted promises for *operae*, which freedpersons then repeated under oath after manumission.

38 See *Dig.* 12.6.26.12, Ulpian (referring to Julian), *natura enim operas patrono libertus debet*. In this example, a freedman who has performed duties for his patron in the mistaken belief that he owes them as *operae*, cannot bring action for payment. Cf. Treggiari (1969): 75–76.

39 *Dig.* 38.1.6.pr, Ulpian; 38.1.9.1, Ulpian. In addition, jurists often made descriptive distinctions between types of labor. For example, Julian classifies *operae* as artistic services and trade services (*veluti pictoriae fabriles, Dig.* 38.1.24.pr; cf. *Dig.* 12.6.26.12, Ulpian; Waldstein 1986: 226).

40 *Dig.* 38.1.16.pr-1, Paul; 38.1.17.pr, Paul; 38.1.38.pr, Callistratus; 38.1.50.pr, Neratius.

41 Ulpian ruled that *operae officiales* were nontransferable and could only be owed to one's patron because their value lay only in the person performing the services and person receiving them (*Sed officiales quidem futurae nec cuiquam alii deberi possunt quam patrono, cum propietas earum et in edentis persona et in eius cui eduntur constitit, Dig.* 38.1.9.1). The distinction between *operae officiales* and *obsequium* is not always clear, and modern scholars often connect and conflate these categories. Gardner proposes that the concept of *operae officiales* as contracted duties arose after the edict of Rutilius denied patrons the right to require unlimited personal services (1993: 29).

42 *Dig.* 38.1.25, Julian.

43 As McGinn rightly notes, there was nothing to prevent patrons from exploiting and profiting from the sex of their freedwomen (e.g., continuing to act as their pimps). The law only restricted this work from being required as *operae*. He suggests that one possible aim of this ruling was to discourage the manumission of prostitutes, whom Romans would have perceived as less desirable citizens. By limiting access to their professional services, jurists removed some of the economic incentive for manumission (1998: 330–331); cf. Waldstein (1986): 244–245, esp. 245n.30.

44 McGinn also characterizes this as the separation of *patronus* and pimp (1990: 339n.86; 1998: 330).

45 Many modern scholars have suggested that either law or social norms obligated (or expected) freedpersons to provide sexual duties for their patron primarily on the basis of the famous quote attributed to the orator Q. Haterius: "A lack of *pudicitia* in a freeborn individual is a crime, in a slave is a necessity, and in a freedperson is a duty" (*inpudicitia in ingenuo crimen est, in servo necessitas, in liberto officium*, Sen. *Contr.* 4.pr.10). Some simply reference the statement without consideration of the context:

namely, that Seneca cited this case as an example of Haterius's making a ridiculous statement (*quae derisum effugere non possent*) and noted that the term *officium* became the basis for popular witticisms (*res in iocos abiit*). Examples include Mattingly (2011): 109; Williams (2010): 107–108; Langlands (2006): 22; Friedl (1996): 206; Richlin (1992): 225, 258–259n.11; Fabre (1981): 259–260. Other scholars take into consideration the ensuing jokes but nonetheless still see this statement as proof of mandated sexual services. For example, Cantarella understands the joke as having been at the expense of the freedman who was compelled to provide sexual duties to his patron (1992: 245–246n.77). However, such an opinion does not seem to resonate with Seneca's primary statement about Haterius's penchant for making ridiculous statements. McGinn reads the jokes as resulting from an unfortunate choice of words (*officium*), but not an error of "sociological description." He believes that the statement supports the sexual exploitation of freedpersons (1991: 353n.77). I would argue that Haterius's statement does not reflect either popular opinion or legal reality. Rather, it was a deliberate (and ultimately unsuccessful) attempt to redefine – and thus mitigate – a freedman's sexual offense by categorizing it as part of the unique hierarchical bond between patrons and their ex-slaves (Perry 2011).

46 Gardner suggests that this rule arose from interpretation of the Augustan marriage laws. Since these laws concerned only women in a specific age range, there was no need to use the exemption from *operae* as an incentive for marriage for older women (1986: 227). Although some scholars have suggested the existence of a similar ruling for freedmen at the age of sixty (e.g., Treggiari 1991: 69), Waldstein found no evidence to support such an assertion (1986: 175).

47 Cf. *CJ* 6.6.2, Alexander Severus (223 CE). In this case, the law declared that freedwomen who married with the consent of their patron should not be compelled to perform *officium*. A freedwoman who became her patron's wife or concubine should no longer perform *operae* (*Dig.* 38.1.46.pr, Valens; *CJ* 6.3.9, Alexander Severus (225 CE)).

48 *pace* Duff (1958): 46.

49 *CJ* 6.3.11.1, Gordianus (238 CE) explicitly states that although patrons were no longer allowed to exact *operae* from married freedwomen, they did not lose their other patronal rights.

50 The root *decus* conveys a sense of honor and esteem and, for women, is closely tied to *pudicitia*. Livy writes of Tarquinius Superbus and the rape of Lucretia: "after lust had conquered her unwilling virtue (*pudicitia*), just as a victorious fighter, fierce Tarquinius departed from that

place with the woman's honor (*decus*) having been defeated" (*cum vicis-set obstinatam pudicitiam velut victrix libido, profectusque inde Tarquinius ferox expugnato decore muliebri esset*, 1.58.5). In this example, *pudicitia* and *decus* are clearly parallel qualities, both of which were "conquered" by Tarquinius. Cf. Sen. *Dial.* 12.16.4.

51 Although none of these passages explicitly mentions the Augustan leg-islation, one opinion was from a commentary on the *lex Iulia et Papia* (*Dig.* 38.1.14, Terentius Clemens). From this, Waldstein believes that these juristic opinions were in some accord with sentiments expressed in these laws (1986: 167, 170).

52 *Dig.* 38.1.14.pr, Terentius Clemens (*omnes fere consentiunt*); 38.1.48.1, Hermogenian. In these situations, the jurists treated marriage not so much as an incentive, but rather a state that is fundamentally opposed to the rendering of *operae*. Compare this law to a similar statute concern-ing freedmen. During the rule of Augustus, legislation released freed-men from the obligation to perform *operae* if they possessed two or more children in *sua potestate* or one child who reached the age of five (*Dig.* 38.1.37.pr-1, Paul). According to Paul, deceased children would still count toward satisfying these conditions. In contrast, women who ceased to be married were once again bound to complete any owed services.

53 Waldstein (1986): 170. Celsus wrote that action for services due before her marriage would be given against a freedwoman who married with the consent of her patron (*Dig.* 38.1.30.1). Cf. *Dig.* 38.1.8.pr, Pomponius (*semper praeterita opera, quae iam dari non possit, petatur*).

54 Hermogenian believed that releasing a married woman from the per-formance of *operae* was an ideal situation, but not a necessary one. He indicated that freedwomen should be (*debet*) in the *officium* of their husbands rather than their patrons.

55 *Sed si liberta, quae operas promisit, ad eam dignitatem perveniat, ut incon-veniens sit praestare patrono operas, ipso iure hae intercident* (*Dig.* 38.1.34, Pomponius).

56 Waldstein (1986): 276. He bases this proposal on *CJ* 6.3.9, Alexander Severus (225 CE) (*Libertae tuae ducendo eam uxorem dignitatem auxisti*). If Waldstein's proposal is true, Pomponius's opinion was necessary because only freedwomen who married with the consent of their patron were automatically exempt from the performance of *operae*.

57 Since *tutores* had to be male, a freedwoman with a female patron had a guardian appointed by a magistrate (Gaius 1.195). This was not a unique provision for freedwomen, but rather fell under the provi-sions of the *lex Atilia* (in Rome) or *lex Iulia et Titia* (in the provinces), which established procedures for the appointment of guardians. See

Buckland (1963): 147–149. If a freedwoman had multiple patrons, all of them were her *tutores*. However, if one of the patrons died, *tutela* would not pass to his son, but instead would be consolidated among the remaining *tutores* (*Dig*. 26.4.3.4–5, Ulpian).

58 Dixon argues that lawmakers designed *tutela mulierum* to protect family property, not the women themselves (2001b: 73–88). On *tutela* in general, see Buckland (1963): 142–167; Watson (1967): 102–154.

59 Buckland (1963): 167; Watson (1967): 149; Gardner (1986): 18–20. More will be said about *tutores* and marriage *cum manu* in the section on marriage consents later.

60 Gaius 190–192. At some point, women acquired the means to compel guardians' (other than *tutores legitimi*) consent through application to the praetor. Buckland (1963): 167; Gardner (1986): 19–20.

61 Gaius 1.165.

62 Gaius 1.179. Although there is no evidence from the Republic, Watson argues from imperial sources that *impuberes* could not normally inherit agnatic guardianship. He believes that the right of an underage son to hold *tutela legitima* over his father's freedwomen was a direct result of the legal connection between guardianship and a patron's succession rights (1967: 118n.1). This connection is discussed in the following paragraph.

63 Gaius 1.173–174. This rule also applied to parents who were serving as the *tutores* of their emancipated children (Gaius 1.175).

64 Livy notes that the freedwoman Hispala Faecenia had applied to the magistrates for a new *tutor* after her patron died (39.9.7). Later, the Senate granted her the right of choosing her own *tutor* as a reward for her service in suppressing the Bacchanalian rites (39.19.5).

65 Roman law did permit patrons to transfer the guardianship of a freedwoman to another individual, if they desired (Gaius 1.168; cf. Watson 1967: 149).

66 Gaius recorded the evolution of the practice of granting patrons a share of their deceased freedpersons' estates (3.39–42; cf. *Tit. Ulp*. 29.1–3; *Dig*. 50.16.195.1, Ulpian; Crawford 1996: 646–648).

67 Gardner (1993): 21.

68 Cf. *Dig*. 26.4.3.pr, Ulpian.

69 Watson cautiously dates the edict to between 118 BCE and 74 BCE (1967: 231–232). Waldstein believes that the increase in patronal property rights was a recoil against the concessions made by Rutilius (1986: 149–153).

70 The edict did not extend this privilege to female patrons or female descendants of a male patron (Gaius 3.46, 49).

71 Buckland (1963): 88. Treggiari adopts a moderate view, representing the edict as a more equitable recognition of the patron's paternal role and his role in founding the freedperson's fortunes (1969: 79). In either case, it is clear that Roman lawmakers and jurists believed that patrons deserved additional compensation for manumitting their slaves.

72 Gaius 3.42. It is possible that this exemption only applied to freedmen and not to freedwomen. A later paragraph suggests that a patron would receive a share even if a freedwoman had four children (3.44). However, this section of the paragraph is almost completely illegible and the exact statement is unclear.

73 Gaius 3.46–52. Many of the new rights were conditional on having three or four children.

74 Gaius 1.194.

75 Cf. Gardner (1993): 23; Watson (1987): 38. The practice of granting legal exemptions and concessions to women as incentives for desirable actions would continue throughout the Principate. For example, Claudius gave women who invested in the corn trade the right of four children (Suet. *Cl.* 18–19). The fact that the reward for women was the right of four children demonstrates that Claudius's measure was aimed, at least in part, at freedwomen (since freeborn women only needed three children to gain exemption from the *tutela*). See Sirks (1980).

76 Gaius listed several ways that a freedwoman could have a guardian other than her patron: Her patron was a woman, her patron gave himself in adoption, or her patron died leaving no male descendants. The most interesting case involved a woman manumitted by a man, who then made a contrived sale of herself at his suggestion and was then reemancipated and manumitted again (1.195).

77 Gaius 3.44.

78 *Tit. Ulp.* 26.7; Just. *Inst.* 3.4. Scholars have debated whether or not the *senatus consultum* itself actually allowed the children of freedwomen to inherit (e.g., Buckland 1963: 373n.8), or whether this right was the product of juristic interpretation (e.g., Gardner 1986: 200). Clearly, the jurists chose to interpret the law as excluding patrons. Ulpian explicitly remarked that children of a freedwoman could succeed to the estate of their mother (*Dig.* 38.17.1.1). If it is true that the *senatus consultum Orphitianum* did not mention the children of freedwomen, Gardner suggests that jurists may have developed this interpretation through analogy to the children of an emancipated freeborn woman (1986: 200).

79 Dixon asserts that there is no evidence to suggest that Roman law-
    makers ever believed women to have been incapable of managing their
    financial affairs. She argues that jurists in the late Republic developed
    the idea of an ancestral belief in "womanly weakness" to explain the
    existence of *tutela mulierum* (2001b: 73–88; cf. n.58).

80 See also Cic. *Mur.* 27.

81 See n.60.

82 Gaius 1.157, 171; *Tit. Ulp.* 11.8. The only way that *tutela legitima*
    could now occur for a freeborn woman was in the case of a father and
    his emancipated daughter (Buckland 1963: 166).

83 During the Republic, Roman law considered informally freed women
    still to be in a legal state of servitude, despite the protections pro-
    vided to them by the praetor (see Chapter 2). As a result, all of their
    property reverted to their patrons after they died, just as if it had been
    a *peculium*. After the *lex Iunia*, their status as Junian Latins meant
    that they now died free, and therefore their estates could no longer
    be considered *peculium*. However, the drafters of the law inserted a
    provision declaring that the estates of Junian Latins should revert to
    their patrons as if they were *peculia* (Gaius 3.56). This was also true
    for freedpersons whom lawmakers had classified as *dediticii* (Gaius
    3.74–76).

84 Roman lawmakers did not prohibit marriage between freedmen and
    freeborn women, but jurists discouraged these unions (e.g., *Dig.*
    40.2.14.1, Marcian). Evans Grubbs contends, rightly I think, that
    most *patrona-libertus* unions were cases where a female slave was freed
    first and then purchased her *contubernalis* (1993: 131).

85 There is evidence to suggest that this mode of marriage, which was
    the prevalent form of matrimony until the late Republic, was of par-
    ticular relevance to freedwomen. Commenting on the praetor's edict
    concerning the estates of intestate freedpersons, Gaius listed wives *in
    manu* as an example of legal heirs not deserving to inherit ahead of
    patrons (3.39–41, 46; cf. *Tit. Ulp.* 29.1; Treggiari 1991: 30). Modern
    scholars have postulated that this was not simply an academic exam-
    ple, but rather a legal response to actual behavior. Gardner suggests
    that older freedmen may have frequently resorted to taking their
    wives into *manus* in order to secure an heir of their own choosing
    (1993: 22). She bases her theory on Treggiari's assertions about the
    small size of freedperson families resulting from their older ages at
    marriage (1969: 213–215). It appears then that marriage *cum manu*
    for freedwomen was not unusual, at least during the republican

era. For the prevalence of marriage *cum manu* in general in the early and middle Republic, see Watson (1967): 19, 25; Treggiari (1991): 16, 30–32.

86 Watson (1967): 46, 149.

87 Fabre (1981): 211.

88 *Dig.* 37.14.6.4, Paul; cf. *Dig.* 40.9.32.pr, Terentius Clemens. It is impossible to determine whether the Augustan laws were the first to invalidate such behavior, or rather whether they reconfirmed or strengthened existent regulations.

89 Waldstein believes that the *lex Aelia Sentia* strengthened the provision outlined in the *lex Iulia de maritandis ordinibus* and specified punishments for patrons who violated these laws (1986: 164). This rule was part of a larger effort to prevent private individuals from limiting the marriage opportunities of others. Cf. Treggiari (1991): 64–65.

90 *Dig.* 38.16.3.5, Ulpian. However, Ulpian noted that patrons who had their freedwomen swear not to marry illegally (*ne illicite nubat*) were not in violation of this law.

91 *Dig.* 37.14.15, Paul; 38.16.3.5, Ulpian. *Dig.* 37.14.15 reads, "*Qui contra legem Aeliam Sentiam ad iurandum libertum adegit, nihil iuris habet nec ipse nec liberi eius.*"

92 The use of *liberta* implies that the woman in question was an ex-slave of Trimalchio.

93 Fabre (1981): 211.

94 *Dig.* 38.16.3.5, Ulpian.

95 Jurists also used the phrase *patroni voluntate nubere* (*Dig.* 38.1.13.4, Ulpian; 38.1.28.pr, Paul). Jurists included some form of the phrase "marriage with a patron's consent" in every opinion considering a married freedwoman's release from *operae*. In his analysis of the phrase *invito patrono*, Ulpian suggests that "consent" depended on an active act of granting approval. See n.106.

96 *Si impubes sit patronus, voluntate eius non videtur liberta nupta, nisi tutoris auctoritas voluntati accesserit. Rati quoque habitio patrono obest in nuptiis libertae* (*Dig.* 38.1.13.4–5, Ulpian).

97 As Duff notes, there would have been no need for jurists explicitly to outline specific situations in which consent was necessary if Roman law always required patronal approval (1958: 47–48; cf. Fabre 1981: 211). Furthermore, if patrons could have invalidated marriages by withholding their approval, it is unlikely that there would have been

so much concern about compelling freedwomen to swear oaths to remain unmarried. Cf. Gardner (1986): 226.

98 If a freedwoman's marriage was valid, then there must have been more to patronal consent than a simple expression of yea or nay. If not, then there would have been nothing to stop patrons from ever consenting to a marriage and thereby retaining the right to services from their freedwomen. Gardner suggests that a patron might have resorted to issuing a legal charge that a freedwoman who married without his or her consent failed in her duty of *obsequium* (1986: 226). While the need for initiating legal proceedings may have made "refusing consent" more difficult, it still raises the same problems.

99 Duff theorizes that the release from *operae* may have provided incentive for freedwomen to obtain their patrons' consent before marriage (1958: 47). Gardner adopts a similar view, arguing that the exemption from *operae* served as an incentive to encourage freedwomen to marry (1986: 227). Hopkins maintains that the lawmakers' willingness to curtail these obligations indicates that the economic benefit received from *operae* was marginal (1978: 131).

100 See Chapter 2.

101 *Dig.* 37.14.6.3, Paul. A patron who forced a freedwoman to swear such an oath with no intention of marrying her would have been in violation of the *lex Aelia Sentia*, forbidding patrons to prohibit marriage.

102 *Dig.* 23.2.28, Marcian; 23.2.29, Ulpian; 23.2.51.pr, Licinnius Rufinus; 40.2.13, Ulpian; 40.9.21, Modestinus.

103 For patrons' inability to compel marriage, see *Dig.* 23.2.28.pr, Marcian. Ulpian remarked that this was decreed by Ateius Capito during his consulship (5 CE) (*Dig.* 23.2.29.pr).

104 *Dig.* 23.2.45, Ulpian; 24.2.11.pr-2, Ulpian. Ulpian noted that this prohibition only applied to freedwomen who had been married to their patrons, not merely betrothed (*Dig.* 23.2.45.4). If a married freedwoman's patron/husband ceased to be her patron, she was then permitted to initiate a divorce without his consent (*Dig.* 24.2.11.1, Ulpian).

105 Cf. Watson (1987): 143n.15.

106 *Dig.* 23.2.45.pr, Ulpian; 24.2.11.pr, Ulpian; 38.11.1.1, Ulpian. In this case, Ulpian explained the phrase *invito patrono* as meaning not consenting to a divorce (*non consentit ad divortium, Dig.* 23.2.45.5). Ulpian preferred the term *invitus* because the statute covered patrons considered to be unwilling to divorce their freedwomen, even if they could not explicitly refuse consent. The two examples he used were a

patron with diminished mental capacity (*furiosus*) and a patron who
was divorced without his knowledge (*Dig.* 23.2.45.5).

107 Similarly, a freedwoman did not need consent to divorce her husband
if he had manumitted her under a *fideicommissum* (*Dig.* 24.2.10.pr,
Modestinus). The *lex Iulia de maritandis ordinibus* did give the patron's
son who married his father's freedwoman the same marital rights as a
patron (*Dig.* 23.2.48.pr, Terentius Clemens).

108 Ulpian, however, disagreed, arguing that since Roman law likened
captivity to death, a freedwoman was allowed to remarry just as she
would be if her patron/husband had died (*Dig.* 23.2.45.6).

109 *Dig.* 24.2.11.2, Ulpian; 32.49.4, Ulpian; 48.5.14.pr, Ulpian;
50.16.144, Paul; *PS* 2.20.1. Jurists indicated that a man should
not have a wife and a concubine at the same time (*PS* 2.20.1; *Dig.*
45.1.121.1, Papinian; cf. *CJ* 7.15.3.2, Justinian (531 CE), which
refers to the existence of *antiqua iura*). For the prohibition of marriage between men of the senatorial order and freedwomen, see *Dig.*
23.2.23, Celsus; 23.2.44, Paul; 24.1.3.1, Ulpian (Chapter 5 will
address this issue in more detail). In addition, see Saller (1987: 74–76)
and Friedl (1996: 150–184) for the motives for upper-class Roman
men to take concubines. For concubinage in general, see B. Rawson
(1974); Treggiari (1981a); Saller (1987): 71–76; McGinn (1991);
Friedl (1996).

110 McGinn (1991). He argues that there is fragmentary evidence that the
Augustan legislation addressed concubinage directly, giving license
to jurists to incorporate these categories of women into the framework
of respectable concubinage (343–347); cf. Treggiari (1981a): 75–76;
Friedl (1996): 193–198.

111 Treggiari (1981a: 74–75). But *contra* Treggiari (1982): 25, where the
same examples are cited seemingly to argue that a freedwoman in
concubinage with her patron did not have the honor due to a matron.
While a concubine lacked the *dignitas* of a married woman (as envisioned by elite males in relation to her partner), jurists seem to have
agreed that a freedwoman in concubinage with her patron possessed
the legal status of a *mater familias*. The title/status of *mater familias*
will be discussed in greater detail in Chapter 5.

112 *Dig.* 38.1.46, Valens.

113 In some cases, modern scholars read this opinion as a literal statement that it was more honorable *in general* for freedwomen to be the
concubines of their patrons than their wives. Such a reading seems
implausible to me given the promotion (and valorization) of patron-
freedwoman marriages by the *lex Aelia Sentia*. In addition, many

patrons would have possessed social standing equal to their freedwomen's (and many patrons would have been freedmen themselves).
Thus, it seems unlikely that it was *always* more honorable for a freedwoman to be her patron's concubine rather than his wife (i.e., that the
role of concubine was better suited for freedwomen than the role of
wife). Instead, I believe Ulpian used the *cum* in a more circumstantial
than causative sense: In cases where concubinage was more honorable
than marriage (i.e., when the patron possessed a much higher social
status than his freedwoman), patrons should possess the same rights
to marriage consent that they would have if they were married to
their freedwomen (cf. Friedl 1996: 180; McGinn 1991: 350; Gardner
1986: 57; Treggiari 1981a: 72). McGinn argues that, in this opinion,
mater familias should be translated as "wife" rather than "woman of
respectable status" – the strict legal meaning of the title – since the
latter technically applied to all freedwomen in general. He suggests
that Ulpian deliberately used *mater familias* instead of the more standard *uxor* to emphasize the difference in social status between a concubine and a wife (1991: 350).

114 A similar issue was the freeing of slaves by testamentary manumission
in order to attend one's funeral procession. There was only a short-
term relationship between manumitter and ex-slave, who would still
owe certain obligations to the manumitter's children, but it conveys
similar sense of duty and obligation.

115 The significance and substance of this relationship are indicated by
the *lex Irnitana* (Flavian Municipal Law), which outlined the gover-
nance of the Roman municipality of Irni in Spain. The code stated
that in cases where either a patron or a freedperson received Roman
citizenship, the patron would retain his patronal rights (23, 97). Such
a statement was necessary because the acquisition of Roman citizenship technically dissolved existing legal relationships (as the individual's status under and relationship to the law had changed). See
González (1986): 204; cf. Plin. *Ep.* 10.11.2.

4 THE PATRON-FREEDWOMAN RELATIONSHIP IN FUNERARY INSCRIPTIONS

1 See Chapters 2 and 3.

2 Some of the more valuable examples investigating the lives of freedwomen include B. Rawson (1966, 1974); Weaver (1972, 1991);
Huttunen (1974); Treggiari (1975a, 1975b, 1976, 1979a, 1981a);

Saller and Shaw (1984); Joshel (1992); Dixon (2001a); D'Ambra
and Métraux (2006); Hernandez Guerra (2008). For the Roman
"epigraphic habit," see MacMullen (1982); Meyer (1990); Morris
(1992): 167–173; Cherry (1995); Woolf (1996); Hope (2001). These
scholars have tied the epigraphic culture of the Romans to issues of
social mobility, especially the receipt of citizenship (the relevance of
this conclusion for the study of freedpersons will be discussed later).
Mouritsen accepts this premise, but cautions that it is only one aspect
of a much more complex system of epigraphic "habits" in Roman
culture (2005). For epigraphic evidence as means of "listening" to
silence, see Joshel (1992): 3–24; Dixon (2001a): 122.

3 Ulpian defined a *monumentum* as "something that exists for the sake
of preserving a memory" (*quod memoriae servandae gratia existat*, Dig.
11.7.2.6). See also *Dig.* 11.7.42, Florentius; Hor. *Carm.* 3.30.1–9;
Petron. *Sat.* 71; Hope (2009): 34–37. Funerary commemoration
was primarily undertaken by members of the nuclear family, most
commonly a spouse or a parent (Saller and Shaw 1984; cf. Herrmann-
Otto 1994: 80). Commemorations between patrons and freedpersons
appear in a smaller, yet still significant, portion of these inscriptions.
In Saller and Shaw's "Rome: Lower Orders" sample from *CIL* 6 (every
50th inscription), patron-freedperson relationships make up 14 percent of the named relationships (1984: 147). In Sigismund Nielsen's
sample from *CIL* 6 (every 5th inscription), they are 8 percent of
named relationships (1997: 172). A substantial number of inscriptions do not indicate the nature of the relationship between commemorated individuals (Sigismund Nielsen notes that one-quarter of the
funerary epitaphs from her Roman sample – the largest percentage
of any category – do not describe the relationship between dedicator
and dedicatee, 1997: 172). Saller and Shaw believe that these must
still be familial commemorations because no other patterns of commemoration are evident among inscriptions with known relationships
(1984: 132–133). Hopkins also reminds that epitaphs were often just
as much about commemorating the dedicator as commemorating the
deceased (1983: 207n.6). For Roman burial and commemoration in
general, see Toynbee (1971); Carroll (2006); Hope (2009).

4 There is always a question of authorship when considering funerary
epitaphs, as it is unclear who actually wrote the text and chose the
imagery, even if the dedicator and dedicatee are apparent. For example,
in a famous scene from the *Satyrica*, Trimalchio publicly composes his
own epitaph (71). For the purposes of clarity, this chapter will treat

the dedicator (when known) as the writer or author of the epitaph. Hope stresses that the epitaph was only one aspect of a tomb/burial space and thus only provides an incomplete (or limited) view of the larger commemorative message that would have been communicated by experiencing the tomb in toto (Hope 2001, esp. 7–8, 74–78); cf. Koortbojian (1996): 218–219; Davies (2007).

5 See Sigismund Nielsen (1997) for a discussion of the meanings of particular epithets.

6 The intended readership of an epitaph was largely tied to its location. Whereas simple grave markers and inscriptions erected on the outside of tombs would have had served a more public purpose, inscriptions located in the interior of tombs were almost certainly intended to be read only by family members, as these buildings were not usually accessible for entry to the general public (Eck 1984: 133n.34; Petersen 2006: 210–215). However, Petersen observes that tomb interiors were never entirely private spaces, as passersby might catch a glimpse of interior décor when doorways were opened for family celebrations (2006: 213).

7 This is a fundamental assumption in Sigismund Nielsen's study of epithets from Roman funerary epitaphs (1997: 167–170).

8 The methodology and aggregate numbers of this sample are discussed later.

9 Taylor (1961): 122; Huttunen (1974): 129; cf. Rawson (1966); Herrmann-Otto (1994), esp. 404–411. For the numbers of inscriptions with freeborn and freed status indicators, see Huttunen (1974): 139; Sigismund Nielsen (1997): 203.

10 Taylor (1961): 129–132; Huttunen (1974): 31; Zanker (1975); Kleiner (1977); Hope (1997a); Carroll (2006): 146. Joshel remarks that the sheer number of individuals employing status indicators makes it unlikely that a significant portion of the population found these terms shameful. Thus, she assumes that most *incerti* were freeborn rather than freedpersons "ashamed of their servile origin" (1992: 167–168, 183–186).

11 However, Weaver has shown that the use of the *tria nomina* does not automatically indicate Roman citizenship, as Junian Latins could adopt such a nomenclature (1990, 1997).

12 Zanker (1975); Kleiner (1977); Frenz (1985); Shaw (1991): 86–87; Kockel (1993), esp. 50; Koortbojian (1996); D'Ambra (2002): 224–230; George (2004, 2006); Petersen (2006), esp. 184–226; Mouritsen (2011): 285–299. These studies read the emphasis on family as a

statement in contrast to previous servitude, where Roman law denied the legal existence of slave families. Mouritsen persuasively asserts that the commemoration of family bonds was perhaps the most important goal of these monuments, given the precariousness of slave families (2011: 285–287). While the prevalence of freedpersons in funerary monuments containing group portraits has led to identification of this style as "freedman art," as Petersen rightly notes, ex-slaves were not the only individuals to adopt this mode of representation (2006: 96). Accordingly, she cautions against trying to understand nonelite art as an expression of the tastes or desires of a particular group (2006, esp. 227–230; cf. Clarke 2003, esp. 273–274; Mouritsen 2011: 284). Sigismund Nielsen, however, raises questions about the relationship between an individual's freed status and a desire to commemorate his or her family. In her sample of inscriptions from *CIL* 6, she found that only 26 percent of dedications to individuals marked as ex-slaves involved close family, compared with 53 percent in the sample as a whole (1997: 203–204).

13   In her sample from *CIL* 6, Sigismund Nielsen calculated that only 28 percent of those commemorated (excluding self-commemorations) and 18 percent of the dedicators have an explicit status indication (1997: 203). Huttunen found that 31 percent of those commemorated and 13 percent of dedicators included precise status indicators (1974: 129). In her study of concubinage, Rawson notes that less than 20 percent of the persons examined explicitly declared their legal status (1974: 283). Taylor persuasively demonstrates that use of formal libertination declined over the first two centuries CE by ex-slaves outside the *familia Caesaris* (1961). Such a shift highlights the importance of social convention to individual choice.

14   Joshel (1992); Sigismund Nielsen (1997): 204. Both argue that inscription writers only mentioned legal status when it was important to defining social relationships. Cf. Petersen, who explores how freedperson tombs (identified by explicit formal status markers) from Isola Sacra use art and architecture to reinforce ideas of family and community (2006: 184–226).

15   All inscriptions in this chapter are from *CIL* 6 unless otherwise noted.

16   Weaver has repeatedly maintained that the number of free individuals whose praenomen and/or *nomen gentilicium* was omitted from their epitaphs (for whatever reason) should not be discounted (1972: 83; 2001: 104).

17   This style of commemoration may also reflect the perceived tension between a woman's social roles as wife and freedwomen. See Chapter 3 and later discussion.

18 Barbieri has proposed a reading of *purpurari a Marianeis* instead of *purpuraria Marianeis* (*ILLRP* 809).
19 Oddly, Veturia Fedra omits the *nomen gentilicium* of Nicepor on the monument.
20 See Joshel (1992): 136, 140; Dixon (2001a): 116–117. Dixon qualifies this assessment, noting that such a commemoration also stresses the patronal links and the marriage bond (which is also indicated by the size of the lettering describing Fedra's union with Nicepor, 117n.5).
21 For a detailed description of the tomb, see Calza (1940): 345–348; Sigismund Nielsen (1996): 45–46; Petersen (2006): 184–226, esp. 203–210.
22 The wording on the plaque over the doorway to the burial chamber is the same as that on the exterior plaque, but the layout of the text is slightly different:
    P(ublius) Varius Ampelus
    et Varia Ennuchis
    fecerunt sibi et
    Variae P(ubli) f(iliae) Servandae patronae
    et libert(is) libertab(us) posterisq(ue) eorum
    ita ne in hoc monimento
    sarcophagum in feratur
    h(oc) m(onumentum) h(eredem) f(amiliae) ex(terae) non s(equetur)
    in fronte p(edes) xs in agro p(edes) xxxiii (Thylander A 269).
23 Interestingly, the inscribed names of Ampelus and Ennuchis would have been the most visible, as they were written in the largest letters and were located at the top of the plaques. In comparison, the name of their deceased patron was written in smaller letters and located in the middle of the inscription. Petersen notes that a passerby casually glancing at the monument could have easily misinterpreted the family hierarchy (2006: 216). This contrasts with the hierarchical organization of the tomb itself, where the remains of Varia Servanda were the only ones marked by a monument and occupied the "prime space" of the central niche (Hope 1997b: 81).
24 Sigismund Nielsen (1996): 46; Petersen (2006): 212–215. See also n.6.
25 Petersen suggests that the mythic scenes painted on the interior walls of the tomb (the stories of Pyramus and Thisbe and of Ajax and Cassandra) may have called attention to the harsh unfairness of life and that the bucolic floor mosaic depicting Endymion and Selene may have portrayed death (or an "eternal sleep") as a welcome remedy. In this respect, the tomb décor may have been purposely chosen by the dedicators to console grieving visitors (2006: 210). If true, then the

conscious desire to minister to the emotional well-being of the living may also suggest a close and powerful bond.

26 It is unclear exactly how the third name, Gaius Iulius Messius, fits into the inscription. The layout of the text suggests that it was not part of the original inscription, but one cannot know for certain.

27 Sigismund Nielsen argues that inscriptions in columbaria must have been intended only for relatives of the deceased, given the nature of the physical space and the immense effort needed to access and view a specific epitaph (1996: 37–38). See also Hasegawa (2005): 4–29.

28 See n.3.

29 For the legal relationship between patrons and their freedwomen, see Chapter 3.

30 Inscriptions where a freedwoman's patron was also her spouse will be discussed further later.

31 *Dig.* 11.7.4, Ulpian; 11.7.14.8, Ulpian. See Saller and Shaw (1984): 126; Meyer (1990): 76–77.

32 Other examples of freedwomen explicitly described as "heir" include 19886, 22123.

33 In the epitaph, Seia Veneria inverted the traditional onomastic word order, describing herself as "Veneria Luci liberta Seia." Such practice was not uncommon and seems to have been simply a personal/stylistic decision (Salway 1994: 130).

34 Alternatively, the *colliberti* may have given their permission to include this burial in a site allocated to the freedpersons.

35 Sometime during the late second or early third century CE, Papinian ruled that freedpersons could neither be buried nor bury others in a household tomb unless they had been named heirs to their patron (11.7.6.pr, Ulpian). This opinion seems to be restricting the use of the generic *libertis libertabusque posterisque eorum* formula (Duff 1958: 100).

36 12459, 27681.

37 Sigismund Nielsen notes that there was less variation in the actual epithets chosen for patrons and freedpersons, who were generally described as *bene merens*. She argues that this phrase characterized relationships based on obligation and gratitude, but also comments on its frequent use to describe familial relationships (1997: 178–185). This evidence seems to suggest not that inscription writers viewed patron-freedperson relationships as being inherently different from familial relationships, but rather that they had less inclination to personalize the epitaphs.

38 Cf. Corbier (2008): 319–320.
39 For example, 8014 and 15375.
40 Fabre (1981): 191–192. 20170 is a similar example. Hopkins sur-
    mises that dedicators who included the length of a marriage did so
    because they were proud of the long-lasting union (1965: 323).
41 Sigismund Nielsen (1997): 180, 185–198. In her sample, a patron is
    described as *pientissimus* only once and never as *dulcissimus*.
42 For a description and images of the altar, see Kleiner (1987): 107–
    109 and plates VI 1–2. Kleiner also identifies the image as *dextrarum
    iunctio*.
43 Cf. Davies (2007): 55–58. For *dextrarum iunctio* as an indication of
    marriage, see Kleiner (1977): 23–24. Dixon examines a monument
    commemorating two individuals represented only as *colliberti* (9489)
    that includes a visual motif suggesting marriage, or at least a quasi-
    marital relationship (2001a:120). Hughes makes a similar argument
    about marriage indicated by visual imagery rather than text in her
    analysis of the relief of the Gessii (inscription reproduced in *ILLRP*
    503). She bases her argument on nomenclature and the relative age of
    individuals conveyed by the portraits (2003).
44 Several other inscriptions include the phrase, which may suggest
    mutual descendants (e.g., 16394, 21397, 22561, 27712, 27799).
45 Other examples include 5046 and 5047, 16185, 16395, 22561,
    28113.
46 It is possible that Trophime's freedman Phoebus is the father of the
    children, but this seems less plausible given the order of the names.
    But consider 28055, where a freed couple names their freeborn child
    after their patron.
47 See Chapter 3.
48 These are inscriptions where one individual is explicitly commem-
    orated as "patron" and another as "husband." This sample does not
    include epitaphs dedicated to a single individual described as both
    "patron" and "husband." In fourteen of the inscriptions the patron is
    male, in three female, and the last is dedicated to a couple, who are
    titled *patroni*. The full list of inscriptions is located in Appendix B. A
    total of eighteen inscriptions among the tens of thousand epitaphs in
    CIL 6 suggests that commemorating both patron and husband on the
    same monument was not common. However, dedications to multiple
    individuals in general were less common. In his sample of every 5th
    epitaph from *CIL* 6, Huttunen found that 83 percent (N 4,050) com-
    memorated only one person (1974: 30).

49 This trend also continues in examples where a woman is commemo-
     rated by her patron and her husband; the name of the patron was
     generally mentioned first (see 15645, 16752, 37454).

50 Consider the earlier example of 12331, where the women (two of
     whom have the title *coniunx*) alone lack libertination. Yet one would
     also expect to see an increased number of epitaphs where a freed-
     woman commemorates her female patron and her husband, since
     there was less perceived incompatibility. However, only 22 percent
     (N = 4) commemorate female patrons.

51 This count includes Donatus, an imperial freedman (or possibly slave)
     named as the husband of Claudia Ge, who was herself the freedwoman
     of an imperial freedman (8829), and the imperial slave Lucanus,
     whom the imperial freedwoman Flavia Helpis named as her husband
     (18042).

52 Four writers commemorate their patrons with epithets but not their
     husbands (15540, 19234, 23665, 34401) and five commemorate their
     husbands but not their patrons (6194, 6612, 16744, 17562, 20819).
     In 18042, the epithet *bene merens* follows the name of the husband
     but may also apply to the patron. In two examples, the freedwoman
     describes both her husband and her patron using epithets (16956,
     19239).

53 See Kleiner (1987): 168–170 for analysis of the altar.

54 Corbier characterizes the image of the patron as occupying the place
     of the ancestor (2008: 319, 319n.33).

55 Joshel remarks that even as Cameria Iarine articulates the hierarchical
     links between patron and ex-slave, she essentially bestows the same
     social identity upon all of the commemorated individuals – that of
     freedperson and tailor (1992: 138–139).

56 In this sample, I have only included inscriptions that used an explicit
     title for husband (*coniunx*, *maritus*, etc.). I excluded inscriptions that
     could imply a marital (or marriage-like) relationship between a patron
     and his freedwoman (see earlier discussion). There is one inscription
     where the phrases "freedwoman and wife" and "patron and husband"
     are both used in describing one couple (13491); I have included this
     inscription in both the "patron and husband" count and the "freed-
     woman and wife" count. The full list of inscriptions is included in
     Appendix C. It bears noting that 171 inscriptions represent a small
     percentage of the total corpus (cf. Mouritsen 2011: 192). Nonetheless,
     I believe that these epitaphs are still quite useful as they demonstrate
     the possible range of meanings contained in the titles of "patron" and

"freedperson." Inscriptions including the phrases "freedman and husband" and "patron and wife" are less common, but still visible in the epigraphic record (see Weber 2008).

57   The sample includes only women explicitly described as "freedwoman" and "wife," excluding cases where women with libertination are also described as wives. Many of these latter examples arguably indicate marital unions between freedwomen and their patrons, yet (I believe) reflect a different style of commemoration.

58   For example, Huttunen seems to assume a natural inclination to subsume patronal identity to spousal (1974: 153). Interestingly, compared to the 171 inscriptions that reference "patron/freedwoman and husband/wife", I found only 65 inscriptions that reference a *"collibertus/a* and husband/wife" – an identity that one might expect to have been more visible.

59   The most likely explanation for the different *nomina* is that Pollis was owned jointly and received the *nomen* of her other patron. See Weaver (1972): 62; cf. Buckland (1908): 575–578.

60   I have only found only a few examples (N = 15) of inscriptions with "split status," where one partner is described with the marital title (*coniunx, uxor*, etc.) and the other with the patronal title. For example, *"D(is) M(anibus) / M(arci) Luccei M(arci) l(iberti) / Chresti / Lucceia Ionis / co(n)iunx patrono / bene merenti"* (21531). All of this seems to stem from the general trend of ascribing titles and epithets to the individual being commemorated (see n.61).

61   Of individuals described as patron-husbands, 95 percent were being commemorated; 89 percent of the freedwoman-wives were.

62   The *CIL* 6 commentary suggests that the dedicator created side B as a replacement for the inscription on side A on account of errors of unpolished craftsmanship (cf. Frascati 1997: 102), adding that the death of Primitiva and an ensuing change of heart regarding the status of Eutychus may have prompted an update.

63   It is worth noting that Verecundus also identified his parents as his patrons, clearly highlighting the significance of patronal links to the author.

64   Weaver believes that Nymphodotus manumitted Claudia Stepte at the age of twenty-six, *"matrimonii causa"* (1972: 109). However, Treggiari prefers a later manumission date, as Nymphodotus's use of the title *contubernalis* strongly suggests that the forty-six-year relationship began when Stepte was still a slave (1981b: 48–49). See also Boulvert (1974): 284; Weaver (1986): 168n.10; Gardner (1986): 58–59.

65 For the *univira*, see Treggiari (1991): 233–234; Williams (1958), esp. 23–24.
66 *nulla nisi spectatae pudicitiae matrona et quae uni uiro nupta fuisset ius sacrificandi haberet;* (10.23).

5 THE SLAVISH FREE WOMAN AND THE CITIZEN COMMUNITY

1 Mouritsen reaches a similar conclusion, stating: "It could be argued that the category of the freedman was essentially artificial, a legal and ideological construct which had little real bearing on the lives of ordinary people" (2011: 296).
2 Kunkel, *RE* 14.2 (1930): 2183–2184; Treggiari (1991): 34–35; McGinn (1998): 151–152; Saller (1999): 193–196. Although the title *mater familias* technically presupposes marriage and motherhood, a woman did not necessarily need to be a mother nor even married to be deemed a *mater familias*. This was especially true for legal commentators, who used the term *mater familias* to denote the category of respectable women (see later discussion).
3 Mommsen (1899): 691–692; McGinn (1998): 194–199. McGinn believes that the exempt status of actresses may have been a postclassical addition.
4 McGinn (1998): 147–156. He argues that the status of *mater familias* or *matrona* was the only positive criterion for establishing a woman's liability under the *lex Iulia*.
5 See also *Dig.* 43.30.3.6, Ulpian. This passage defines a *mater familias* as "a woman of known repute" (*notae auctoritatis femina*). McGinn persuasively argues that the legal term *vidua* included women who had never married (1998: 150–151); cf. *Dig.* 48.5.11(10).pr, Papinian.
6 Olson (2008): 27–29; Sebesta (1994): 48–49. Festus defined a *matrona* as a woman who possesses "the right to wear a *stola*" (*stolas habendi ius*, 112L). For the *vestis longa (stola)* as a public declaration of moral status, see Olson (2002); Sebesta (1997). Veyne argues that, as the *stola* became more of a ceremonial costume than everyday dress it also began to be seen as a sign of social superiority. Thus, references to a *stolata matrona* were about class/rank as well as respectability (1988: 73). Cf. Zanker (1988): 162–166; Kockel (1993): 51–52; Olson (2002): 389–391; Edmondson (2008): 24.

7   This is seemingly corroborated by an inscription most likely dating to the first century BCE, which also indicates a freedwoman's ability to wear the *stola* (*CIL* I².1570 = 10.6009 = *ILLRP* 977 = *CLE* 56).

8   Monuments frequently depict freedwomen in the characteristic garb of the Roman matron (Zanker 1975; Kockel 1993: 50–51, 77; George 2004, esp. 44–50: Corbier 2008; cf. Fabre 1981: 193–194). Corbier rightly critiques those modern scholars who describe freedwomen as "usurping" the trappings of the Roman matron (2008: 320–321). In his commentary on Horace's *Satire* 1.2.62–66, the scholiast Pseudo-Acro noted that freedwomen wore the toga rather than the *stola*. However, all other evidence seems to contradict his assertion. Indeed, the commentator may be following the lead of the poet, who melded freedwomen and prostitutes (see later discussion).

9   Servius refers to Feronia as a goddess of freedpersons (*libertorum dea*) and notes that her temple was a popular site for manumissions (*A.* 8.564). The exact connection between Feronia and freedpersons is unknown.

10 *utique ei ingenuo nubere liceret, neu quid ei qui eam duxisset ob id fraudi ignominiaeue esset* (39.19). The character of Hispala Faecenia is discussed in more detail later.

11 There has been lengthy academic discussion about the exact terms of the republican marriage prohibition between freeborn and freed individuals. For a synopsis and analysis of the debate, see Watson (1967): 32–37; Treggiari (1969): 82–86; Humbert (1987); Treggiari (1991): 63–64; McGinn (1998): 85–91. Most scholars now seem to agree with the view I have stated, although concurrence on specific details is far from universal. In addition to Livy's account of Hispala Faecenia, scholars analyzing this issue consider sources on the Augustan marriage legislation as evidence for a ban. Most notably, Cassius Dio twice remarks that Augustus "allowed" freeborn men from outside the senatorial order to marry freedwomen, implying that previously they were unable to wed (54.16.2, 56.7.2). As evidence that marriages between freeborn men and freedwomen were not void under republican law, scholars primarily point to Cicero's reference to Poplicola and his freedwoman wife (*Sest.* 110).

12 The degree to which Romans actively prohibited the marriage between freeborn persons and ex-slaves is unclear. A speaker in one of Seneca's *Controversiae* asserts that many illustrious senators had married freedwomen but is attacked by another orator for failing to provide any

supporting evidence. The only example that the first speaker is able to muster is Cato the Elder's marriage to a freeborn woman of low status (7.6.17). Treggiari argues that censors would have been less likely to proceed against unions between freedwomen and lower-class freeborn men (1971: 198).

13   Freedmen did not have access to the institutions that imbued individuals with elite status: enrollment in senatorial and equestrian orders, political magistracies, and legionary service. For a freedman's disabilities under public and civil law, see Mommsen (1887): 3.440, 518; Duff (1958): 50–71; Treggiari (1969): 51; MacMullen (1974): 105; Mouritsen (2011): 71-80, 90-92. Under the earliest regulations governing manumission, there appear to have been no statutory limitations placed on freedpersons as most civic inequalities seem to have been extralegal (Treggiari 1969: 62–63; Sherwin-White 1973: 322–331). The only direct statement on the illegality of freedmen holding political office in the Republic is that of Valerius Maximus, who comments on the illegal tribunician campaign of L. Equitius, a man of the "freedman rank" (which may also mean that he was the son of a freedperson). However, Valerius does not explicitly connect the illegality of the campaign to the man's legal status (9.7.1, cf. Treggiari 1969: 58–59).

14   See Treggiari (1969): 37–67; Nicolet (1980): 227–230.

15   *Dig.* 23.2.44.pr, Paul; cf. *Dig.* 23.2.23, Celsus (referencing the *lex Papia*). The term "actress" is a loose translation of "*artem ludicram facit fecerit.*" The law also restricted a female member of the senatorial class from marrying a freedman, an actor, or the son of an actor/actress. It is notable that the *lex Iulia* forbade marriage to the children of actors/actresses, but not to the children of freedpersons. Marriages between freedwomen and senators would not have been voided under the law. Treggiari argues that Augustan law inflicted punishment for noncompliance but did not invalidate an act. Thus the participants would technically remain married but would not receive the legal benefits of a legitimate marriage (1991: 63–64).

16   *Tit. Ulp.* 13.2. McGinn details the full range of evidence for this prohibition and relevant scholarly criticism (1998: 91–93); cf. Treggiari (1991): 62.

17   This degradation carried legal consequences of its own, given the importance of status in Roman law (see Garnsey 1970). As low(er)-status individuals, freedwomen would have suffered legal disabilities in comparison to elite women.

18 The explicit mention of the senatorial class suggests that other free-born individuals were now able to marry freedwomen without the official mark of disgrace. The jurist Celsus interpreted the *lex Papia* in this fashion (*Lege Papia cavetur omnibus ingenuis praeter senatores eorumque liberos libertinam uxorem habere licere*, Dig. 23.2.23). Cf. Watson (1967): 33–34; McGinn (2004b). Duff argues that marriages between freed-women and freeborn men were very common during the Principate (although he focuses primarily on relationships between freedwomen and their patrons) (1958: 61–62); cf. B. Rawson (1966): 72.

19 For the changing notion of citizenship in the Principate, see Garnsey (1970), esp. 260–280; Sherwin-White (1973): 313. Both scholars acknowledge evolving ideas of Roman citizenship but caution against dismissing the continued value of the institution. Cf. Mouritsen (2011): 89-90. For the growing power and influence of freedpersons in the late Republic and early Principate, see Treggiari (1969): 239–241; Weaver (1972) [for the *familia Caesaris* and the rise of the freed-person "civil service"]; Łoś (1995); Mouritsen (2011): 93-119.

20 One of the many disabilities caused by slavery was the official severing of agnatic ties – freedwomen had no legally-recognized relationship with their blood kin (for the purposes of inheritance). It is very impor-tant to note that Romans would not have viewed parent-daughter and patron-freedwoman relationships as functioning in the same manner, but rather that they understood the types of obligations and fiscal interactions as being structured similarly from a legal perspective.

21 In the case of a female agnate/patron, a magistrate would appoint a tutor for the woman. Gaius refers to these tutors as Atilian tutors, after the *lex Atilia,* which governed this process (1.195).

22 See Chapter 3 for more details on the patron-freedwoman relationship outlined in Roman law.

23 Gaius 1.145, 194; 3.44; *PS.* 4.9; *Tit. Ulp.* 29.3.

24 Ex-slaves were already at a disadvantage because any children born before manumission did not count toward the required total. Furthermore, the minimum age limits created earlier by the *lex Aelia Sentia* suggest that Roman legislators expected the standard age of manumission for freedwomen to be thirty years (see Gaius 1.18–19). However, as Gaius notes, there were many exceptions to this rule. One factor partially mitigating this obstacle was that the *lex Papia* appears to have granted the *ius liberorum* on the basis of the number of live births, as opposed to the number of surviving children. The evi-dence for this is from the *Pauli Sententiae* discussing the *ius liberorum*

in the context of the *senatus consultum Tertullianum* (4.9), which passed
during the reign of Hadrian (Just. *Inst.* 3.3.1). From the text, one
cannot absolutely determine whether the classification of live births
as children for the purposes of the *lex Papia* dated to the original
Augustan legislation, or rather was a more recent development by the
sc Tertullianum.

25 Gaius 3.44. The presence of this law is clear from Gaius, but some
    of the details are uncertain owing to problems with the transmit-
    ted text. The *lex Papia* contained a similar provision for freedmen,
    but with two important differences: It only applied to wealthy freed-
    men, who possessed estates in excess of 100,000 *sesterces*, and freedmen
    could exclude the patron completely by having three or more chil-
    dren (Gaius 3.42). In contrast, the regulation governing freedwomen
    appears to have applied to all freedwomen, and no number of children
    would have allowed for the complete exclusion of the patron.

26 Roman law still required freeborn women to have guardians but
    largely stripped these administrators of their power by allowing
    women the ability to compel approval of desired transactions (Gaius
    1.190–192). Freedwomen with female patrons would have tutors
    appointed by a magistrate, thus placing them in the same situation as
    freeborn women in *tutela* (see Gaius 1.194–195).

27 For a similar assessment, see Gardner (1993): 50–51. *Pace* MacMullen,
    who describes these obligations as elites "punishing" the socially infe-
    rior freedpersons (1974: 104).

28 Tac. *Ann.* 12.53; Gaius 1.84, 91, 160; *CTh* 4.12; *CJ* 7.24.1, Justinian
    (531 CE); cf. *PS* 2.21.11. Until the time of Hadrian, children pro-
    duced from such a union would become slaves of their father's owner, a
    custom that differed from the standard practice, in which illegitimate
    children took the status of their mother (Gaius 1.84). Both Weaver
    and Herrmann-Otto believe the impetus for this edict arose, at least
    in part, from the desire to control offspring of the *familia Caesaris*
    (Weaver 1972: 162–169; Herrmann-Otto 1994: 28–34, 110–119).
    For the *senatus consultum Claudianum*, see also Crook (1967): 62–63;
    Evans Grubbs (1993): 128; Sirks (1994, 2005); Mouritsen (2011):
    21–22.

29 The underlying assumption was that it was more acceptable for a
    freedwoman to be in a sexual relationship with a male slave than it
    was for a freeborn woman. Interestingly, this second provision is not
    mentioned in any of the surviving legal sources; it only appears in
    Tacitus's account. As Mouritsen notes, this was the only example in

Roman law where an individual could become a freedperson without ever having been a slave (2011: 22).

30 Veyne wants to dismiss the idea of an equal civic body as a fiction because of the actual inequalities of real life – especially as they appear in literature (1988: 67–84, esp. 73). While his criticisms of actual societal equity are justified, the assertions of civic equality in Roman law should not be discounted.

31 Perhaps the best evidence of the pervasiveness of this degraded image of freedwomen in literature is the conclusions reached in modern studies of Roman women that rely almost exclusively on literary sources. For example, J. P. V. D. Balsdon categorizes all freedwomen together with prostitutes, courtesans, and concubines in a chapter entitled "Less Reputable Women" (1962: 224–234). Accordingly, the sexual nature attributed to several women mentioned in elegiac poetry prompted scholars to identify these individuals as freedwomen. Some even used these elegiac representations to argue that freedwomen were in fact condemned to less honorable social positions because Roman law denied them the right to marry. See Williams (1968): 525–542; Treggiari (1971). In response, Williams notes the lack of evidence supporting the classification of individuals such as Cynthia and Delia as freedwomen (542). Treggiari calls attention to the fact that classifying licentious women as "freedwomen" only reinforces an underlying conception that all freedwomen were in fact licentious (198). Only as historians began drawing on nonliterary sources did freedwomen lose this stigma of licentiousness.

32 As simple examples Horace mentions garment length – one man wears his tunic too low, another too high – and body odor – one man smells strongly of perfume; another smells like a goat (25–28).

33 Brown suggests that the term *classis* evokes Servius Tullius's political division of citizens (1993: 106) – and thus literally describes freedwomen as second-class citizens.

34 Treggiari remarks that in this satire Horace makes the freedwoman "the mistress and harlot *par excellence*" (1969: 142).

35 It is possible to read Pyrgopolinices' preference for freeborn women as a joke at the expense of his pompous nature, especially given Palaestrio's earlier dismissal of the importance of a courtesan's legal status (784). Nonetheless, such a joke would work only if the audience recognized that a perceived sexual hierarchy did exist among some sexual elitists.

36 Quoted and discussed in Chapter 1.

37 See the specific examples discussed later. In addition, every use of
the term "freedwoman" in Roman comedy refers to a female slave
who, in the course of the narrative, acts or has acted as a courtesan/
prostitute (*meretrix*, Plaut. *Cist.* 38; *Epidi.* 465; *Mil.* 784, 962; *Per.*
82, 484, 737, 789, 797; *Poen.* 164; *Pseud.* 176). However, there is an
important distinction made between these women serving as private
courtesans and those working as common prostitutes (Plaut. *Pseud.*
176). The only freedwoman who appears in the surviving corpus of
Latin poetry and is not branded as a prostitute/courtesan is the *liberta*
who kills her miserly patron Ummidius (Hor. *Sat.* 1.1.99). Even the
very few historical figures explicitly described as "freedwomen" often
have some connection to disreputable sexual activity. For example,
Cicero reports that one of Verres' unfortunate victims was a wealthy
freedwoman of Venus Erycina, whose worship was closely linked to
cultic sexual activity and prostitution (*Caecin.* 55; cf. Wilson 1990:
283–284).

38 *OLD* 5c.

39 Nisbet and Hubbard read *"melior ... Venus"* as a reference to the high-
class courtesans mentioned in elegy (1970: 374). Mankin notes that
the phrase *nec uno contenta* appears elsewhere (Ter. *Eun.* 122; Catull.
68.135) and seems to be a deliberate inversion of the traditional praise
of the *matrona* as *univira* (1995: 233).

40 Cf. Treggiari (1969): 211. *Libido* was a very sexually charged term,
suggesting an intense physical desire or passion (see *OLD* 3).

41 *amicitia*: *OLD amica* 2; *cognitus*: *OLD* 2b, Adams (1982): 190.

42 *OLD* 2, 4.

43 For the *ancilla* as the facilitator of her mistress's illicit sexual behavior,
see Chapter 1.

44 See also Cic. *Att.* 15.22; *Fam.* 9.26.2, 14.16.1; *Phil.* 2.20, 61, 69;
Plin. *NH* 8.55. Interestingly, in the surviving literature, Cicero never
referred to Volumnia Cytheris as a "freedwoman." When he chose to
insult Anthony by calling attention to her low status, he emphasized
the fact that she had been an actress (*mima*, *Att.* 10.10.5; *Phil.* 2.20,
58, 61, 69).

45 After mentioning Nero's general practice of seducing young boys
and married women, Suetonius listed the following specific offenses:
debauching a Vestal Virgin, attempting to "marry" Acte, castrating a
boy and then "marrying" him, and having incestuous relations with
his mother (*Ner.* 28).

46 See n.62.

47 Moreover, the use of the term *libertina* implies that Gellius was not her patron, thus making the relationship even more socially unacceptable.

48 Horace recounts the famous story of Cato the Elder, who complimented a young man exiting a brothel because the young man chose prostitutes over adulterous affairs with married women (*Sat.* 1.2.31–35); cf. Cic. *Cael.* 48–50.

49 Livy 39.9–15.

50 *Scortum nobile libertina Hispala Faecenia, non digna quaestu cui ancillula adsuerat, etiam postquam manumissa erat eodem se genere tuebatur* (39.9.5).

51 Only by learning that she is actually freeborn can a woman hope to achieve marriage and a more-elevated social standing.

52 Cf. *HA* Ant. Pius 8.9, where the freedwoman Lysistrata, the concubine of the emperor Pius, supposedly aided the prefect Repentinus in obtaining his position.

53 For the impact of genre on reading representations of Roman women, see Dixon (2001b), esp. 18–22.

54 For freedwomen as a significant percentage of prostitutes in ancient Rome, see Treggiari (1969): 142; (1971): 197; Fabre (1981): 354; McGinn (2004a): 59–60. Evans accepts the fact that many prostitutes were slaves and freedwomen but argues that they did not dominate the profession as other scholars have suggested (1991: 139–142).

55 As literature was the product of an elite male culture, it generally reproduced and advanced the interests of this same group. See Habinek (1998), esp. 3; Roller (2001): 6–7. Bloomer provides an excellent example of the pervasiveness of the elite voice in his study of the writings of the freedman author Phaedrus, who, despite his own legal status, reinforced dominant (that is to say, elite) views on language and social status (1997): 73–109. The exclusionary nature of Roman literature in part resulted from the financial and time constraints required to attain the necessary level of literacy (Harris 1989). While other scholars have questioned some elements of Harris's conclusions, nearly all agree that only wealthy individuals had access to a level of literacy needed to read and produce literature (for example, see articles in Humphrey 1991).

56 For example, scholars have noted how literature uses depictions of women in an implicit discussion about masculine social norms. For this argument and its origins in French feminist theory, see Hallet (1989); Gold (1993).

57 An apt analogy to this silence may be found in Scheidel's analysis of female rural labor. He surmises that a profound lack of personal

interest among upper-class Romans contributes to the scarcity of evidence concerning free female rural laborers (1996: 3).

58 See Dixon (2001b): 43.

59 Veyne examines several of the criteria used to create and define the stereotypes that commonly describe these categories (1988: 219n.19).

60 The lack of (or indifference to) precision is clearly evident in the case of Ovid, who, after his exile to Tomis, defended the appropriateness of his *Ars Amatoria* by reinterpreting the scope of its intended audience (*Pont.* 3.3.49–52; *Tr.* 2.243–244, 303–304).

61 Veyne sees a deliberateness in the mapping that occurs in Roman poetry; he argues that courtesans and freedwomen functioned as literary stereotypes that allowed Roman elites not to believe that other women had lax morals (1988: 72). I would argue that poets used these stereotypes to speak more about the accessibility and liabilities of sexual partners than about morality. Elegiac immorality seems to exist independent of class.

62 The only two positive examples of ordinary, married freedwomen in Roman literature are the ex-mistress of the deceased Scipio Africanus, whom his widow freed and gave in marriage to a freedman (V. Max. 6.7.1), and Fortunata, the former courtesan and singing girl (*ambubaia*) who was married to Trimalchio (Petron. *Sat.* 74). Interestingly, although both women are described as ex-slaves, neither is explicitly labeled as a "freedwoman" (*libertina* or *liberta*). In contrast, Cicero attempted to discredit Poplicola by mentioning his "freedwoman" (*libertina*) wife (*Sest.* 110).

63 One quotation from Plautus suggests that freedwomen might have been constrained in some way by a lack of financial options. Syra claims that she and another woman became prostitutes (*meretrices*) because they were freedwomen, later suggesting that she directed her daughter into the same profession because of financial concerns (*Cist.* 38); cf. Epict. *Diss.* 4.1.35.37.

64 See Chapter 3 for more details on these provisions. The significance of marriage as a means of achieving respectability is also indicated by the legal recognition and benefits granted to female slaves in quasi-marital relationships (see Chapter 2).

65 For the details of respectable concubinage, especially relationships between freedwomen and their patrons, see Chapter 3. It seems that the *lex Papia* made a positive reference to respectable concubinage, but the exact text does not survive (see McGinn 1991: 343–345).

66 Marcellus ruled that a freedwoman living with her patron as his con-
    cubine was a *mater familias* (*Dig.* 23.2.41.1; cf. 48.5.14(13).pr). For
    Ulpian's juxtaposition of *concubina* and *mater familias* in *Dig.* 25.7.1.pr,
    see McGinn (1991): 350. While all jurists agreed that concubinage
    between a man and his ex-slave was honorable, they disagreed about
    whether or not the *lex Iulia et Papia* allowed for respectable concu-
    binage between a man and a freedwoman of another (see McGinn
    1991).

67 Earlier in the story, a dinner guest had described the slave Fortunata as
    someone from whose hand you would not want to take a piece of bread
    (37.13). Another freedman uses the same phrase (*homo inter homines*)
    proudly to describe his own status in Roman society (57).

68 Discussed in n.62 and Chapter 1.

69 Cohen (1991a): 114. Similarly, one can examine the importance of
    the Vestal Virgins' chastity to the perceived well-being of the Roman
    state. See Beard (1995): 171–173 for the significance of virginity to
    this cult.

70 Edwards (1993): 42–47; Fischler (1994); Joshel (1997).

71 According to Tacitus, Augustus went so far as to call sexual mis-
    conduct "sacrilege and treason" (*nomine laesarum religionum ac viola-
    tae maiestatis*), even though, as the historian notes, this classification
    surpassed the strict letter of his laws (*Ann.* 3.24); cf. Severy (2003):
    180–184.

72 The *lex Iulia de adulteriis coercendis* mandated many of these expecta-
    tions (see *Dig.* 4.4.37.1, Tryphoninus; 48.5.2.2, Ulpian; 48.5.30(29).
    pr, Ulpian; cf. Crawford (1996): 781–786).

73 Dixon argues that in reality Roman norms governing female chas-
    tity were more flexible than strict, having none of the "life-and-death
    force" of the honor/shame system of classical Athens (2001b: 35–36).
    Regardless, Roman law insists that citizenship and morality were
    inextricably linked, especially for women.

74 This emphasis on sexual norms in determining a woman's legal
    standing in the community is clearly evident in the civic position of
    the prostitute: the definitive low-status social role for a free Roman
    woman. See Chapter 1 for details.

75 *Dig.* 23.2.26.pr, Modestinus; cf. *Tit. Ulp.* 13.2, which prohibits free-
    born men from marrying convicted adulteresses. See also Edwards
    (1993): 40.

76 In a much later decision, the emperor Justinian emphasized the
    heinousness of the crime of rape with the explanation that "virginity

and chastity having been corrupted are not able to be restored" (*cum virginitas vel castitas corrupta restitui non potest*, *CJ* 9.13.1 (533 CE)).

77 See Evans Grubbs on *raptus* marriage (1989); also see James, who has a similar, but slightly different interpretation of the relationship between sexual assault and marriage. Rather than seeing marriage as a means to repair sexual assault, she notes a prevalent view of rape being decriminalized so long as it led to marriage (1998: 36).

78 Gaius 1.13. See Chapter 2.

79 This rescript must be addressing the situation of freedwomen who had been prostituted during slavery.

80 See Chapters 3 and 4.

81 Petron. *Sat.* 74.13. See also *CIL* 5.1071. A freedwoman from Aquileia wrote in her epitaph, "I was well-reputed enough and pleased a good man, who brought me to the highest honor from the lowest rank" (*satis fui probata quae viro placui bono qui me ab imo ordine ad summum perduxit honorem*).

82 By regarding the honorable concubine as *mater familias*, and thus liable for prosecution for adultery and *stuprum*, jurists allotted her the same moral responsibility as a wife.

83 Ovid expressed a contradictory opinion in the *Ars Amatoria*, when he prioritized the social status of freedwomen – and thus their sexual availability – over their marital status (3.611–616, see earlier quote). Yet, Ovid's exile and subsequent apologetic writings indicate that some Roman elites saw the poet's views as contradictory to the Augustan moral program.

84 The Augustan legislation created a few exceptions, permanently or temporarily denying certain freedpersons citizen status. However, in designing these restrictions, lawmakers were interrogating the types of slaves gaining access to citizenship, rather than manumission as a citizen-building process.

CONCLUSION

1 As an example of moral worth, consider the fact that an owner of a slave prostitute did not have access to an *actio servi corrupti* – slave prostitutes could not be made worse (see Chapter 1).

Bibliography

Adams, J. N. (1982). *The Latin Sexual Vocabulary*. Baltimore: Johns Hopkins University Press.

Alföldy, Géza. (1972). "Die Freilassung von Sklaven und die Struktur der Sklaverei in der römischen Kaiserzeit." *RSA* 2: 97–129.

Andreau, Jean. (1993). "The Freedman." In Andrea Giardina, ed., *The Romans*, 175–198. Translated by Lydia Cochrane. Chicago: University of Chicago Press.

Armstrong, David. (1989). *Horace*. New Haven, CT: Yale University Press.

Atkinson, K. M. T. (1966). "The Purpose of the Manumission Laws of Augustus." *Irish Jurist* n.s. 1: 356–374.

Aubert, J.-J. (1994). *Business Managers in Ancient Rome: A Social and Economic Study of Institores, 200 B.C.–A.D. 250*. Leiden: E. J. Brill.

Bagnall, Roger. (1997). "Missing Females in Roman Egypt." *SCI* 16: 121–138.

Bagnall, Roger and Bruce Frier. (1994). *The Demography of Roman Egypt*. Cambridge: Cambridge University Press.

Balsdon, J. P. V. D. (1962). *Roman Women: Their History and Habits*. New York: John Day Company.

Barrow, R. H. (1928). *Slavery in the Roman Empire*. New York: Barnes & Noble.

Barton, Carlin A. (2001). *Roman Honor: The Fire in the Bones*. Berkeley and Los Angeles: University of California Press.

Basanoff, Vsevolod. (1929). *Partus Ancillae*. Paris: Librairie du Recueil Sirey.

Bauman, Richard. (1996). *Crime and Punishment in Ancient Rome*. London and New York: Routledge.

Beard, Mary. (1995). "Re-reading (Vestal) Virginity." In Richard Hawley and Barbara Levick, eds., *Women in Antiquity: New Assessments*, 166–177. London and New York: Routledge.

Biezunska-Malowist, Iza and Marian Malowist. (1966). "La procréation des esclaves comme source de l'esclavage (quelques observations sur l'esclavage dans l'antiquité, au moyen-âge et au cours des temps modernes)." In *Mélanges offerts à Kazimierz Michałowski*, 275–280. Warsaw: PWN.

Bloomer, W. Martin. (1997). *Latinity and Literary Society at Rome.* Philadelphia: University of Pennsylvania Press.

Bonfiglio, Barbara. (1998). *Corruptio Servi.* Milan: A. Giuffrè.

Boulvert, Gérard. (1970). *Esclaves et affranchis impériaux sous le Haut-Empire romain: Rôle politique et administratif.* Naples: Jovene.

    (1974). *Domestique et fonctionnaire sous le Haut-Empire romain: La condition de l'affranchi et de l'esclave du prince.* Paris: Les Belles Lettres.

Bradley, Keith R. (1978). "The Age at Time of Sale of Female Slaves." *Arethusa* 11: 243–251.

    (1984). *Slaves and Masters in the Roman Empire: A Study in Social Control.* Oxford: Oxford University Press.

    (1986). "Wet-Nursing at Rome: A Study in Social Relations." In Beryl Rawson, ed., *The Family in Ancient Rome*, 201–229. Ithaca, NY: Cornell University Press.

    (1987). "On the Roman Slave Supply and Slavebreeding." *Slavery and Abolition* 8: 42–64.

    (1991). *Discovering the Roman Family: Studies in Roman Social History.* Oxford: Oxford University Press.

    (1993). "Review Article: Writing the History of the Roman Family." *CPh* 88.3: 237–250.

    (1994). *Slavery and Society at Rome.* Cambridge: Cambridge University Press.

    (2000). "Animalizing the Slave: The Truth of Fiction." *JRS* 90: 110–125.

Brennan, T. Corey. (2000). *The Praetorship in the Roman Republic*, Volume 2. Oxford: Oxford University Press.

Broughton, T. Robert S. (1951). *The Magistrates of the Roman Republic*, Volume 1. New York: American Philological Association.

Brown, P. Michael. (1993). *Horace: Satires I.* Warminster: Aris & Phillips.

Brunt, P. A. (1971). *Italian Manpower, 225 B.C. – A.D. 14.* Oxford: Oxford University Press.

    (1993). *Studies in Greek History and Thought.* Oxford: Oxford University Press.

Buckland, W. W. (1908). *The Roman Law of Slavery.* New York: AMS Press.

    (1963). *A Textbook of Roman Law from Augustus to Justinian*, third edition. Cambridge: Cambridge University Press.

Calza, Guido. (1940). *La necropoli del Porto di Roma nell'Isola Sacra*. Rome: Libreria dello Stato.

Cantarella, Eva. (1991). "Homicides of Honor: The Development of Italian Adultery Law over Two Millennia." In David I. Kertzer and Richard P. Saller, eds., *The Family in Italy from Antiquity to Present*, 229–244. New Haven, CT: Yale University Press.

(1992). *Bisexuality in the Ancient World*. Translated by Cormac Ó Cuilleanáin. New Haven, CT: Yale University Press.

Carlsen, Jesper. (1993). "The *Vilica* and Roman Estate Management." In Heleen Sancisi-Weerdenburgm ed., *De Agricultura: In Memoriam Pieter Willem de Neeve*, Dutch Monographs on Ancient History and Archaeology 10, 197–205. Amsterdam: J. C. Gieben.

(1995). *Vilici and Roman Estate Managers until AD 284*. Rome: L'Erma di Bretschneider.

Carroll, Maureen. (2006). *Spirits of the Dead: Roman Funerary Commemoration in Western Europe*. Oxford: Oxford University Press.

Chantraine, Heinrich. (1967). *Freigelassene und Sklaven im Dienst der römischen Kaiser: Studien zu ihrer Nomenklatur*. Wiesbaden: Steiner.

Cherry, David. (1995). "Re-Figuring the Roman Epigraphic Habit." *AHB* 9: 143–156.

Clarke, John R. (2003). *Art in the Lives of Ordinary Romans: Visual Representation and Non-Elite Viewers in Italy, 100 B.C. – A.D. 315*. Berkeley and Los Angeles: University of California Press.

Cohen, David. (1991a). "The Augustan Law on Adultery: The Social and Cultural Context." In David I. Kertzer and Richard P. Saller, eds., *The Family in Italy from Antiquity to Present*, 109–126. New Haven, CT: Yale University Press.

(1991b). *Law, Sexuality, and Society: The Enforcement of Morals in Classical Athens*. Cambridge: Cambridge University Press.

Conte, Gian Biagio (1994). *Latin Literature: A History*. Translated by Joseph B. Solodow, revised by Don Fowler and Glenn W. Most. Baltimore: Johns Hopkins University Press.

Corbier, Mireille. (2008). "Famille et intégration sociale: la trajectoire des affranchi(e)s." In Antonio Gonzalès, ed., *La fin du statut servile? Affranchissement, libération, abolition*, 313–327. Besançon: Presses universitaires de Franche-Comté.

Crawford, M. H., ed. (1996). *Roman Statutes*. Bulletin of the Institute of Classical Studies Supplement 64. London: Institute of Classical Studies.

Crook, J. A. (1967). *Law and Life of Rome, 90 B.C. – A.D. 212*. Ithaca, NY: Cornell University Press.

(1984). "Lex Aquilia." *Athenaeum* n.s. **62**: 67–77.

Crook, Zeba. (2009). "Honor, Shame, and Social Status Revisited." *JBL* **128**.3: 591–611.

Dalby, Andrew. (1979). "On Female Slaves in Roman Egypt." *Arethusa* 12: 255–263.

D'Ambra, Eve. (2002). "Acquiring an Ancestor: The Importance of Funerary Statuary among the Non-Elite Orders of Rome." In Jakob Munk Højte, ed., *Images of Ancestors*, 223–246. Aarhus: Aarhus University Press.

D'Ambra, Eve and Guy P. R. Métraux, eds. (2006). *The Art of Citizens, Soldiers and Freedmen in the Roman World*. BAR International Series 1526. Oxford: Archeopress.

D'Arms, John H. (1981). *Commerce and Social Standing in Ancient Rome*. Cambridge, MA: Harvard University Press.

Dasen, Véronique and Thomas Späth, eds. (2010). *Children, Memory, and Family Identity in Roman Culture*. Oxford: Oxford University Press.

Daube, David. (1946). "Two Early Patterns of Manumission." *JRS* **36**: 57–75.

Davies, Glenys. (2007). *"Idem Ego Sum Discumbens, Ut Me Videtis*: Inscription and Image on Roman Ash Chests." In Zahra Newby and Ruth Leader-Newby, eds., *Art and Inscriptions in the Ancient World*, 38–59. Cambridge: Cambridge University Press.

Dixon, Suzanne. (2000–2001). "How Do You Count Them If They're Not There? New Perspectives on Roman Cloth Production." *ORom* **25–26**: 7–17.

    (2001a). *"Familia Veturia*: Towards a Lower-Class Economic Prosopography." In Suzanne Dixon, ed., *Childhood, Class and Kin in the Roman World*, 115–127. London and New York: Routledge.

    (2001b). *Reading Roman Women*. London: Duckworth.

    (2004). "Exemplary Housewife or Luxurious Slut? Cultural Representations of Women in the Roman Economy." In Fiona McHardy and Eireann Marshall, eds., *Women's Influence on Classical Civilization*, 56–74. London and New York: Routledge.

Duff, A. M. (1958). *Freedmen in the Early Roman Empire*. 1928. Reprint with addenda. Cambridge: W. Heffer & Sons.

Eck, Werner. (1984). "Senatorial Self-Representation: Developments in the Augustan Period." In Fergus Millar and Erich Segal, eds., *Caesar Augustus: Seven Aspects*, 129–167. Oxford: Clarendon Press.

Edmondson, Jonathan. (2008). "Public Dress and Social Control in Late Republican and Early Imperial Rome." In Jonathan Edmondson and

Alison Keith, eds., *Roman Dress and the Fabrics of Roman Culture*, 27–46. Toronto: University of Toronto Press.

(2011). "Slavery and the Roman Family." In Keith Bradley and Paul Cartledge, eds., *The Cambridge World History of Slavery*. Volume 1: The Ancient Mediterranean World, 337–361. Cambridge: Cambridge University Press.

Edwards, Catharine. (1993). *The Politics of Immorality in Ancient Rome*. Cambridge: Cambridge University Press.

Erdkamp, Paul. (1999). "Agriculture, Underemployment, and the Cost of Rural Labour in the Roman World." *CQ* 49.2: 556–572.

Evans, John K. (1991). *War, Women and Children in Ancient Rome*. London and New York: Routledge.

Evans Grubbs, Judith. (1989). "Abduction Marriage in Antiquity: A Law of Constantine (CTh IX.24.1) and Its Social Context." *JRS* 79: 59–83.

(1993). "Marriage More Shameful than Adultery: Slave-Mistress Relationships, 'Mixed Marriages,' and Late Roman Law." *Phoenix* 47: 125–154.

(1995). *Law and Family in Late Antiquity: The Emperor Constantine's Marriage Legislation*. Oxford: Oxford University Press.

(2002). "*Stigmata Aeterna*: A Husband's Curse." In John F. Miller, Cynthia Damon, and K. Sara Myers, eds., *Vertis in usum*: *Studies in Honor of Edward Courtney*, 230–242. Munich and Leipzig: K. G. Saur.

Fabre, Georges. (1981). *Libertus: Recerches sur les rapports patron-affranchi à la fin de la république romaine*. Paris and Rome: École française de Rome.

Fantham, Elaine. (1991). "*Stuprum: Public Attitudes and Penalties for Sexual Offences in Republican Rome*." *EMC* 35, n.s. 10: 267–291.

Finley, Moses I. (1998). *Ancient Slavery and Modern Ideology*. 1980. Expanded edition edited by Brent D. Shaw. Princeton, NJ: Markus Wiener.

Fischler, Susan. (1994). "Social Stereotypes and Historical Analysis: The Case of the Imperial Women at Rome." In Leonie J. Archer, Susan Fischler, and Maria Wyke, eds., *Women in Ancient Societies*, 115–133. New York: Routledge.

Flemming, Rebecca. (1999). "*Quae Corpore Quaestum Facit*: The Sexual Economy of Female Prostitution in the Roman Empire." *JRS* 89: 38–61.

Flory, Marleen Bourdreau. (1978). "Family in Familia: Kinship and Community in Slavery." *AJAH* 3: 78–95.

Frascati, Simona. (1997). *La collezione epigrafica di Giovanni Battista de Rossi*. Vatican City: Pontificio Istituto di Archeologia Cristiana.

Frenz, Hans G. (1985). *Römische Grabreliefs in Mittel- und Süditalien.* Rome: Giorgio Bretschneider.

Friedl, Raimund. (1996). *Der Konkubinat im kaiserzeitlichen Rom.* Stuttgart: Franz Steiner.

Galinsky, Karl. (1981). "Augustus's Legislation on Morals and Marriage." *Philologus* 125: 126–144.

———. (1996). *Augustan Culture: An Interpretive Introduction.* Princeton, NJ: Princeton University Press.

Gardner, Jane F. (1986). *Women in Roman Law and Society.* Bloomington: Indiana University Press.

———. (1993). *Being a Roman Citizen.* London and New York: Routledge.

———. (1995). "Gender-Role Assumptions in Roman Law." *EMC* 39, n.s. 14: 377–400.

Garnsey, Peter. (1970). *Social Status and Legal Privilege in the Roman Empire.* Oxford: Oxford University Press.

———. (1996). *Ideas of Slavery from Aristotle to Augustine.* Cambridge: Cambridge University Press.

Garrido-Hory, Marguerite. (1999). "Femmes, femmes-esclaves et processus de feminisation dans les oeuvres de Martial et Juvénal." In Francesca Reduzzi Merola and Alfredina Storchi Marino, eds., *Femmes-esclaves: Modèles d'interprétation anthropologique, économique, juridique,* 303–313. Naples: Jovene.

George, Michele. (2004). "Family Imagery and Family Values in Roman Italy." In Michele George, ed., *The Roman Family in the Empire: Rome, Italy, and Beyond,* 37–66. Oxford: Oxford University Press.

———. (2006). "Social Identity and the Dignity of Work in Freedmen's Reliefs." In Eve D'Ambra and Guy P. R. Métraux, eds., *The Art of Citizens, Soldiers and Freedmen in the Roman World,* BAR International Series 1526, 19–29. Oxford: Archeopress.

Gilmore, David D., ed. (1987a). *Honor and Shame and the Unity of the Mediterranean.* Washington, DC: American Anthropological Association.

———. (1987b). "Introduction: The Shame of Dishonor." In David D. Gilmore, ed., *Honor and Shame and the Unity of the Mediterranean,* 2–21. Washington, DC: American Anthropological Association.

Gold, Barbara K. (1993). "'But Ariadne Was Never There in the First Place': Finding the Female in Roman Poetry." In Nancy Sorkin Rabinowitz and Amy Richlin, eds., *Feminist Theory and the Classics,* 75–101. London and New York: Routledge.

Golden, Mark. (1992). "The Uses of Cross-Cultural Comparison in Ancient Social History." *EMC* 36 n.s. 11: 309–331.

González, Julián. (1986). "The Lex Irnitana: A New Copy of the Flavian Municipal Law." *JRS* 76: 147–243.

Gordon, Mary L. (1931). "The Freedman's Son in Municipal Life." *JRS* 21: 65–77.

Günther, Rosmarie. (1987). *Frauenarbeit – Frauenbindung: Untersuchungen zu unfreien und freigelassenen Frauen in den stadtrömischen Inschriften*. Munich: W. Fink.

Habinek, Thomas N. (1998). *The Politics of Latin Literature*. Princeton, NJ: Princeton University Press.

Hallet, Judith P. (1989). "Women as Same and Other in Classical Roman Elite." *Helios* 16.1: 59–78.

Harper, James. (1972). "Slaves and Freedmen in Imperial Rome." *AJPh* 93.2: 341–342.

Harries, Jill. (2007). *Law and Crime in the Roman World*. Cambridge: Cambridge University Press.

Harris, William V. (1989). *Ancient Literacy*. Cambridge, MA: Harvard University Press.

(1999). "Demography, Geography and the Sources of Roman Slaves." *JRS* 89: 62–75.

Hasegawa, Kinuko. (2005). *The Familia Urbana during the Early Empire: A Study of Columbaria Inscriptions*. BAR International Series 1440. Oxford: Archaeopress.

Hernández Guerra, Liborio. (2008). "La liberta en Hispanie. Manifestations épigraphiques de la province tarraconense." In Antonio Gonzalès, ed., *La fin du statut servile?: Affranchissement, libération, abolition*, 329–359. Besançon: Presses universitaires de Franche-Comté.

Herrmann-Otto, Elisabeth. (1994). *Ex Ancilla Natus: Untersuchungen zu den "hausgeborenen" Sklaven und Sklavinnen im Westen des römischen Kaiserreiches*. Stuttgart: Franz Steiner.

Herzfeld, Michael. (1980). "Honor and Shame: Some Problems in the Comparative Analysis of Moral Systems." *Man* n.s.15: 339–351.

(1984). "The Horns of the Mediterraneanist Dilemma." *American Ethnologist* 11: 439–454.

(1987). "'As in Your Own House': Hospitality, Ethnography, and the Stereotype of Mediterranean Society." In David D. Gilmore, ed., *Honor and Shame and the Unity of the Mediterranean*, 75–89. Washington, DC: American Anthropological Association.

Hope, Valerie M. (1997a). "Constructing Roman Identity: Funerary Monuments and Social Structure in the Roman World." *Mortality* 2: 103–121.

(1997b). "A Roof over the Dead: Communal Tombs and Family Structure." In Ray Laurence and Andrew Wallace-Hadrill, eds., *Domestic Space in the Roman World: Pompeii and Beyond.* JRA Supplementary Series Number 22, 69–88. Portsmouth, RI: Journal of Roman Archaeology.

(2001). *Constructing Identity: The Roman Funerary Monuments of Aquileia, Mainz and Nimes.* BAR International Series 960. Oxford: John and Erica Hedges and Archaeopress.

(2009). *Roman Death: The Dying and the Dead in Ancient Rome.* New York: Continuum.

Hopkins, Keith. (1965). "The Age of Roman Girls at Marriage." *Population Studies* 18: 309–327.

(1978). *Conquerors and Slaves: Sociological Studies in Roman History*, Volume 1. Cambridge: Cambridge University Press.

(1983). *Death and Renewal: Sociological Studies in Roman History*, Volume 2. Cambridge: Cambridge University Press.

(1991). "Conquest by the Book." In J. H. Humphrey, ed., *Literacy in the Roman World.* JRA Supplementary Series Number 3, 133–158. Ann Arbor, MI: Journal of Roman Archaeology.

Horden, Peregrine and Nicholas Purcell. (2000). *The Corrupting Sea: A Study of Mediterranean History.* Malden, MA: Blackwell Publishers.

Hughes, Lisa A. (2003). "More than Just Another Piece of Pretty Portraiture: A Note of the Relief of the Gessii." *Mouseion* 3: 147–160.

Humbert, Michel. (1987). "Hispala Faecenia et l'endogamie des affranchis sous la République." *Index* 15: 131–148.

Humphrey, J. H., ed. (1991). *Literacy in the Roman World.* Ann Arbor: JRA Supplementary Series #3.

Huttunen, Pertti. (1974). *The Social Strata in the Imperial City of Rome.* Oulu: Acta Universitatis Oluensis.

James, Sharon L. (1998). "From Boys to Men: Rape and Developing Masculinity in Terence's *Hecyra* and *Eunuchus*." *Helios* 25: 31–47.

(2003). *Learned Girls and Male Persuasion: Gender and Reading in Roman Love Elegy.* Berkeley and Los Angeles: University of California Press.

Jolowicz, H. F. and Barry Nicholas. (1972). *Historical Introduction to the Study of Roman Law.* Cambridge: Cambridge University Press.

Joshel, Sandra R. (1986). "Nurturing the Master's Child: Slavery and the Roman Child-Nurse." *Signs* 12: 3–22.

(1992). *Work, Identity, and Legal Status at Rome: A Study of the Occupational Inscriptions.* Norman: University of Oklahoma Press.

(1997) "Female Desire and the Discourse of Empire." In Judith P. Hallet and Marilyn B. Skinner, eds., *Roman Sexualities*, 221–254. Princeton, NJ: Princeton University Press.

Just, Roger. (2001). "On the Ontological Status of Honour." In Joy Hendry and C. W. Watson, eds., *An Anthropology of Indirect Communication*, 34–50. London and New York: Routledge.

Kamen, Deborah. (2011). "Slave Agency and Resistance in Martial." In Richard Alston, Edith Hall, and Laura Proffitt, eds., *Reading Ancient Slavery*, 192–203. London: Bristol Classical Press.

Kampen, Natalie. (1981). *Image and Status: Roman Working Women in Ostia*. Berlin: Gebr. Mann.

Karras, Ruth Mazo and David Lorenzo Boyd. (1996). "*Ut cum muliere*: A Male Transvestite Prostitute in Fourteenth-Century London." In Louise Fradenburg and Carla Freccero, eds., *Premodern Sexualities*, 101–116. London and New York: Routledge.

Kaster, Robert A. (2005). *Emotion, Restraint, and Community in Ancient Rome*. Oxford: Oxford University Press.

Kirschenbaum, Aaron. (1987). *Sons, Slaves and Freedmen in Roman Commerce*. Jerusalem and Washington, DC: Magnes Press and Catholic University of America Press.

Klees, Hans. (2002). "Die römische Einbürgerung der Freigelassenen und ihre naturrechtliche Begründung bei Dionysios von Halikarnassos." *Laverna* 13: 91–117.

Kleijwegt, Marc, ed. (2006) *The Faces of Freedom: The Manumission and Emancipation of Slaves in Old World and New World Slavery*. Leiden: Brill.

(2012). "Deciphering Freedwomen in the Roman Empire." In Sinclair Bell and Teresa Ramsby, eds., *Free at Last: The Impact of Freed Slaves on the Roman Empire*, 110–129. London: Bristol Classical Press.

Kleiner, Diana E. E. (1977). *Roman Group Portraiture: The Funerary Reliefs of the Late Republic and Early Empire*. New York: Garland Publishing.

(1987). *Roman Imperial Funerary Altars with Portraits*. Rome: Giorgio Bretschneider.

Kockel, Valentin. (1993). *Porträtreliefs stadtrömischer Grabbauten: Ein Beitrag zur Geschichte und zum Verständnis des spätrepublikanisch-frühkaiserzeitlichen Privatporträts*. Mainz: Philipp von Zabern.

Kolendo, Jerzy. (1981). "L'esclavage et la vie sexuelle des hommes libres à Rome." *Index* 10: 288–297.

Koortbojian, Michael. (1996). "*In Commemorationem Mortuorum*: Text and Image along the 'Street of Tombs.'" In Jaś Elsner, ed., *Art and Text in Roman Culture*, 210–233. Cambridge: Cambridge University Press.

Laes, Christian. (2003). "Desperately Different? *Delicia* Children in the Roman Household." In David L. Balch and Carolyn Osiek, eds. *Early Christian Families in Context*, 298–326. Grand Rapids, MI: William B. Eerdmans.

    (2010). "*Delicia*-Children Revisited: The Evidence of Statius' Silvae." In Véronique Dasen and Thomas Späth, eds. *Children, Memory, and Family Identity in Roman Culture*, 245–272. Oxford: Oxford University Press.

Lambert, Jacques. (1934). *Les operae liberti: Contribution à l'histoire des droits de patronat.* Paris: Dalloz.

Langlands, Rebecca. (2006). *Sexual Morality in Ancient Rome.* Cambridge: Cambridge University Press.

Last, H. (1934). "The Social Policy of Augustus." *CAH* 10: 425–64.

Lendon, J. E. (1997). *Empire of Honour: The Art of Government in the Roman World.* Oxford: Oxford University Press.

López Baria de Quiroga, Pedro. (2008) "Las leyes augusteas sobre manumissión." In Antonio Gonzalès, ed., *La fin du statut servile? Affranchissement, libération, abolition*, 219–227. Besançon: Presses universitaires de Franche-Comté.

Łoś, Andrzej. (1995). "La condition sociale des affranchis privés au 1er siècle après J.-C." *Annales HSS* 50: 1011–1043.

MacMullen, Ramsey. (1974). *Roman Social Relations: 50 B.C. to A.D. 284.* New Haven, CT: Yale University Press.

    (1982). "The Epigraphic Habit in the Roman Empire." *AJPh* 103: 233–246.

Mankin, David. (1995). *Horace: Epodes.* Cambridge: Cambridge University Press.

Masi Doria, Carla. (1989). "Die Societas Rutiliana und die Ursprünge der prätorischen Erbfolge der Freigelassenen." *ZRG* 106: 358–403.

Mattingly, David J. (2011). *Imperialism, Power, and Identity: Experiencing the Roman Empire.* Princeton, NJ: Princeton University Press.

McGinn, Thomas. (1990). "*Ne Serva Prostituatur*: Restrictive Covenants in the Sale of Slaves." *ZRG* 107: 315–353.

    (1991). "Concubinage and the *Lex Iulia* on Adultery." *TAPhA* 121: 335–375.

    (1997). "The Legal Definition of Prostitute in Late Antiquity." *MAAR* 42: 73–116.

    (1998). *Prostitution, Sexuality, and the Law in Ancient Rome.* Oxford: Oxford University Press.

    (2004a). *The Economy of Prostitution in the Roman World.* Ann Arbor: University of Michigan Press.

(2004b). "Missing Females? Augustus' Encouragement of Marriage between Freeborn Males and Freedwomen." *Historia* 53.2: 200–208.

McKeown, J. C. (1998). *Ovid: Amores*, Volume 3. Leeds: Francis Cairns .

Meyer, Elizabeth A. (1990). "Explaining the Epigraphic Habit in the Roman Empire: The Evidence of Epitaphs." *JRS* 80: 74–96.

Milnor, Kristina. (2005). *Gender, Domesticity, and the Age of Augustus: Inventing Private Life*. Oxford: Oxford University Press.

(2007). "Augustus, History, and the Landscape of the Law." *Arethusa* 40.1: 7–23.

Mommsen, T. (1887) *Römisches Straatsrecht* (3 volumes). Volumes 1 and 2.1, Leipzig: S. Hirzel. Volumes 2.2 and 3 (1969 reprint), Graz: Akademische Druck- u. Verlagsanstalt.

(1899). *Römisches Strafrecht*. Leipzig: Duncker & Humblot.

Morabito, Marcel. (1981). *Les réalités de l'esclavage d'après le Digeste*. Paris: Annales Littéraires de l'Université de Besançon.

Morris, Ian. (1992). *Death-Ritual and Social Structure in Classical Antiquity*. Cambridge: Cambridge University Press.

Mouritsen, Henrik. (2004). "Freedmen and Freeborn in the Necropolis of Imperial Ostia." *ZPE* 150: 281–304.

(2005). "Freedmen and Decurions: Epitaphs and Social History in Imperial Italy." *JRS* 95: 38–63.

(2011). *The Freedman in the Roman World*. Cambridge: Cambridge University Press.

Mueller, Hans-Friedrich. (1998). "Vita, Pudicitia, Libertas: Juno, Gender, and Religious Politics in Valerius Maximus." *TAPhA* 128: 221–263.

Nicolet, C. (1980). *The World of the Citizen in Republican Rome*. Translated by P. S. Falla. Berkeley and Los Angeles: University of California Press.

Nisbet, R. G. M. and Margaret Hubbard. (1970). *Horace: Odes Book 1*. Oxford: Clarendon Press.

Olson, Kelly. (2002). "*Matrona* and Whore: The Clothing of Women in Roman Antiquity." *Fashion Theory* 6.4: 387–420.

(2008). *Dress and the Roman Woman*. London and New York: Routledge.

Osiek, Carolyn. (2003). "Female Slaves, *Porneia*, and the Limits of Obedience." In David L. Balch and Carolyn Osiek, eds., *Early Christian Families in Context*, 255–274. Grand Rapids, MI: William B. Eerdmans.

(2008). "Women, Honor, and Context in Mediterranean Antiquity." *HTS Teologiese Studies / Theological Studies* [online] 64.1: 323–337.

Papadis, Dimitris. (2001). "Das Problem des 'Sklaven von Natur' bei Aristoteles." *Gymnasium* **108**: 345–365.

Parker, Holt. (1998). "Loyal Slaves and Loyal Wives." In Sandra R. Joshel and Sheila Murnaghan, eds., *Women and Slaves in Greco-Roman Culture: Differential Equations*, 152–173. London and New York: Routledge.

Patterson, Orlando. (1982). *Slavery and Social Death*. Cambridge, MA: Harvard University Press.

Peristiany, J. G., ed. (1966). *Honour and Shame: The Values of Mediterranean Society*. Chicago: The University of Chicago Press.

Perry, Matthew J. (2011). "Quintus Haterius and the 'Dutiful' Freedman: The Consideration of Sexual Conduct between Patrons and Freedpersons in Roman Law." *AHB* 25.3–4: 133–148.

Petersen, Lauren Hackworth. (2006). *The Freedman in Roman Art and Art History*. Cambridge: Cambridge University Press.

Pitt-Rivers, Julian. (1966). "Honour and Social Status." In J. G. Peristiany, ed. *Honour and Shame: The Values of Mediterranean Society*. Chicago: University of Chicago Press.

(1977). *The Fate of Shechem, or the Politics of Sex*. Cambridge: Cambridge University Press.

Pomeroy, Sarah B. (1975). *Goddesses, Whores, Wives, and Slaves*. New York: Shocken Books.

Rawson, Beryl. (1966). "Family Life among the Lower Classes at Rome in the First Two Centuries of the Empire." *CPh* **61**.2: 71–82.

(1974). "Roman Concubinage and Other De Facto Marriages." *TAPhA* **104**: 279–305.

(1986). "Children in the Roman *Familia*." In Beryl Rawson, ed., *The Family in Ancient Rome*, 201–229. Ithaca, NY: Cornell University Press.

(1989). "*Spurii* and the Roman View of Illegitimacy." *Antichthon* **23**: 10–41.

(2010). "Degrees of Freedom: Vernae and Junian Latins in the Roman Family." In Véronique Dasen and Thomas Späth, eds. *Children, Memory, and Family Identity in Roman Culture*, 195–221. Oxford: Oxford University Press.

Rawson, Elizabeth. (1993). "Freedmen in Roman Comedy." In Ruth Scodel, ed. *Theater and Society in the Classical World*, 215–233. Ann Arbor: University of Michigan Press.

Richlin, Amy. (1992). *The Garden of Priapus: Sexuality & Aggression in Roman Humor*, revised edition. Oxford: Oxford University Press.

Robinson, Olivia. (1981). "Slaves and the Criminal Law." *ZRG* **98**: 213–254.

(1995). *The Criminal Law of Ancient Rome*. Baltimore: Johns Hopkins University Press.

Rodger, Alan. (2007). "A Very Good Reason for Buying a Slave Woman?" *Law Quarterly Review* **123**: 446–454.

Roller, Matthew B. (2001). *Constructing Autocracy: Aristocrats and Emperors in Julio-Claudian Rome*. Princeton, NJ: Princeton University Press.

Roth, Ulrike. (2002). "Food Rations in Cato's *de Agri Cultura* and Female Slave Labour." *Ostraka* **11**: 195–213.

(2004). "Inscribed Meaning: The *Vilica* and the Villa Economy." *PBSR* **72**: 101–124.

(2005). "Food, Status, and the *Peculium* of Agricultural Slaves." *JRA* **18**: 278–292.

(2007). *Thinking Tools: Agricultural Slavery between Evidence and Models*. Bulletin of the Institute of Classical Studies Supplement 92. London: Institute of Classical Studies.

(2008). "Cicero, a Legal Dispute, and a *Terminus Ante Quem* for the Large-Scale Exploitation of Female Slaves in Roman Italy." *Index* **36**: 557–565.

(2010). "*Peculium*, Freedom, Citizenship: Golden Triangle or Vicious Circle? An Act in Two Parts." In U. Roth, ed. *By the Sweat of Your Brow: Roman Slavery in Its Socio-Economic Setting*. London: Institute of Classical Studies.

Ryan, F. X. (1994). "The *Lex Scantinia* and the Prosecution of Censors and Aediles." *CPh* **89**.2: 159–162.

Ste. Croix, G. E. M de. (1981). *The Class Struggle in the Ancient Greek World*. Ithaca, NY: Cornell University Press.

Saller, Richard. (1982). *Personal Patronage under the Early Empire*. Cambridge: Cambridge University Press.

(1987). "Slavery and the Roman Family." *Slavery and Abolition* **8**: 65–87.

(1991). "Corporal Punishment, Authority, and Obedience in the Roman Household." In Beryl Rawson, ed., *Marriage, Divorce, and Children in Ancient Rome*, 144–165. Oxford: Oxford University Press.

(1994). *Patriarchy, Property and Death in the Roman Family*. Cambridge: Cambridge University Press.

(1998). "Symbols of Gender and Status Hierarchies in the Roman Household." In Sandra R. Joshel and Sheila Murnaghan, eds., *Women and*

Slaves in Greco-Roman Culture: Differential Equations, 85–91. London and New York: Routledge.

(1999). "*Pater Familias, Mater Familias*, and the Gendered Semantics of the Roman Household." *CPh* 94: 182–197.

(2003). "Women, Slaves, and the Economy of the Roman Household." In David L. Balch and Carolyn Osiek, eds., *Early Christian Families in Context*, 185–204. Grand Rapids, MI: William B. Eerdmans.

(2007). "Household and Gender." In Walter Scheidel, Ian Morris, and Richard Saller, eds., *The Cambridge Economic History of the Greco-Roman World*, 87–112. Cambridge: Cambridge University Press.

(2011). "The Roman Slave Supply." In Keith Bradley and Paul Cartledge, eds., *The Cambridge World History of Slavery*. Volume 1: *The Ancient Mediterranean World*, 287–310. Cambridge: Cambridge University Press.

(2012). "Human Capital and Economic Growth." In Walter Scheidel, ed., *The Cambridge Companion to the Roman Economy*, 71–86. Cambridge: Cambridge University Press.

Saller, Richard P. and Brent D. Shaw. (1984). "Tombstones and Roman Family Relations in the Principate: Civilians, Soldiers and Slaves." *JRS* 74: 124–156.

Salway, Benet. (1994). "What's in a Name? A Survey of Roman Onomastic Practice from c. 700 B.C. to A.D. 700." *JRS* 84: 124–145.

Scafuro, Adele. (1989). "Livy's Comic Narrative of the Bacchanalia." *Helios* 16.2: 119–142.

Scheidel, Walter. (1995). "The Most Silent Women of Greece and Rome: Rural Labour and Women's Life in the Ancient World (I)." *G&R* 42: 202–217.

(1996). "The Most Silent Women of Greece and Rome: Rural Labour and Women's Life in the Ancient World (II)." *G&R* 43: 1–10.

(1997). "Quantifying the Sources of Slaves in the Early Roman Empire." *JRS* 87: 156–169.

(2005). "Human Mobility in Roman Italy. II: The Slave Population." *JRS* 95: 64–79.

Scullard, H. H. (1981). *Festivals and Ceremonies of the Roman Republic*. Ithaca, NY: Cornell University Press.

Sebesta, Judith Lynn. (1994). "Symbolism in the Costume of the Roman Woman." In Judith Lynn Sebesta and Larissa Bonfante, eds., *The World of Roman Costume*, 46–53. Madison: University of Wisconsin Press.

(1997). "Women's Costume and Feminine Civic Morality in Augustan Rome." *Gender and History* **9**.3: 529–541.

Setälä, Päivi. (1998). "Female Property and Power in Imperial Rome." In Lena Larsson Lovén and Agneta Strömberg, eds., *Aspects of Women in Antiquity: Proceedings of the First Nordic Symposium on Women's Lives in Antiquity*, 96–110. Sweden: Paul Åströms.

Severy, Beth. (2003). *Augustus and the Family at the Birth of the Roman Empire.* New York and London: Routledge.

Shaw, Brent. (1991). "The Cultural Meaning of Death." In David I. Kertzer and Richard P. Saller, eds., *The Family in Italy from Antiquity to the Present*, 66–90. New Haven, CT: Yale University Press.

Sherwin-White, A. N. (1973). *The Roman Citizenship*, second edition. Oxford: Oxford University Press.

Sigismund Nielsen, Hanne. (1996). "The Physical Context of Roman Epitaphs and the Structure of the Roman Family." *ARID* **23**: 35–60.

    (1997). "Interpreting Epithets in Roman Epitaphs." In Beryl Rawson and Paul Weaver, eds., *The Roman Family in Italy: Status, Sentiment, Space*, 169–204. Oxford: Oxford University Press.

Sirks, A. J. B. (1980). "A Favour to Rich Freed Women (*libertinae*) in 51 A.D.: On Sue. Cl. 19 and the Lex Papia." *RIDA* **27**: 283–294.

    (1981). "Informal Manumission and the Lex Junia." *RIDA* **28**: 247–276.

    (1994). "Ad senatus consultum Claudianum." *ZRG* **111**: 436–437.

    (2005). "Der Zweck des Senatus Consultum Claudianum von 52 n. Chr." *ZRG* **122**: 138–149.

Smadja, Elisabeth. (1999). "L'affranchissement des femmes esclaves à Rome." In Francesca Reduzzi Merola and Alfredina Storchi Marino, eds., *Femmes-esclaves: Modèles d'interprétation anthropologique, économique, juridique*, 355–368. Naples: Jovene.

Spelman, Elizabeth V. (1988). *Inessential Woman: Problems of Exclusion in Feminist Thought.* Boston: Beacon Press.

Stewart, Frank Henderson. (1994). *Honor.* Chicago: University of Chicago Press.

Taylor, Lily Ross. (1961). "Freedmen and Freeborn in the Epitaphs of Imperial Rome." *AJPh* **82**.2: 113–132.

Thalmann, William G. (1998). "Female Slaves in the *Odyssey*." In Sandra R. Joshel and Sheila Murnaghan, eds., *Women and Slaves in Greco-Roman Culture: Differential Equations*, 22–34. London and New York: Routledge.

Thomas, Yan. (1982). "Droit domestique et droit politique à Rome: Remarques sur le pécule et les *honores* des fils de famille," *MEFRA* 94: 527–580.

Thylander, Hilding. (1952). *Inscriptions du Port d'Ostie*. Lund: C. W. K. Gleerup.

Toynbee, J. M. C. (1971). *Death and Burial in the Roman World*. Ithaca, NY: Cornell University Press.

Treggiari, Susan. (1969). *Roman Freedmen during the Late Republic*. Oxford: Oxford University Press.

    (1971). "Libertine Ladies." *CW* 64: 196–198.

    (1975a). "Family Life among the Staff of the Volusii." *TAPhA* 105: 393–401.

    (1975b). "Jobs in the Household of Livia." *PBSR* 43: 48–77.

    (1976). "Jobs for Women." *AJAH* 1: 76–104.

    (1979a). "Lower Class Women in the Roman Economy." *Florilegium* 1: 65–86.

    (1979b). "Questions on Women Domestics in the Roman West." In Maria Capozza, ed., *Schiavitù, manomissione e classi dipendenti nel mondo antico*, 185–201. Rome: L'Erma di Bretschneider.

    (1981a). "*Concubinae*." *PBSR* 49: 59–81.

    (1981b). "*Contubernales* in *CIL* 6." *Phoenix* 35: 42–69.

    (1982). "Woman as Property in the Early Roman Empire." In D. Kelly Weisberg, ed., *Women and the Law: A Social History Perspective*, Volume 2, 7–33. Cambridge, MA: Schenkman.

    (1991). *Roman Marriage: Iusti Coniuges from the Time of Cicero to the Time of Ulpian*. Oxford: Oxford University Press.

Tucker, C. Wayne. (1982). "Women in the Manumission Inscriptions at Delphi." *TAPhA* 112: 225–236.

Verboven, Konrad. (2012). "The Freedman Economy of Roman Italy." In Sinclair Bell and Teresa Ramsby, eds., *Free at Last: The Impact of Freed Slaves on the Roman Empire*, 88–109. London: Bristol Classical Press.

Veyne, Paul. (1961). "*Vie de Trimalchion*." *Annales ESC* 16.2: 213–247.

    (1988). *Roman Erotic Elegy: Love, Poetry, and the West*. Translated by David Pellauer. Chicago: University of Chicago Press.

Wacke, Andreas. (2001). "*Manumissio matrimonii causa*: Die Freilassung zwecks Heirat nach den Ehegesetzen des Augustus." In Heinz Bellen and Heinz Heinen, eds., *Fünfzig Jahre Forschungen zur antiken Sklaverei an der Mainzer Akademie 1950–2000*, 133–158. Stuttgart: Franz Steiner.

Waldstein, Wolfgang. (1986). *Operae Libertorum: Untersuchungen zur Dienstpflicht freigelassener Sklaven.* Stuttgart: Franz Steiner.

Wallace-Hadrill, Andrew. (1989). "Patronage in Roman Society: From Republic to Empire." In Andrew Wallace-Hadrill, ed., *Patronage in Ancient Society*, 63–87. London and New York: Routledge.

Watson, Alan. (1965). *The Law of Obligations in the Later Roman Republic.* Oxford: Oxford University Press.

(1967). *The Law of Persons in the Later Roman Republic.* Oxford: Oxford University Press.

(1975). *Rome of the XII Tables.* Princeton, NJ: Princeton University Press.

ed. (1985). *The Digest of Justinian* (4 volumes). Philadelphia: University of Pennsylvania Press.

(1987). *Roman Slave Law.* Baltimore: Johns Hopkins University Press.

Weaver, Paul R. C. (1972). *Familia Caesaris: A Social Study of the Emperor's Freedmen and Slaves.* Cambridge: Cambridge University Press.

(1986). "The Status of Children in Mixed Marriages." In Beryl Rawson ed., *The Family in Ancient Rome*, 145–169. Ithaca, NY: Cornell University Press.

(1990). "Where Have All the Junian Latins Gone? Nomenclature and Status in the Early Empire." *Chiron* 20: 275–305.

(1991). "Children of Freedmen (and Freedwomen)." In Beryl Rawson, ed., *Marriage, Divorce and Children in Ancient Rome*, 166–190. Oxford: Oxford University Press.

(1997). "Children of Junian Latins." In Beryl Rawson and Paul Weaver, eds., *The Roman Family in Italy: Status, Sentiment, Space*, 54–72. Oxford: Oxford University Press.

(2001). "Reconstructing Lower-Class Roman Families." In Suzanne Dixon, ed., *Childhood, Class and Kin in the Roman World*, 101–114. London and New York: Routledge.

Weber, Ekkehard. (2008). "*Libertus et coniunx.*" In Peter Mauritsch, Werner Petermandl, Robert Rollinger, and Christoph Ulf, eds., *Antike Lebenswelten Konstanz-Wandel-Wirkungsmacht: Festschrift für Ingomar Weiler zum 70. Geburtstag*, 367–379. Wiesbaden: Harrassowitz.

Weiler, Ingomar. (2001). "Eine Sklavin wird frei: Zur Rolle des Geschlechts bei der Freilassung." In Heinz Bellen and Heinz Heinen, eds., *Fünfzig Jahre Forschungenzur antiken Sklaverei an der Mainzer Akademie 1950–2000*, 113–132. Stuttgart: Franz Steiner.

(2003). *Die Beendigung des Sklavenstatus im Altertum: Ein Beitrag zur vergleichenden Sozialgeschichte.* Stuttgart: Franz Steiner.

Welch, Katherine. (1999). "Subura." In E. M. Steinby, ed., *Lexicon Topographicum Urbis Romae*, Volume IV, 379–383. Rome: Edizioni Quasar.

Wiedemann, Thomas E. J. (1985). "The Regularity of Manumission at Rome." *CQ* **35**: 162–175.

Williams, Craig. (2010). *Roman Homosexuality: Ideologies of Masculinity in Classical Antiquity*, second edition. Oxford: Oxford University Press.

Williams, Gordon. (1958). "Some Aspects of Roman Marriage Ceremonies and Ideals." *JRS* **48**: 16–29.

(1968). *Tradition and Originality in Roman Poetry.* Oxford: Clarendon Press.

Wilson, R. J. A. (1990). *Sicily under the Roman Empire: The Archaeology of a Roman Province, 36 BC-AD 535.* Warminster: Aris and Phillips.

Wlassak, Moriz. (1905). "Die prätorische Freilassungen," *ZRG* **26**: 367–431.

Woolf, Greg. (1996). "Monumental Writing and the Expansion of Roman Society in the Early Empire." *JRS* **86**: 22–39.

Wyke, Maria. (2002). *The Roman Mistress: Ancient and Modern Representations.* Oxford: Oxford University Press.

Yardley, J. C. (1974). "Propertius' Lycinna." *TAPhA* **104**: 429–434.

Zanker, P. (1975). "Grabreliefs römischer Freigelassener." *JDAI* **90**: 267–315.

(1988). *The Power of Images in the Age of Augustus.* Translated by Alan Shapiro. Ann Arbor: University of Michigan Press.

Żeber, Ireneusz. (1981). *A Study of the Peculium of a Slave in Pre-Classical and Classical Roman Law.* Wroclaw: Wydawn. Uniwersytetu Wrocławskiego.

Zelnick-Abramovitz, Rachel. (2005). *Not Wholly Free: The Concept of Manumission and the Status of Manumitted Slaves in the Ancient Greek World.* Boston: Brill.

Index of Sources

[Acro]
  Hor. Epist.
    1.18.75, 182n103
  Hor. Sat.
    1.2.62–66, 227n8
Ammianus Marcellinus
  28.1.49, 192n50
Anthologia Palatina
  5.18, 14
  5.18.7–8, 173n33
Appian
  BC
    4.24, 54
Apuleius
  Met.
    2.6, 182n101
    2.7, 182n101
    2.16, 182n101
    3.13, 182n101
Aristaenetus
  2.7, 181n101
[Aristotle]
  Oik.
    1.1344a3–6, 184n2
Aulus Gellius
  NA
    2.23.10, 183n110

4.1.17, 189n28
12.1.17, 191n41

Calpurnius Flaccus
  Decl.
    5, 179n87
Cassius Dio
  54.16.2, 227n11
  55.13.7, 202n112
  56.7.2, 227n11
  66.14.3, 145
Cato the Elder
  Agr.
    10–11, 48, 187n10, 189n26
    143, 45, 186n9, 192n48
Catullus
  47.41–42, 173n35
  68.135, 232n39
Cicero
  Att.
    10.10.5, 142, 232n44
    15.22, 232n44
  Balb.
    24, 61, 200n94, 200n96
  Caecin.
    55, 232n37
    96, 200n94

Cicero (*cont.*)
  Cael.
    42, 26
    48–50, 232n48
  Fam.
    9.26.2, 232n44
    14.16.1, 232n44
  Fin.
    5.64, 172n24, 172n25
  Mur.
    27, 213n80
  Phil.
    2.20, 232n44, 232n44
    2.58, 142, 232n44
    2.61, 232n44, 232n44
    2.69, 232n44, 232n44
  Q. fr.
    1.1.13, 205n10
  Rosc. Com.
    23, 196n72
  Sest.
    110, 140, 143, 227n11, 234n62
  Top.
    2.10, 200n94
Codex Iustinianus (CJ)
  4.56.1, 180n95
  5.35.1, 184n2
  6.3.9, 209n47, 210n56
  6.3.11.1, 209n49
  6.6.1, 207n29
  6.6.2, 209n47
  6.6.6, 206n24
  7.15.3.2, 216n109
  7.24.1, 230n28
  7.66.5, 189n23
  9.9.23, 178n76, 184n117
  9.9.24(25), 177n74
  9.13.1, 235n76
Codex Theodosianus
  4.12, 230n28

Columella
  1.8.5, 192n48
  1.8.19, 49, 58
  8.2.7, 187n14
  12.pref.1–6, 184n1
  12.pref.8–10, 186n9, 203n119
  12.1–3, 186n9
  12.3.6, 46
  12.3.6–8, 187n13
  12.4.3, 187n13
Corpus Inscriptionum Latinarum
  (CIL)
  1².1570 (= 10.6009 = *ILLRP*
    977 = *CLE* 56), 226n7
  5.1071, 236n81
  6.2211, 195n67
  6.5047, 223n45
  6.5254, 106
  6.6194, 224n52
  6.6612, 224n52
  6.8014, 223n39
  6.8829, 224n51
  6.8951 (= *ILS* 1783), 123
  6.9675 (= *ILS* 7577), 102–103
  6.10096 (= *CIL* 1².1214 = *ILLRP*
    803 = *ILS* 5213 = *CLE* 55),
    196n72
  6.12331, 102–103, 224n50
  6.12459, 222n36
  6.13491, 120, 224n56
  6.13498, 114
  6.14529, 123–124
  6.14930, 120–122, 194n60
  6.14991, 114
  6.15003, 111–112
  6.15004, 111–112
  6.15375, 223n39
  6.15540, 224n52
  6.15598, 125
  6.15645, 224n49

6.16066, 101
6.16185, 223n45
6.16394, 223n44
6.16395, 223n45
6.16744, 224n52
6.16752, 224n49
6.16794, 108
6.16956, 224n52
6.17562, 224n52
6.18042, 224n51, 224n52
6.19234, 224n52
6.19239, 224n52
6.19793, 101–102
6.20449, 115
6.20819, 116–117, 224n52
6.20905, 56
6.21397, 223n44
6.21531, 225n60
6.21607, 40, 183n113
6.22561, 223n44, 223n45
6.23665, 224n52
6.24049, 123–124
6.24739, 109
6.25319, 120
6.26115, 109
6.26868, 108
6.27681, 222n36
6.27712, 223n44
6.27799, 223n44
6.28055, 223n46
6.28063, 110–111
6.28113, 223n45
6.28439, 111
6.29009, 114
6.34401, 224n52
6.34890, 126–127
6.37454, 224n49
6.37820 (= *ILLRP* 809), 104
6.37826, 117–118, 196n76
6.5046, 223n45

Curtius Rufus
8.4.26, 173n33
10.2.20, 175n48
Digesta
1.5.3, 173n40
1.5.15, 57, 196n74, 196n79, 199n85
1.6.2, 181n100
1.6.2.pr, 28
1.12.1.8, 37, 175n48
1.18.21, 176n61, 177n74
2.4.4.1, 207n29
2.4.10.1, 180n95
3.2.4.2, 34
3.2.24, 236n79
3.5.13(14).pr, 47
4.3.7.8, 196n75
4.4.37.1, 235n72
5.3.27.pr, 50, 190n37
7.1.68, 190n37
9.2.2.2, 175n57
9.2.18, 179n84
11.3, 176n60
11.3.1.pr, 176n60
11.3.1.4, 25
11.3.1.5, 25, 176n64, 176n65
11.3.2, 176n63, 176n65, 177n74
11.3.14.4, 179n84
11.7.2.6, 218n3
11.7.4, 222n31
11.7.6.pr, 222n35
11.7.14.8, 222n31
11.7.42, 218n3
12.6.26.12, 208n38, 208n39
13.6.3.4, 188n23
13.7.24.3, 31
14.3.7, 46
15.1.27.pr, 47
16.1.13.pr, 57, 196n75
18.1.11.1, 18, 173n38
18.1.42, 181n99

Digesta (cont.)

18.1.56, 180n94

18.7.6.pr, 35, 180n93

18.7.9, 35

19.1.11.5, 173n38

19.1.21.pr, 191n38

21.1, 49, 190n34

21.1.14.1, 190n34, 191n38

21.1.23.pr, 176n61, 176n63

21.1.23.4, 188n23

21.1.35, 184n118

21.2.34.pr, 180n95

22.1.28.1, 190n37

22.5.4.pr, 206n18

23.2.23, 216n109, 228n15, 228n18

23.2.26.pr, 235n75

23.2.28, 215n102

23.2.28.pr, 215n103

23.2.29, 215n102

23.2.29.pr, 215n103

23.2.41.pr, 180n94

23.2.41.1, 92, 234n66

23.2.43.pr-3, 29

23.2.43.4–5, 151

23.2.43.9, 180n91

23.2.44, 216n109

23.2.44.pr, 228n15

23.2.45, 215n104

23.2.45.pr, 215n106

23.2.45.4, 215n104

23.2.45.5, 216n106

23.2.45.6, 216n108

23.2.48.pr, 216n107

23.2.50.pr, 91

23.2.51.pr, 195n68, 215n102

23.3.39.pr, 189n23

24.1.3.1, 216n109

24.1.31.1, 191n40

24.2.10.pr, 216n107

24.2.11.pr, 91, 215n106

24.2.11.pr-2, 215n104

24.2.11.1, 215n104

24.2.11.2, 216n109

25.3.5.18–26, 206n19

25.3.6.1, 206n21, 206n22

25.3.9, 206n19

25.7.1.pr, 93, 234n66

26.4.3.pr, 211n68

26.4.3.4–5, 211n57

32.41.2, 58, 197n82

32.49.4, 149, 216n109

32.62, 18

32.65.1, 189n24

33.5.21, 50

33.7, 187n11

33.7.12.5, 53, 193n52

33.7.12.6, 187n13

33.7.12.6–7, 53, 184n118

33.7.12.7, 187n12, 192n47

33.7.12.33, 187n12, 193n51

33.7.20.4, 193n51

33.8.3, 190n33

33.8.8, 190n33

33.9.3.pr, 48

33.9.3.6, 48, 189n29

34.1.20.pr, 197n82

35.1.59.1, 174n42

37.14.5, 206n22

37.14.5.1, 206n23

37.14.6.pr, 89

37.14.6.3, 215n101

37.14.6.4, 214n88

37.14.7.pr, 180n93, 180n94

37.14.15, 214n91

37.14.19.pr, 206n19

37.15, 206n15

37.15.2, 206n17

37.15.11, 73

38.1.1.pr, 207n36

38.1.6.pr, 208n39

38.1.7.4, 204n6

38.1.8.pr, 210n53

38.1.9.1, 208n39, 208n41

38.1.13.pr-1, 204n6

38.1.13.4, 90, 214n95

38.1.13.4–5, 214n96

38.1.14, 210n51

38.1.14.pr, 210n52

38.1.16.pr-1, 208n40

38.1.17.pr, 208n40

38.1.24.pr, 208n39

38.1.25, 208n42

38.1.28.pr, 90, 214n95

38.1.30.1, 210n53

38.1.34, 210n55

38.1.35.pr, 80

38.1.36.pr, 205n13

38.1.37.pr-1, 210n52

38.1.38.pr, 79–80, 208n40

38.1.46, 216n112

38.1.46.pr, 209n47

38.1.48, 82

38.1.48.pr, 90, 210n54, 214n95

38.1.48.1, 210n52

38.1.50.pr, 208n40

38.2.1, 72

38.2.1.pr, 200n94

38.2.1.2, 205n13

38.2.9.pr, 206n25

38.2.29.pr, 204n6

38.2.33.pr, 206n23

38.11.1.1, 215n106

38.16.3.5, 214n90, 214n91, 214n94

38.17.1.1, 213n78

40.1, 199n84

40.2.11–13, 201n107

40.2.13, 202n108, 215n102

40.2.14.1, 201n107, 213n84

40.2.15, 201n107

40.2.16, 202n111

40.4.59.pr, 192n48, 193n53

40.5.26.2, 190n33

40.5.41.15, 186n9

40.7.3.16, 196n79, 197n80

40.8.7, 180n95

40.9.21, 215n102

40.9.30, 204n6

40.9.32.pr, 214n88

43.30.3.6, 226n5

45.1.121.1, 216n109

47.1.2, 176n62

47.1.2.5, 25, 175n57, 176n62,
    176n64

47.2.39, 33

47.2.83(82).2, 32

47.10.1.2, 172n23

47.10.1.3, 207n27

47.10.7.2, 74, 75, 77, 207n32

47.10.9.4, 25, 28, 178n75

47.10.10, 25, 28, 178n75, 178n77

47.10.11.7, 76, 77

47.10.11.8, 77, 207n34

47.10.15–23, 177n68

47.10.15.3, 77

47.10.15.5–6, 77

47.10.15.12, 207n33

47.10.15.15, 23, 26, 32, 78, 172n23,
    177n66, 177n68, 178n77,
    179n85

47.10.15.15–16, 171n17

47.10.15.20, 26, 177n68, 178n77

47.10.15.35, 177n67

47.10.15.44, 175n53, 177n66,
    177n67

47.10.25, 26, 175n59, 177n74

48.5.2.2, 235n72

48.5.6.pr, 23, 171n20, 175n47,
    184n117

48.5.6.pr-1, 27, 177n73

48.5.11(10).pr, 226n5

Digesta (*cont.*)
   48.5.13(12), 171n20, 176n64
   48.5.14(13).pr, 92, 234n66
   48.5.14.pr, 216n109
   48.5.30(29).pr, 235n72
   48.5.30(29).9, 172n27
   48.5.35(34), 177n73
   48.5.40(39).pr, 172n27
   48.6.3.4, 172n27
   48.8.11.1–2, 181n99, 181n99
   50.4.3.3, 184n2
   50.16.46.1, 132, 133
   50.16.101.pr, 177n73
   50.16.144, 216n109
   50.16.195.1, 211n66
   50.17.32, 174n42
   50.17.207, 174n42

Dio Cassius. *See* Cassius Dio
Dionysius of Halicarnassus
   4.22, 62, 200n99
   4.24.3–4, 61, 63
   4.24.4, 32, 57, 63, 66
   4.24.4–8, 63
   4.24.7, 63

Epictetus
   Diss.
      4.1.35–37, 234n63

Festus
   112L, 226n6
Fontes Iuris Romani AnteIustiniani (FIRA)
   3.11, 196n75

Gaius
   Inst.
      1.9, 173n40
      1.13, 202n110, 235n78
      1.18–19, 201n106, 229n24
      1.19, 201n107

   1.22, 60
   1.23, 202n114
   1.26–27, 202n110
   1.28–34, 203n117
   1.29, 203n116
   1.34, 203n118
   1.36–41, 201n106
   1.39, 201n107
   1.40–46, 201n105
   1.44, 199n87
   1.55–56, 202n114
   1.67–71, 203n116
   1.79–80, 203n116
   1.84, 230n28, 230n28
   1.91, 230n28
   1.144, 87, 184n2
   1.145, 229n23
   1.157, 213n82
   1.160, 230n28
   1.165, 84, 211n61
   1.168, 211n65
   1.171, 213n82
   1.173–174, 211n63
   1.175, 211n63
   1.176–181, 84
   1.179, 211n62
   1.190, 87, 184n2
   1.190–192, 211n60, 230n26
   1.194, 212n74, 229n23
   1.194–195, 230n26
   1.195, 211n57, 212n76, 229n21
   3.39–41, 213n85
   3.39–42, 211n66
   3.40–41, 85
   3.42, 86, 230n25
   3.43, 85
   3.44, 86, 212n72, 229n23,
      230n25
   3.46, 212n70
   3.46–52, 212n73
   3.49, 212n70

3.56, 199n88, 213n83
3.74–76, 213n83
3.220, 77, 172n23
3.221, 207n27
Historia Augusta
  Ant. Pius
    8.9, 233n52
  Aurel.
    49.4, 178n76, 184n117
    49.5, 184n117
  Hadr.
    18.8, 36

Horace
  Carm.
    1.33.13–15, 140
    2.4, 16
    3.30.1–9, 218n3
  Epist.
    1.18.72–75, 38, 177n70
  Epod.
    14.15, 140
  Sat.
    1.1.99, 232n37
    1.2, 139, 140, 147, 179n88
    1.2.114–119, 14
    1.2.25–28, 231n32
    1.2.31–35, 232n48
    1.2.47, 139
    1.2.48, 139
    1.2.55–63, 139
    Institutiones (Justinian)
    3.3.1, 229n24
    3.4, 212n78

Jerome
  Ep.
    77.3, 173n32, 174n45, 179n88
  lex Irnitana (Flavian Municipal Law)
    23, 217n115
    97, 217n115

Livy
  1.58, 12, 172n24
  1.58.5, 210n50
  2.4–5, 61, 63
  3.50.6, 20
  10.23, 126
  22.1.18, 133
  39.9–15, 232n49
  39.9.5, 143, 233n50
  39.9.6–7, 144
  39.9.7, 211n64
  39.12.1, 143
  39.19, 134, 227n10
  39.19.5, 211n64
  45.14.1–7, 201n102
  45.14.3–4, 201n102

Macrobius
  Sat.
    1.6.13, 132
    1.11.36, 175n52
    1.11.36–40, 175n49
Martial
  1.84, 51
  2.63, 182n102
  3.33, 13, 139
  4.13, 192n50
  6.66, 179n84
  6.71, 51, 182n102
  11.23, 191n40
  11.27, 191n40
  12.58, 173n32
Musonius Rufus
  fr. 12, 182n108, 183n110

Nepos
  Att.
    13.4, 190n36

Ovid
  Am.

1.11, 173n35, 191n40
2.7–8, 181n101
2.7.21–22, 15, 172n31
2.8.9–10, 15, 172n31
2.8.11–14, 16
2.19.41, 173n35
Ars am.
  1.351–398, 173n34
  1.383–386, 181n101
  2.257–258, 175n49
  3.611–616, 142, 236n83
  3.615, 198n84
  3.665–666, 181n101
Fast.
  2.741–834, 172n24
Pont.
  3.3.49–52, 234n60
Tr.
  2.243–244, 234n60
  2.303–304, 234n60
Pauli Sententiae
  1.13a.6, 175n57
  2.19.6, 183n114
  2.20.1, 216n109, 216n109
  2.21.11, 230n28
  2.26.16, 23, 175n54, 177n74
  2.31.31, 32
  3.6.38, 52, 187n12
  4.9, 229n23, 229n24

Petronius
Sat.
  16, 173n35
  37, 235n67
  53, 89
  53.10, 143
  57, 235n67
  71, 218n3, 218n4
  74, 234n62, 236n81
  74.13, 149

75–76, 191n43
75.11, 22
111–112, 16, 173n34, 191n40
126, 173n35, 182n105
Plautus
Cas.
  67–78, 192n50
Cist.
  38, 231n37, 234n63
Epidi.
  463–466, 182n102, 183n112
  465, 231n37
Men.
  1034, 199n90
Merc.
  415, 171n17
Mil.
  784, 231n35, 231n37
  962, 139, 198n84, 231n37
Per.
  82, 231n37
  474–475, 62, 201n101
  484, 231n37
  487, 201n101
  737, 231n37
  789, 231n37
  797, 231n37
Poen.
  102–103, 182n102
  164, 231n37
Pseud.
  176, 231n37
Truc.
  94, 181n101
Pliny the Elder
  NH
    8.55, 232n44
Pliny the Younger
  Ep.
    4.11.11, 141

5.86, 190n36
7.32, 62, 201n100
10.5.2, 203n117
10.11.2, 217n115
Plutarch
  Cam.
    33, 175n49
  Cat. Mai.
    21.1, 192n48
  Mor.
    140B, 15
    267C, 171n17
  Rom.
    29, 175n49
Priapea
  40, 57
Propertius
  1.9.4, 183n111
  3.15, 181n101

Quintilian
  Inst.
    5.11.34–35, 191n43
    8.4.1–2, 31
[Quintilian]
  Dec. Min
    301.7, 14, 172n30
    301.17, 39, 177n70, 182n104
    311.9, 200n98

Salvian
  Ad ecc.
    3.7.31, 203n115
Seneca the Elder
  Contr.
    1.2, 152
    1.2.8, 152
    4.pr.10, 208n45
    6.6, 173n35
    7.6.17, 227n12

Seneca the Younger
  Ben.
    1.9.3–4, 15
    6.32.1, 31
  Dial.
    12.16.4, 210n50
  Ep.
    94.26, 183n110
    95.37, 183n110
    123.10, 183n110
  Ira
    2.28.7, 177n70
Servius
  A.
    8.564, 227n9
Statius
  Silv.
    5.5.66–70, 190n36
Suetonius
  Aug.
    40.3–4, 202n112
    65.2, 141
  Cl.
    18–19, 212n75
    18.2–19, 203n117
  Ner.
    28, 232n45
    28.1, 142
  Vesp.
    3.1, 145
Sylloge Inscriptionum Graecarum
    (SIG3)
    543, 62, 200n99

Tacitus
  Ann.
    3.24, 235n71
    12.53, 230n28
    13.26, 206n21
    13.27, 64, 201n102, 203n115

Tacitus (*cont.*)
    15.51, 141
    15.72, 143
  Ger.
    25, 189n26
Terence
  Eun.
    122, 232n39
  Haut.
    130, 191n40
    142–143, 189n30
Tertullian
  Ad ux.
    2.8.1, 192n50
Thylander, *Inscriptions du Port d'Ostie*
  A 268, 105
  A 269, 221n22
  A 270, 106
Tituli ex corpore Ulpiani
  1.6, 200n94
  1.24, 201n105
  3.1, 203n118
  3.1–6, 203n117
  3.3, 203n116

5.5, 183n114
11.8, 213n82
11.16, 202n114
13.2, 228n16, 235n75
20.14, 203n115
26.7, 212n78
29.1, 213n85
29.1–3, 211n66
29.3, 229n23

Valerius Maximus
  6.1.pr, 174n47
  6.1.1, 172n24, 172n25
  6.3.10, 171n17
  6.3.11, 140
  6.7.1, 54, 149, 183n108, 183n110,
    234n62
  9.7.1, 228n13
Varro
  Rust.
    1.17.5, 52
    1.18, 187n10
Vitruvius
  2.9.1, 190n34

Subject Index

Acte (Claudia Acte, freedwoman, mistress of Nero), 142, 232n45
actio iniuriarum, 23–24, 25–26, 74–78, 177n67. *See also iniuria*
actio legis Aquiliae. See lex: Aquilia
actio servi corrupti, 24–25, 26, 31
adultery (*adulterium*), 12, 30, 131, 151, 171n14, 171n20, 182n101, 236n82.
  See also stuprum
  associated with slave behavior, 27–28, 38, 184n117
  not applicable to freedwomen, 139
  not applicable to slaves, 23, 27, 178n76
Alföldy, Géza, 193n54
ancillarum feriae, 21
anniculi probatio, 66, 203n116
Augustus (emperor), 30, 141, 148, 170n11, 235n71
  social reforms of, 12, 23, 29, 62–63, 64–67, 80, 88, 92, 150, 196n78, 198n84, 202n112, 227n11
Aurelian (emperor), 184n117

Bagnall, Roger, 197n83
Barton, Carlin, 174n45
Boyd, David Lorenzo, 178n80
Bradley, Keith, 190n34, 190n38, 192n50

Caenis (Antonia Caenis, freedwoman, mistress/concubine of Vespasian), 144
Cantarella, Eva, 208n45
Cato the Elder, 45, 48, 186n6, 187n10, 187n14, 189n26, 192n48, 228n12, 233n48
citizenship (Roman), 30, 100, 229n19
  deservingness of, 6, 63–64, 65, 154
  gendered understandings of, 2, 66–67, 150, 153
  limitations on, 57, 60, 135, 179n82
  and manumission, 3–4, 6, 59–67, 154, 200n94, 217n2
  and marriage, 90, 149, 154
  and morality, 150, 235n73
Claudius (emperor), 87, 203n117, 206n22, 212n77
colliberti, 99, 104, 109, 195n64, 223n43, 225n58

Columella, 45, 49, 58, 186n9,
    187n14, 187n14, 196n78,
    203n119
Commodus (emperor), 206n22
Compitalia, 19
concubinage/concubines, 40, 92–93,
    144, 149
Constantine (emperor), 192n50
contubernium/contubernales, 35, 41, 45,
    52–53, 58, 125, 197n81
Corbier, Mireille, 224n54
Corinna (mistress of Ovid), 15,
    173n35
Cornelius Scipio Africanus, P., 54,
    149, 182n108, 234n62
Cytheris. *See* Volumnia Cytheris
    (freedwoman, mistress of M.
    Antonius)

dediticii, 65, 151
dextrarum iunctio, 112
Dixon, Suzanne, 171n14, 185n2,
    221n20

edict of Rutilius. *See* Rutilius Rufus, P.
Epicharis (freedwoman, conspirator
    against Nero), 140
epigraphic practices
    of freedpersons, 99–100,
    219n12
    of Romans, 97, 217n2
    and the use of status indicators,
    99–106
Evans Grubbs, Judith, 56, 170n11,
    213n84

Fabre, Georges, 204n9, 204n10
Faecenia Hispala. *See* Hispala
    Faecenia
familia Caesaris, 186n5, 187n18,

    190n35, 197n83, 220n13
Feronia (goddess), 133
Flemming, Rebecca, 181n100
Fortunata (wife of Trimalchio), 149,
    152, 234n62, 235n67
fructus, 50

Gardner, Jane, 4, 70, 199n86,
    203n116, 204n4, 207n31,
    207n36, 208n41, 209n47,
    213n85
Garrido-Hory, Marguerite, 186n9

Hadrian (emperor), 34, 36, 180n95
Harper, James, 193n54
Harris, William, 187n14, 190n38
Haterius, Q. (orator), 208n45
Herrmann-Otto, Elisabeth, 190n35,
    190n38
Hispala Faecenia (Faecenia Hispala),
    133, 143–144, 211n63
honor and shame, 16–17, 35, 40,
    150, 151
    applicability to slaves, 20–22, 36
    freedwomen's right to, 70–71, 80–83
    in Roman society, 8–13
Hope, Valerie, 218n4
Hopkins, Keith, 186n6, 193n54,
    196n77, 197n83, 218n3, 223n40
Hughes, Lisa, 223n43

impudicitia. *See pudicitia*
incerti (in inscriptions), 99
iniuria, 23–24, 25–26, 33, 34, 36,
    74–78, 85, 183n110, 207n27,
    207n28
inscriptions. *See* epigraphic practices

Joshel, Sandra, 219n10, 220n14,
    224n55